ON
THIN
ICE

The **STORY** *and* **DIARY** *of a*
MALE ANOREXIC

a memoir

CHRIS HENRIE
A FOREWORD BY **KARIN SCHOENFELD, LCSW**

Copyright © 2022, 2024 by Chris Henrie

All rights reserved.

No part of this book may be reproduced in any form or by any electronic or mechanical means, including information storage and retrieval systems, without written permission from the author, except for the use of brief quotations in a book review.

2 1

Second edition

Author's Note

On Thin Ice is a deeply personal memoir predominantly composed of the journal entries I kept during my two-month stay in inpatient treatment for anorexia nervosa when I was fifteen and sixteen years old.

I want to emphasize that *On Thin Ice* is not intended to offer an all-encompassing account or universal experience of individuals grappling with eating disorders. Instead, through the publication of this work, my aspiration is to offer an intimate insight, particularly as a teenage boy, embarking on the arduous journey of recovery from an eating disorder while navigating difficult family dynamics, first romances, friendships, and personal identity. I also aim to shed light on and explore facets of my personal narrative that may have played a role in its development.

To safeguard privacy and address legal concerns, all names, places, locations, relationships, and defining characteristics of the individuals and locations portrayed in *On Thin Ice* have been altered. Any resemblance to real-life individuals, locations, or events is purely coincidental.

It's important to note that *On Thin Ice* delves into the

intricate and distressing realm of eating-disordered thoughts and behaviors. This content may be triggering to some readers, and I strongly advise exercising caution while engaging with the material.

Sensitivity Warning

On Thin Ice contains vivid depictions of eating-disordered thoughts and behaviors that may be distressing and triggering to some readers.

Additionally, *On Thin Ice* touches upon themes of bullying, domestic abuse, and drug use.

Please engage with this material responsibly.

Disclaimer

On Thin Ice is not intended to be read as a "self-help" or "how-to-recover" book. Any insights or suggestions offered by Henrie within the book are derived solely from the author's personal experiences within recovery. They should not be construed as medical advice or as a replacement for professional treatment.

On Thin Ice reflects the thought processes of a child in the early stages of recovery while still deeply immersed in the throes of an eating disorder. The book illuminates the transformative journey that occurs within the mind of an individual beginning recovery from an eating disorder. It is not indicative of the author's present thoughts or interpretations.

This book is dedicated to my mom.

Foreword

BY KARIN SCHOENFELD, LCSW

When a fellow therapist asks you to see their child, you do so without hesitation. What comes next can be uncomfortable, confusing, or even combative. No one ever wants to believe that their child is so deeply embedded in an eating disorder because they then must admit to themselves that they were blind to the suffering that happened right before their eyes. Even the most seasoned professionals can miss the blaring signs of anorexia when it is attached to someone they love. In the case of Christopher, this couldn't be more evident.

The day I met Christopher is forever seared in my brain. As I opened my office door, I saw this statuesque figure of a young man who appeared nervous, frail, and inviting all at once. He had a gentle voice and a kindness that permeated the room. Traditionally, clients would sit on the couch across from me, but Chris opted to sit in the chair right beside me. I knew from the moment we began our session that by the end of the hour, I would be recommending he immediately go to a hospital for inpatient treatment, something I had never done in all my years of practice.

We had the typical first session, the back and forth get-to-know-you conversation, but something was different about

Chris. I could see the despair in his eyes and felt an energy of need that, without saying a word, this young man was put before me so that I could be his voice to his family that he was in desperate need of life-saving treatment.

After a few brief moments, I turned to him and informed him that I was recommending he go to a hospital immediately, or my fear was he would not survive this battle much longer. Prior experience with eating disordered patients had me prepared for a fight—the typical manipulation by a client so deep in their disorder that they will say anything not to go inpatient. Chris was different. He let out a sigh of relief and looked at me in a way I wasn't prepared for.

"Thank you. I know this is what I need," he said. I thought to myself in that brief moment that Chris was ready to fight for himself. All he needed was someone to validate what he already knew, and I will forever be grateful for the courage it took that he allowed me to be that person.

That was the easy part. Chris and I agreed without any difficulty that if he was going to beat this disease, he needed intensive inpatient treatment. Convincing his family of this wasn't as easy as I had hoped. Just because a family member doesn't admit or want to see how serious a situation is, it is not indicative of their love or commitment to their child. The love was never in question. The understanding of the seriousness was.

"Are you sure we can't do this on an outpatient basis?" I was floored to hear his father ask me the following day. I paused to stop myself from going into full-blown aggressive advocate mode. This was a colleague of mine who worked in the same building. I remembered who I was fighting for. I didn't care who got mad at me, whether I hurt someone's feelings or even stepped over the line for someone I only spent one hour with. My job was clear, and even more so, my heart was fully committed to finding a way to save this young man from a disease that would take his life before he even got a chance to live.

The battle Chris faced was intense, but he found the strength within the darkness of this insidious disease to fight for himself and face all the challenges along the way. His continued fight for his recovery and his advocacy for others who struggle, oftentimes in silence, is a testament to the bravery and determination he possesses to make sure that no person ever feels like they are alone on their journey. I will forever be grateful to Chris for allowing me to be a part of his recovery, for trusting the process, and for his willingness to see that he was worth the fight.

ON THIN ICE

The **STORY** *and* **DIARY** *of a*
MALE ANOREXIC

a memoir

Before

"So, what have you eaten today?"

Nothing. I gulped and placed both of my hands underneath my thighs. The entire room turned ice cold and my mind began to race. The silence in the room was resounding as the stranger sitting next to me looked into my eyes. It was as if she were searching for any spark of life to wash across my face. The urge to lie to her was overwhelming. With the right choice of words, I could be walking out of this woman's office as the same person I was when I walked in. The *wrong* choice of words could sabotage any goals my disordered mind had manipulated me to believe were best.

"A few veggie chips and some lemonade," I muttered, which wasn't a complete lie. The night prior, I allowed myself to indulge in a few of those greasy, straw-shaped vegetable-flavored chips—my eating disorder's definition of a binge—under the condition that I would no longer eat anything for the rest of the week. It was only Thursday.

The pain I saw in the woman's eyes looking back at me was comforting. It finally felt like someone understood what I had been going through for the past few years of my life, and that simple acknowledgement wasn't something I experienced before. It shouldn't have felt as liberating as it did.

The woman's name was Cori, and she was a social worker who specialized in the treatment of eating disorders among teenagers and young adults. This was my first time meeting with her, and ironically enough, she worked in the same office building as my father, who was a clinical psychologist.

Cori's office was small and quaint with school-like posters plastered upon every wall—posters that gave you the same encouragement your mom would give when you were a child about to stand up to the class bully. *You can do it! Believe in yourself!* In this situation, the only bully in the room was the overwhelming stench coming from the air vents in the ceiling. It was awful.

Perhaps it was all in my head. It probably was. My mind was too distracted thinking about the amount of people who sat in the same chair I was in before me. I wondered how many of them were still alive. Maybe that's what smelled so bad.

I had a funny thought. *This is where eating disorders come to die. And all those people who sat here before me looking for help were nothing but failures.*

I didn't want to be like them. I didn't want to be a failure. A failure, that is, in my eating disorder's eyes.

Another thought danced in my mind. *What if this room wasn't just a graveyard for eating disorders, but a sanctuary where life without an eating disorder seemed possible? A place where struggles were acknowledged, battles were fought, and, yes, some were lost, but others emerged victorious.*

My mind went back and forth.

It had taken me more than three weeks to get an appointment with Cori. It wasn't because she was busy with other clients or taking a tropical vacation in Bermuda. My parents took their time determining what the best route was for me to begin seeking help for what I believed to be an eating disorder. I understood my parents' desire to be thorough when diving into a world they knew very little about, but I grew more and more frustrated as each day went by that nothing changed and little progress was being made toward what should've been me receiving help as quickly as possible.

It was the same routine every day, from the earliest memories of my childhood to my most recent teenage years. My dad would come home from work and lock himself in his room until my sister and I were in bed. My mom, who bent herself backward to give me and my sister the best chance at a normal childhood, struggled to do things and make decisions without my dad. Unfortunately, the window of opportunity for anyone to talk to my dad was slim. His mood was always changing, and nobody ever knew where they stood with him. In my mom's effort to include my dad in our everyday lives, little, if anything, would get accomplished.

It became a running joke in my family that the Henries never get things done. Either that, or it takes us a long period of time to complete fairly simple tasks that would take other families mere hours. Our attic was still disheveled from that one weekend we began organizing the Christmas decorations but never finished, and empty baseball card binders sat on my father's dresser from that time he wanted to catalog his collection. We went nearly three years without living room furniture because of a bed bug infestation I uncovered in my room, which, by the way, took a month to convince my parents *was* a bed bug infestation.

This way of living caused constant rifts within our family, particularly because of my father. Navigating my relationship with him was like walking through a minefield of silence and uncertainty. There were entire stretches where days passed without a single word was exchanged between us. I couldn't shake the feeling of being constantly tested, as if I were a subject in one of his psychological experiments. At times, I resented the fact that my father was a psychologist because it seemed like he needed one most of all. Other times, I entertained the thought that perhaps scheduling an appointment and assuming the role as one of his patients might finally garner the attention I craved from him.

Even I understood that receiving help for an eating disorder was not something that could wait or be put on hold. It also wasn't something one should take months on to survey which therapists in the area had the best reviews on the Internet. It hurt to think my parents didn't understand the severity of my disorder, but at the same time, I couldn't expect them to. Cori sure understood.

"I am going to recommend to your parents that you enter treatment for your eating disorder as soon as possible," Cori began. She kept her eyes fixated on mine as she pushed the pen and paper in her hands aside. "Never in my career have I referred anyone to treatment the day I met them—until today. This is serious, Chris. I need you and your parents to understand the urgency of this situation. I need you to trust me."

My palms began to sweat. How could I possibly feel confident that a person I've known for no more than thirty minutes knew what was best for me? She had her agenda, and I had mine. Thoughts of regret gently pushed their way to the front of my mind. *Seeing Cori was a mistake. Deciding to begin recovery was a mistake.* I had it all. I had a family that was clueless about my eating disorder. I was so close to my goal weight. I had what it took to complete this.

Trust is a theme I only ever associated with my disorder. Do what it says, and you will feel better. Do what it says, and all of your problems will go away. I didn't listen. My biggest problems were now staring me in the face—Cori and my eating disorder's overwhelming fear of gaining weight.

Cori was quick to bring me back to our conversation. "Whose decision was it for you to see me?"

"Mine."

"Why was that?"

"I am tired."

"Tired of what?"

I sighed. "Everything. I am tired of everything. Tired of not having the energy to get out of bed in the morning. Tired of the excruciating headaches that follow me around all day. Everything hurts. I can't make it stop. I can barely make it through a day at school without fainting."

"You can make it stop. And that tells me all there is to know about you, Chris. You're ready to fight this. I can see it in your eyes. That's why you came to see me, isn't it? Do you want to recover?"

The word itself was intimidating. *Recover.* There was only one word that came to my mind whenever I heard it. *Failure.* Beginning recovery would mean that I failed. I failed to reach my goal weight. I failed to keep my disorder a secret from my parents. I failed to succeed at the only thing I ever knew how to do—further deprecate myself until the person I looked at in the mirror was a complete stranger.

Who am I without my eating disorder? It provided me comfort. It provided me an identity I didn't entirely loathe. It has been there for me through every tough moment in my life, promising a distraction from just about anything. Without it, I didn't know myself. It was all I had.

Yet, I chose recovery. I chose to see Cori. I chose to begin the process of learning how to live a life undefined by the restricting rules of my eating disorder. *Why did I do it?* That is something I have been asking myself for the past three weeks. If I could take it all back, I probably would. I've learned to regret a lot in my life. Most of those feelings come from my eating disorder itself. I eat when I'm not supposed to. I stop exercising when I know I shouldn't. I never live it down.

The tension inside of me was building. My eyes burned as if I had just finished slicing ten raw onions. The words I was about to utter were fateful.

"Yes. I want to recover."

I let out a big sigh.

"Chris, you have already taken the most difficult step in your recovery. Things here on out will be tough, but recognizing you want to change is the hardest part," Cori said.

I've heard this saying a thousand times before. Admitting you need help is the first step to reclaiming your life, whether that be from drugs, alcohol, or an eating disorder. I never understood that well enough until it applied to me—until the burden of my mind finally lifted and opened itself up to the possibility of recovery. It felt good. Scary, but good.

"Now, let's see. Cherry Oak Hospital has an outstanding reputation for their eating disorder recovery program, and it is only an hour and a half away," Cori began again. *Here we go. It was time for Cori to send me away to a prison who'd pump my body with artificial nutrition and supplements until I gained enough weight.* I wasn't going to fall for it.

"I have sent many clients of mine there, and they come back with really great results," Cori told me sternly. I wasn't sure how long Cori had been a therapist, but her tone and expression made it clear that she wasn't one to kid around. She saw the pain in my eyes and in my words. I didn't know how to respond.

"Chris, I'm afraid you don't have much time left. You need to get treatment immediately. I know speaking to me was a big step, but it is not enough. I need you to trust me. Don't let this thing kill you."

I sat thinking about her words. Perhaps death wouldn't be the worst thing in the world. Death would mean that I won. Maybe then my family would notice how badly I was struggling. Maybe then I would prove to myself and everybody else that I *was* sick. My death would have a purpose. Cutting myself off from the world seemed like the greatest prize I could be given.

Cori continued. "I know that Cherry Oak is the best option. What sets them apart from other treatment programs is their dedication to focusing on the *mental* side of eating disorders, not just the physical side. That can be rare to find in other eating disorder treatment facilities. You gain the weight; they kick you out. Cherry Oak is different. Trust me. You will be in good hands."

One part of me was appalled at the idea of going into treatment, but the other part of me was relieved. It was a visceral conflict, a tussle between the familiarity of my private struggles and the daunting prospect of unveiling them to the world. With Cori, I felt validated and heard. Everything that I had been going through for what felt like my entire life was real. The room seemed to expand with the weight of the truth settling in.

I would finally be surrounded by people who understood my needs and what was going on inside my head. The mere thought of stepping into an environment where that was not an elusive concept but a shared theme amongst patients and professionals sent waves of anticipation through me.

I thought long and hard about how to respond. I remembered the night that I told my mom about my eating disorder. The feelings of helplessness, desperation, and pain flooded back. I was curled up in my bed. Everything was still, but the room was loud. Every cell in my brain begged me not to tell her. I knew that if I did, that'd be the end. My coldest, most inscrutable secret would be revealed.

Many of the days prior were similar. My mom would come into my room at night to find me sobbing in my pillow. Each time, I conjured an excuse, a feeble attempt to shield her from the raw truth. Perhaps I didn't feel well that day, or a vague incident at school had upset me. The sound of her footsteps approaching down the hallway became a familiar and comforting noise. She'd sit and lay with me until the moment passed, which was all I needed.

The night I told my mom about my eating disorder was different. She wouldn't leave my room until I told her what was going on. She knew there was something deeper. I just didn't know how to tell her.

I've never had a healthy relationship with food. Growing up

naturally underweight, my size became the unwelcome centerpiece of every family gathering or holiday celebration. Shouts would emanate across the dinner table from curious family members, each with their unsolicited recommendations on what I should or shouldn't be eating. My uncle, with a sense of misguided humor, insisted that I abandon my "bird food" diet. On my father's side, my grandmother was unwavering in her conviction that eggs were the key to me gaining weight. It was like a ritual—the first thing she'd say to me whenever we saw each other.

"Eggs! You need to eat eggs!" she would blurt out.

"It's nice to see you, too," I'd reply.

By the time I turned twelve, I stopped attending most family events altogether. The very gatherings that were meant to foster connection with my relatives became a battleground where I grew to resent myself the most. It was as if no one saw me for who I was, and my appearance was the only topic of conversation people felt comfortable bringing up around me. It felt like nothing else mattered.

Comments on my weight and what I ate didn't end with family. Even my elementary school teachers would call my parents and ask them if they knew their son had only brought in a granola bar or a slice of salami for lunch that day. It was as if my every meal was a matter of collective concern, and I felt my relationship with food had become a spectacle for the public. It was isolating, and it further fueled the discordant relationship I had with my body.

Like many kids, I was a picky eater. I'd find one type of food that I enjoyed, and I would eat it every day until I became tired of it. Then, I'd move on to the next food. Eating always felt like a chore to me. The routine of recommendations from family members and the unnecessary scrutiny on my weight only intensified this struggle. Each suggestion, no matter how casual and innocent, triggered an almost reflexive defiance within me. Whatever was said to me, I'd find myself doing the opposite. If a particular food was offered to me, I simply couldn't bring myself to eat it. My mind twisted even the gentlest gestures into something potentially manipulative or ill-intentioned. The act of eating became less and less enticing. There were too many expectations and perceptions that accompanied it.

Thoughts of intentional food restriction didn't begin overnight. I was in the seventh grade when I learned what a calorie was, and I spent nights in my room memorizing how many of them were in my favorite foods. With a notepad and the dim glow of my desk lamp, I meticulously created an archive of numbers that held a power over me I was only beginning to understand. My biggest fear was someone finding that notepad, so I kept it deep within the sock drawer of my dresser.

"I've been starving myself for the past four years," I told my mom that night. Tears flooded my eyes. The words were painful, but my mom's reaction hurt more. She began crying with me and holding me as if she'd never let go. Minutes passed without us saying a word.

"We are going to get you help," my mom eventually replied. "That is not something any person should be going through. We are going to get you help."

Whether I wanted her to be or not, I knew my mom was there for me from that moment on. I don't think she understood how sick I was. I wasn't even sure she noticed any differences in my behavior. Yet, I knew in my heart that by telling her about my problem, I had taken a big step in taking my life back, even if I was the only one who seemed to notice.

I looked back at Cori and saw the last few years of my life flash before my eyes. I knew a life existed without my eating disorder. Millions of people lived those lives every day. I wasn't sure if that was the life I wanted for myself, but a part of me was willing to take the chance.

"Thank you. I know this is what I need."

THE DAY after being referred by Cori, my mom called the eating disorder unit at Cherry Oak Hospital to figure out what the next steps would be for me to get admitted into their inpatient program. After what felt like hours of insurance talk, we learned that the first thing I needed to have done was a physical exam performed by my pediatrician. My mom picked up her phone again and dialed my doctor.

I had been seeing the same pediatrician since I was a child. His name was Dr. Fischer. He stood nearly seven feet tall, wore dark and chunky-framed glasses, and walked around with a hunch in his back that'd make anyone believe he was carrying a fifty-pound weight on his shoulders. My family had a great, lasting relationship with him. He was all I ever knew a doctor to be. He was kind and funny but never hesitated to share any concerns he had with me. Every time I'd see him, he'd make the same comment about my weight never meeting par with any other boys my age and height. My weight was always an issue, but it was a concern that was commonly dismissed by my parents and me. *That's just the way Chris is.* I got the sense that he would not be surprised to learn why I needed this physical exam so urgently.

"Can you hold on one second, please?" my mom asked the receptionist on the phone. "I would like to discuss some things with my son before making the appointment."

"Of course," I overheard the woman reply.

My mom looked at me with an agitated look in her eyes. I could tell something was wrong. She placed her hand over her phone and held it below her waist.

"The office has an opening tomorrow at two o'clock," she began.

"Oh, that's...that's great," I answered nervously. I didn't realize it would be so soon.

"However," my mom sighed. "Dr. Fischer is on vacation. The only available pediatrician to see you tomorrow is Dr. Stonavich. You probably don't remember her. You only saw her when you were a toddler until we switched to Dr. Fischer." The name didn't ring a bell, but I didn't care. It took practically a month for me to have my first meeting with Cori, and the last thing I wanted was to wait another day for Dr. Fischer. I would see whatever doctor I could find.

"That's fine. I just want to get it over with," I said, rolling my eyes.

"Are you sure, Chris? We can wait until Dr. Fischer gets back," my mom said with a twitch in her eye. It was clear that my mom wanted me to see Dr. Fischer. He was someone we were both familiar with, and I knew my mom didn't want to rush things. Frankly, I would have preferred to see him, too, but it wasn't worth it. I was desperate. Besides, I was now curious why my mom felt the way she did about Dr. Stonavich.

"Why? What happened?"

"You just never know what will come out of that woman's mouth," my mom began. She sat down and went on to explain to me about all the times she had taken me and my sister to see Dr. Stonavich before and how she'd leave each visit regretting it.

"She'd tell me I was doing *this* wrong. She'd tell me I was doing *that* wrong. There was no pleasing that woman," my mom said, resting her hand on the kitchen table. "I can remember her calling me up every day to make sure that I had correctly given you your asthma nebulizer treatments. Mind you, I have a master's in nursing and public health!" My mom laughed. "That's just a silly example. I can't think of anything off the top of my head."

I nodded.

"It's like she didn't trust me. She always talked down to me," my mom continued. "I don't know, Christopher. I don't know." She looked around the room. I didn't know what to say.

"How long will Dr. Fischer be out for?"

"Only two weeks," my mom smiled.

Only two weeks? I began to grow impatient. I did not know how to further convince my mom that I needed to begin treatment as soon as possible. I knew that she was trying her hardest to understand. I knew that I had thrown her and my dad into a world that they knew very little about. Still, I was hurt.

"I'll see Dr. Stonavich. I don't mind," I replied in the hopes of reassuring both my mom and me that I didn't mind seeing someone different. Maybe that is what I needed—a fresh pair of eyes. Nobody in my family suspected I had an eating disorder. Maybe Dr. Fischer would be ignorant to the idea of it, too. "It'll be over before we know it, and then we never have to see her again. Please. I just want to get this done with as soon as possible."

"Of course we can go see her, Chris. I am only looking out for you, and I wouldn't want her to say anything strange or inappropriate to you," my mom said to me, looking concerned. "Again, if I were you, I would wait the two weeks to talk to Dr. Fischer, but I'll make the appointment for tomorrow."

FROM THE MOMENT Dr. Stonavich entered the examination room, I knew I should have listened to my mom. She looked about seventy years old, though it was hard to tell from her short, poorly-colored hair that was curled perfectly at the bottom. She wore a dark, navy-blue, Hillary Clinton-styled pantsuit and a pair of thin, rectangular glasses that hung by a chain around her neck. She was tall and stood with her chin high in the air, giving the impression that she perceived herself as the most important person to walk through the door. She reminded me of my seventh-grade algebra teacher who enjoyed embarrassing her students in front of the entire class for answering questions incorrectly. I immediately felt uneasy.

A few moments before, a nurse led me to a room down a long hallway where she checked my vitals and measured my height and weight. The room was all too familiar. It was the same room I had gone to every year prior for my checkups with Dr. Fischer.

I'd sit on the bed and distract myself by reading every pamphlet on the desk beside me until my checkup finally began. This time, it felt different. I wasn't afraid of any potential shots I had to be given. I didn't need to have my blood drawn. I wasn't even dreading the inevitable exam of things below the waist.

It felt like I was attending a funeral. My mind was black, and I felt an air of loss within the room. The office was a lot colder than I remembered and smelled more like a doctor's office than ever before. Every noise I made sounded louder as if microphones were lining my body. I knew I was there for one reason and one reason only—to receive medical clearance before being placed in the hands of the doctors at Cherry Oak Hospital. My concern was that I was entirely too "normal looking" to be considered for treatment for an eating disorder. Would any discerning eye, especially that of a doctor, take my struggles seriously?

The nurse left the room after instructing me to strip down to my underwear and socks in preparation for my exam. I decided to keep on my white undershirt, as well as my socks and briefs, as I had done every other year. Dr. Fischer never made me take them off. He understood that it was always very cold in the building. Little did he know that the temperature was not the reason why I kept everything on.

Nobody in my life had ever seen me without a shirt on—not at the beach, not strolling to my room after taking a shower, not even in the pool. My body dysmorphia was a constant shadow, following me even into the realm of a doctor's office. The numbers on the scale hardly mattered; the reflection in the mirror remained unchanged. It echoed the distorted image my eating disorder had painted that convinced me that shedding an excessive amount of weight was the only path to some form of acceptability. Thankfully, Dr. Fischer had no problem lifting my shirt to check my spine or listen to my heartbeat. Dr. Fischer was very understanding. Dr. Stonavich, well, not so much.

"What are you still doing with your clothes on?" I looked up, startled by Dr. Stonavich's introduction.

"Oh, I'm sorry," I muttered as I hesitantly began taking off my shirt. I can barely stand to look at my own chest for more than a minute. I had no idea how Dr. Stonavich would react to the sight of it. More thoughts began to flood through my mind. *Was I too big? Was I too thin? Did I look too "normal" to be getting evaluated for an eating disorder?*

"Sorry for not introducing myself. I am Dr. Stonavich. You probably do not remember me. Gosh, I remember checking up on you when you were only a baby! You have gotten so tall. What are you now, over six feet?" she asked while taking a look at her clipboard. "What brings you in today, Christopher? Is something wrong?"

Huh? Does she seriously not know?

"Um, well—"

"Ah yes, that's right," she gleamed, interrupting me. She lowered her clipboard and looked me up and down. "Cherry Oak Hospital! I'm sorry. The nurse only briefed me on your case moments ago. Please, tell me what is going on. What is this about some eating disorder? Do you think you have one?"

"Uh, yes, I believe so," I replied.

"What does that mean? You're not eating?"

"Not really."

"Why not?"

"I don't know."

"You need food to live, Christopher," she said with a chuckle. "You need food to live and continue to grow into the young man I know you are. Are you still growing, even at the height you are!?"

"I think so."

"That's amazing. You have gotten so big, Christopher. Look at yourself in a mirror!" She gestured over to the small mirror above the sink in the corner of the room. I had been trying to ignore it. "Look at what a young man you have become. Your body needs every nutrient it can get. How else will you continue to grow? So, I'm going to ask you again. Why aren't you eating?"

"I don't know."

She looked stumped. She continued to look at me while I saw her mind reeling with more questions she wished to ask. I let out a big sigh. This was exactly what my mom had tried to warn me about. My conversation with Dr. Stonavich was not going to go anywhere, and her attempt at sounding like some sort of motivational life coach was particularly embarrassing.

"When was the last time you ate something?" she asked.

"This morning," I replied. A handful of dried banana chips for breakfast was something, right?

"Oh! So, you *are* eating. That's great to hear," Dr. Stonavich said, grinning at me but still looking confused. She leaned her body against the wall and fixed her eyes on my chest. "I can tell you still have room to grow. You remind me so much of my grandson. He is almost double your weight but just as handsome." She winked. "There is just one thing I am not understanding, Christopher. You say you have an eating disorder, yet you also just said that you ate this morning. Can you please explain that to me? I am a bit confused."

I thought long and hard about how to answer. It was clear Dr. Stonavich failed to understand what eating disorders were. Shouldn't she and all doctors have some basic knowledge about them? I felt like a science experiment, like a freak of nature sitting there anxiously waiting for what would come out of her mouth next. If this was any indication of what treatment would be like, then I was certainly not ready. All of her questions were making my head explode. Not only that, but the questions seemed wildly inappropriate. If there was a list of things *not* to say or ask someone with an eating disorder, I was sure she hit them all.

Dr. Stonavich finally got around to the physical exam. She had me sit up while she removed her metal stethoscope from around her neck. I breathed in and out as she moved it all around my chest and my back. It felt cold on my skin. I noticed my heart beginning to pound, as it always did, which probably hid any signs of a slowing heart rate I may have had.

"Try to calm down, dear. I am almost finished. Then, I will have you lay on your back so I can examine your stomach and abdomen," she stated.

Great. I always dreaded that part. It tickled so much, and I always felt strange for laughing. Dr. Fischer would sometimes laugh with me, but Dr. Stonavich didn't seem interested in any of that. She seemed more interested in touching every bone and muscle on my body. I wondered how much longer I would be able to see them all so clearly. I wished they could stay like that forever.

"Everything looks fantastic. You have grown into such a young man. I remember your mother bringing you in when you were just a baby," she laughed, focusing her eyes on my hips. "What was that, fifteen years ago? You have gotten so tall, Christopher, and yet...," she paused a moment, again touching my dry, lifeless body, "and yet...you are so *skinny*. Please excuse my cold hands."

All I wanted to do was put my clothes back on and run out of the room into my mother's arms. I felt like crying.

It felt like an eternity had gone by since I entered the exam room. I finally stood up as she now wished to examine my spine, my eyes, and my ability to walk in a straight line across the floor. As I returned to where she was standing, she grabbed a few pamphlets from her desk and a pair of clear latex gloves.

"Christopher, I need you to be completely honest with me, alright?" she said, looking at me with her tired, grim eyes. She pulled her chair over to where I was standing and sat down right in front of me. "Are you having any trouble with anything down *there?* Listen, I don't have an answer for why you aren't eating. That's something you're going to have to figure out on your own. I wouldn't want anything hindering your future, though," she said with a wink.

Oh, God. I was used to this question with Dr. Fischer, but I did not think it'd be brought up today. The truth was that I was having some issues down *there*. If Dr. Stonavich didn't understand what an eating disorder was, how on earth was I going to begin explaining a fifteen-year-old boy with a possible case of erectile dysfunction, too? My cheeks must've turned bright red. I hadn't gotten hard in weeks.

"No, not at all," I replied.

Despite my reassurance, Dr. Stonavich slipped on her gloves and pulled down my briefs.

Two weeks passed between my meeting with Dr. Stonavich and my admission to Cherry Oak Hospital. I would be lying if I said I remembered one thing from those fourteen days. The regret my eating disorder made me feel for seeking help was overwhelming. Each day, I battled ideas of somehow taking it all back, of somehow convincing myself and my parents that I no longer needed treatment. I knew it was impossible, but my eating disorder made me feel invincible and in complete control of my life and those around me.

There were days I believed I did not need treatment at all. *My eating disorder was completely fictional. All I had to do was eat, right? Was I just looking for attention? Maybe Dr. Stonavich was right.* It seemed easy to make all sorts of excuses, but who would believe them? My deepest, most obscure secret had been unveiled, and my eating disorder didn't go a day without reminding me.

I became hyperaware of every move I made, especially in front of my family. Were they looking at how much I was eating? Were they critiquing the kind of clothing I was wearing? I became convinced that every action I took would somehow be linked to my eating disorder. It made me want to suppress the things I was feeling even more. Part of me was slightly relieved that those around me knew what I was going through, but an even bigger part of me wished they didn't.

I had gone years without a single person questioning my relationship with food. Sure, I was a picky eater. My family knew that. It never translated as something more. My picky eating was just me being me—nothing more, nothing less. However, in my eyes, it was the only thing that provided my life with any potential value and meaning. It made my life worth living. Having the ability to restrict was something I'd glean over. There was no better feeling than that sense of control. It was what I lived for. Seeking recovery meant that I had pushed all of that aside, including the only identity I had come to accept.

January 30, 2014

Dear ▮▮▮

Thank you for referring Christopher Jane to the Eating Disorders Program, here at ▮▮▮ We appreciate your confidence in our program.

His treatment team during her stay includes:

Primary Therapist: ▮▮▮ LSW
Psychiatrist: ▮▮▮ MD
Nutritionist: ▮▮▮ RD

We look forward to our continued working relationship, and ask that you contact us directly if you have any questions or concerns. Thank you again for your trust and support of our program.

Sincerely,

▮▮▮ MD
Psychiatrist

▮▮▮ LSW
Therapist

Tuesday, January 28, 2014
DAY 1 OF RECOVERY

You lose all concept of time. Days cease to be defined by the ticking hands of a clock or the rising and setting of the sun. Days lose their structure, so much so that waking up and going to bed blend into one continuous stretch. If luck is on your side, you wake up already halfway through the day. You remind yourself that each hour spent asleep is one less hour tethered to the relentless cycle of your eating disorder.

Each day unfolds as a series of blurred scenes, a hazy montage of moments that bare little resemblance to how life used to be—how life *should* be. Your life is now primarily spent resisting any feeling other than regret. That regret, of course, comes only when you consume something you aren't supposed to. *That's* when your day ends.

From there, you are given a choice to make. Are the feelings of regret worth it? Is that regret, in any way, justifiable? The answer is almost never, but you can try. You can fast for the next forty-eight hours to purge every nutrient you placed into your body. You can exercise from night until dawn, praying your parents don't awaken by the nonstop creaking of the wooden floors in your bedroom. If you're feeling up to it, you can trace the middle of your tongue to the back of your throat with your favorite toothbrush until what you ate is laid out in front of you like dog food.

But what's the point? Your day is already over. Tomorrow will be different. That's what you keep telling yourself. *Tomorrow will be different.* It will all be worth it.

You think you have control. You think you have a say in the thoughts that pass in and out of your head. You think you have the ability to overcome every urge and every feeling that sweeps your mind.

You think you have control.

You don't have control.

It has control.

I refuse to look up at the walls. They make me sick. Any indication that a light blue and sea green colored room will somehow soothe the thoughts reeling through my brain makes looking at them even worse. I feel everything and nothing at once, like someone drained every emotion from my brain but left its shell. Every minute I am here hurts. Every minute I am here places me at odds with the crippling voices in my head, telling me it is all a dream. Every minute I am here makes me regret my decision to begin recovery.

This is what I wanted. That's what I keep telling myself. Nobody forced me to be here. Nobody even *knew*. I walked through the doors of Cherry Oak Hospital on my own terms. I am beginning to think that was the worst decision of my life. I could have kept going. I could have kept it all a secret. I could have reached my goal weight within weeks, maybe days. *What have I gotten myself into?*

I wasn't supposed to make it this far. Countless people have told me that today. It didn't scare me, though. Death never scared me.

Yet, here I am, sitting in a hospital room with nothing but two beds, two chairs, and a dresser beside me. It's bigger than I had thought. I have a large window to the left of my bed lined with crossbars and locks, and there is an empty bed a few feet from mine that I am guessing is for my roommate. I have yet to meet him. We also have a small bathroom in our room, which is currently locked. Most impressively, there are at least two cameras in the corners of the room staring at me blank in the face.

It was only yesterday that I found out I would be admitted to Cherry Oak Hospital. It was around 6:00 PM when my mom and I got a call from my dad. He had been on the phone with the hospital and they wanted me to come in the following day for an evaluation, but to be packed and prepared for admission. Everything after that happened quickly.

"For how long should I pack for?"

My parents looked at one another.

"Oh, I don't know," my mom began slowly. "A few days? I can always bring over a few more socks and pairs of underwear for you if you need them."

My dad looked at me with an expression I couldn't quite read. He was either angry, confused, or had just encountered a ghost. "Yeah, Christopher, I wouldn't go too crazy," he said. He always called me by my full name.

I packed a duffel bag with a few sweaters, some of my favorite books and magazines, my iPod, and a few toiletries. I left my room not knowing when I'd see it again.

The hospital is about an hour away from my house, and I slept the entire ride here. It terrified me to look outside the window. I felt like a prisoner. I had no idea what kind of person I would be the next time I stepped foot into that car. The idea made me nauseous.

Once we arrived at the hospital, I checked in and immediately underwent another physical exam, two rounds of blood tests, and an EKG. I was interviewed by four different people, all of whom asked me different types of questions about why I felt like I needed treatment. The questions focused on my mental state, what I had been eating, how my digestive system was working, and so on. Here are some of my favorites:

"Why did it take you so long to start recovery?"

Because I didn't fucking want to. Who fucking wants to? Why the fuck am I here? I want to fucking die.

"I don't know," I said.

"When do you think your eating disorder began?"

I don't fucking know. How the fuck do you think I would know that? What do you think I am, some type of psychic?

"I don't know," I said.

"What is the average amount of food that you eat each day?"

Too fucking much.

"A little bit," I said.

"How much do you *want* to weigh?"

Nothing.

"Much less than I am now," I said.

"Are you sexually active?"

Why is this being asked?

"No, no," I replied quickly.

"When is the last time you had a bowel movement?"

"Yesterday."

"How are you pooping if you aren't eating?"

What—do you think people with eating disorders just don't eat at all?

"I don't know," I replied. I felt defeated.

My mom, dad, and I then spent hours waiting in the hospital cafeteria for my admission to be complete. It seemed like forever. I decided to run to the nearest bathroom even though I wasn't convinced I needed to. After ensuring every stall was empty, I walked up to the mirrors above the sink until my nose was practically touching the glass. I stared at myself and wished I could take back everything I had said and done in the last few weeks to get to where I was standing. It was a terrible feeling.

I don't know who I am without my eating disorder. Looking at myself in the mirror, I saw a stranger.

It was around 3:00 PM when someone from the eating disorder unit came to the cafeteria to bring me upstairs. I had just received a text message from my best friend, Ashley. School let out.

hey, y werent u in school today? missed u! <3

I felt terrible. I hadn't told anyone—not even my best friend—where I was or what was going on. As close as Ashley and I are, I don't think she has a clue that I've been struggling. During the short ride up the elevator, I typed a mile a minute, trying to explain to her what was happening. I knew I could trust Ashley. We had been friends for almost two years. She wasn't just a friend. She was more than that. Whether we chatted every day or once a month, nothing changed between us. We even had a little fling during our freshman year of high school. I still have a bit of a crush on her now. I knew she wouldn't tell a soul where I was.

Before I knew it, the words on the door in front of me read:

EATING DISORDER UNIT
AUTHORIZED PERSONNEL ONLY
CLOSE DOOR AT ALL TIMES
ALARM WILL RING

The same person who escorted me up to the unit snatched my phone from my hand.

"Hey!" I shouted. My voice echoed down the hall behind me.

"Sorry. No phones allowed beyond this point," the woman bluntly responded. She opened the heavy door and immediately brought me behind the nurse's station where I had to undress, get weighed in, and declare any and all items I was carrying. I was given a discharge weight that was nearly sixty pounds heavier than what I am right now. My stomach dropped to the floor. The number almost didn't register in my brain.

She tossed me a packet of papers that appeared to be menus. Except, they looked nothing like menus. There were lists and lists of food items with random numbers and letters next to them. The writing almost looked like another language.

"Fill these out," she said under her breath.

"What exactly are these? What do all these numbers mean?" I asked in a panicked state. I hadn't even gotten the chance to sit down.

"Just pick what you want for dinner. For tomorrow, too. Your dietitian will go over this in detail when you meet her."

"When will that be?" I asked. *Dietitian? I have a dietitian?*

"Soon," the nurse spat. "Probably around the same time you meet your doctor and therapist. They will be sure to go over more of the logistics regarding your weight and what is expected of you while here."

I quickly circled a few things on the menu as the nurse dumped out my duffel bag on her desk. As my items were searched, a different nurse handed me a blue binder filled with hundreds of papers. I was to refer to it if I had any questions about *anything* on the unit. My daily schedule would be in there, along with nutritional information, worksheets, poems, and a whole bunch of articles filled with information about eating disorders. Every rule and guideline for patients is also thoroughly outlined in the binder. I will be sure to go over some of those gems later.

AFTER WHAT FELT LIKE YEARS, I was assigned a room. The unit has six altogether, meaning only twelve patients can live on the unit at one time. My room is at the end of the main hallway, meaning I am farthest from any exit. I'm unsure if that was a strategic move on their part, but I don't mind it. A few nurses did warn me about spending the majority of my free time in my room. Doing so can be seen as me isolating myself.

The toughest part of my day so far has been saying goodbye to my parents. They were forced to leave while I was being given a small tour of the unit. My mom left a note on my bed saying that she and my dad would be back to visit me tonight during visiting hours. Seeing her handwriting alone made me want to cry.

My first meal on the unit wasn't any less strange than I had imagined. Instead of lying in bed watching shitty movies and having meals brought in to you on a tray, like I'd expect in a hospital, every patient on the unit meets in a room called the multipurpose room. It is located right smack in the middle of the unit, about three or four doors away from my room. Upon entering the multipurpose room, you are greeted with a large, rectangular table with fourteen seats. At the ends of the table, there are larger, more comfortable chairs for the nurses who supervise the meal. Their eyes watch you the entire time, and their hands are busy taking notes.

There was a poster on the wall that caught my eye. "Restricted Ritualistic Behaviors" it read, and it was a list of disordered actions one may not do while eating. I jotted down just a *few* of my favorites:

- Over-cutting food into smaller than bite-size pieces
- Picking, playing with, or mixing food in an excessive fashion
- Eating specific food items in a set pattern
- Excessively organizing tray and plate of food
- Deliberately dropping food onto the floor in an attempt to not eat a specific food
- Eating unnaturally slow and in small bites
- Sipping water in between each bite of food
- Intensely staring at another patient's tray of food
- Over-stirring
- Hiding food in napkin or pockets

Do you think those are bad? Little did I know there was an entire set of mealtime guidelines we had to follow that were listed only a few posters down. These guidelines are also outlined in the binder they gave me.

Mealtime Rules & Guidelines

- Mealtime lasts for forty-five minutes. You are not permitted to stand up or leave the dining hall during mealtime.
- It is encouraged that you complete each item on your tray, as previously discussed with your dietitian.
- Each day, you may save up to two (2) food items throughout your three meals—excluding entrees—to eat during designated snack times throughout the day. These snack times are at 11 am and 9 pm. Those above a 2,950 caloric intake may save up to three (3) food items.
- No food or snack is to be taken outside of the dining hall.
- You are encouraged to engage in conversation during meals. Topics must not include anything having to do with weight, food, calories, or numbers.
- You are not permitted to watch television during mealtime. Hospital-approved music is allowed to be played at minimal volume.
- You are allowed to use the microwave once per meal for thirty seconds. This must be done before sitting down at the dining table.
- Do not microwave foods that are meant to be eaten cold. Only microwave foods meant to be eaten warm.
- You are not permitted to fill your water cups during meals. This must be done before mealtime.
- Bagels, sandwiches, apples, pizza, and chicken fingers are to be eaten with your hands. No utensils allowed.
- No blotting pizza with a napkin.
- No mixing different foods together, except: yogurt and bowl of cereal, yogurt and cottage cheese, cottage cheese and any fruit, except oranges, apples, and

grapes, oatmeal and one (1) packet of sugar or honey, and peanut butter on apples, cut in fours
- You can have one (1) cup of coffee or tea during your 9 pm snack time <u>only if</u> all meals were complete for the day.
- It is required that you finish the coffee or tea <u>only if</u> milk is added.
- Lactaid will only be given to patients who experience lactose intolerance.
- No heated, plain water.
- All sandwiches must include two (2) pieces of bread and may only be cut in half. You may not remove any crusts. Cream cheese may not be added to sandwiches. Salad dressings may not be added to sandwiches. Pieces of bread may not be toasted. No condiments are allowed on top of the sandwich. All condiments must be between two (2) pieces of bread and ordered before mealtime during meal planning group. They cannot be added by staff or requested during mealtime.
- No ketchup is to be added on chicken breast. Only honey mustard and barbecue sauce are permitted.
- Only one (1) salt condiment per meal. This includes salt packets, ketchup, and mustard.
- No jelly or mustard in cottage cheese.
- No condiment can be "saved" except jelly. All condiments must be completed if opened and ordered during meal planning.
- No "dunking" foods in any condiment, except: carrots in salad dressing, french fries in honey mustard or barbecue sauce, and chicken fingers in honey mustard or barbecue sauce
- No more than three (3) bowls of cereal per day. Granola is only allowed twice.
- Cereal must be eaten in milk or supplement drink.

- Chickpeas cannot be eaten alone. They must be eaten with salad, rice, or vegetable stir fry.
- Salads must be completed only if salad dressing has been used. No more than two (2) dressing packets per salad. No mixing salad dressings. No leftover dressing must remain in the salad container.
- <u>If meals are completed for the entire day,</u> you may order two (2) extras to eat during your 9:00 pm snack. These may include chocolate cake, carrot cake, vanilla cake, apples, oranges, yogurts, etc. No strange combinations.
- Extras do not have to be completed.

I COULD GO ON, but I think I've made my point.

It was strange reading all the rules. For a place that's supposed to kick you out of all your bad eating habits, it sure does seem to promote a list of its own. *No jelly or mustard in cottage cheese.* What the actual fuck? Trust me, I wasn't planning on mixing those items anyway.

When I was admitted, I was required to fill out menus for breakfast, lunch, and dinner for the upcoming three days. I was also assigned a caloric intake of a number that is still considered a "starvation diet." I almost laughed when I heard that. Every food item is characterized by how many starches, proteins, fats, milks, vegetables, and fruits it contains, and, depending on your caloric intake, there is a certain number of each category you have to fulfill. For example, I was required to have one fruit along with my dinner—macaroni and cheese—which I believe only counted for two proteins.

Panic ran through my body as I walked into the multipurpose room for that first meal. I was so distracted by, well, *everything,* that I acted too slowly to sit in any other chair than the one directly next to a nurse.

"Ah, smart choice," she whispered over to me in a sarcastic

tone. She immediately jotted something down in the notebook she was holding. I pretended not to notice.

"Hi," I said, giving her a quick smile.

"Mhmm."

I almost tripped over the leg of my chair as I sat down. Nobody seemed to notice. I looked around and saw every patient sitting with their heads down and eyes glued to the table. It felt like I was in a dream. Did anybody even notice I was there?

I quickly came to terms with the fact that this would be one of the most difficult meals of my life. The lights above me seemingly pointed directly at me, and I began to sweat almost instantly. I could feel the eyes of the nurse glazing over me. I tried to control my breathing as I peered around the room. Everybody had a cup of water. *Where do I get a cup of water?* I was so thirsty.

Moments later, everybody straightened up in their seats. We began to hear what sounded like one of those wonky box televisions your teacher rolls into your classroom on the day of a class party. What entered the room, however, was far less exciting. It was a blue, seven-foot-tall cart that housed the food trays of every patient.

"Let's get this shit over with," one woman at the end of the table called out. A few others snickered around her as a line began to form in the front of the room.

I stood up and walked around the table so I'd be last in line. Groans came from each patient's mouth as they found their tray on the cart. Some trays looked fuller than others. Some trays looked *a lot* fuller than others. I saw cartons of milk, slices of pizza, all different types of fruit, and supplement drinks cluttering nearly every tray. My eyes glanced at the bottom of the cart, where I saw my name written on one of the trays. Covering half of my name was what appeared to be a bowl of macaroni and cheese. I grabbed my tray and ran back to my seat.

The macaroni was cold, and the cheese was so runny that it

looked like someone had dumped a cup of water on my plate. Even microwavable macaroni and cheese looked better than what they gave me. Without giving it much thought, I began to fork each piece of macaroni into my mouth.

I kept to myself. The only noises I paid attention to were the gentle scraping of my fork on my plate and the unfortunate choice of a Nickelback album that played on a speaker in the corner of the room.

I was able to meet some of the other patients. I can barely remember anyone's name, but I will attempt to describe some of them to you. There are only eight patients currently on the unit, me being the ninth. One girl's name is Liz. Apparently, she is having a lot of trouble with her mother. She was the first to greet me when I walked onto the unit. A nearby nurse warned me not to take her welcome too warmly. Liz had a past of violent behavior toward staff and other patients and rotated from the eating disorder unit to the general psych ward every other week.

Another girl introduced herself to me as a former Breatharian. She described it as a more cosmic, spiritual way of eating. She claimed that she learned about the diet in a theology course she took in college and has since received all of her food and energy from the sun.

"I've never heard of that before. Which religion practices it?" I asked her.

"Oh, honey, I don't have a clue," she chuckled and rolled her eyes. She inched closer to me and whispered in my ear, "Do you know how many times I would go to a McDonald's and do nothing but sit and breathe?"

For some reason, that sounded worse to me than eating the actual food.

Then, there is my roommate, David. Oddly enough, he is really cute, and I think we are the same age. He has medium-length, curly black hair, which was mostly hidden underneath a knitted black beanie. His circular glasses kept getting caught on it during dinner. It was pretty funny. We have not been given much of an opportunity to talk yet, and I feel both nervous and excited to get to know him. I have never shared a room with someone before, and I hope that we connect well.

Many of the other patients looked too intimidating to talk to. One of the older ones kept giving me strange looks from across the table. Others didn't even acknowledge that I was there.

Once everybody finished with their meals, we had to go around the table and say whether we completed our meal or not. In response, everybody else had to either shout "good job" or "good try," depending on whether or not the person finished. It took me a while to catch on to this. No one exactly told me that was a thing we do.

As it was nearing my turn, I noticed everybody's plate was wiped clean. Every supplement drink was empty, every bowl was bare, and there wasn't a piece of food left in sight. Except, of course, for some of my macaroni and cheese. I laughed to myself. *How could I be so naive?* It was then that I realized that completing and eating my meals was the only way I would ever get out of here. I quickly demolished whatever was left of my macaroni. I would say I am proud of myself, but my stomach is telling me otherwise.

"Complete," I announced once it got to my turn. Those around me smiled and clapped their hands together.

After that, I walked all the way back to my room, which is where I am sitting now. I still cannot wrap my head around the fact that I am here. I feel so exhausted and drained, and I could really go for a diet soda. My bed feels like cardboard, and I swear the pillows are stuffed with those Styrofoam peanuts people use to ship something fragile. Everything else feels like nothingness.

<u>*8:35 PM*</u>

It is soon snack time on the unit. Basically, with every meal, you have the option to save either one of your fruits, milks, or cakes (every Tuesday and Thursday—yum) for a later time that day. There are two snack times throughout the day—one between breakfast and lunch and one at night after all meals and groups. I can't remember if I saved anything, so I will go just in case.

9:50 PM

I have nearly finished my first full day here. It was difficult, to say the least. This morning feels like weeks ago, and I know my time here will only become more challenging. I have not even met my assigned therapist, dietitian, or doctor yet.

I am currently sitting in the multipurpose room watching *The Big Bang Theory*. I bet my mom is watching this right now. I bet she is alone. That makes me sad.

Speaking of my mom, she and my dad came all the way back to the hospital during visiting hours. It was a little awkward with my dad there. We've never had the closest relationship, and for him to be this aware of everything I have been dealing with is strange. I don't know. Hopefully, tomorrow will be better. They told me they would visit me every day, which I suppose should make me happy. I haven't decided yet.

The bathroom in my room is locked practically throughout the entire day. We have to ask a nurse to open it for us, and we are not permitted to flush the toilet or wash our hands until our toilet is thoroughly inspected. The "DO NOT FLUSH" sign right above the toilet is the perfect touch to the room.

It's getting late. I find myself overthinking more and more as each hour passes. I am used to the last thoughts in my head for the day being ones of self-loathing and fear. It seems those feelings have only grown stronger. I can't help but think about how the next time I step outside, I will be a whole sixty pounds heavier. I don't even know how to process that. I love being thin. I have always been thin. I've been underweight even when my eating was not so disordered. But was it? Maybe I have been under-eating my whole life. Maybe I have never actually eaten the recommended amount of food for someone my age. Maybe it is not just that I was always a picky eater, but always had some subconscious fear of food? That would explain just about everything. I am sure my therapist—who I meet tomorrow—will have something to say about that.

Wednesday, January 29, 2014
DAY 2 OF RECOVERY

<u>8:50 AM</u>

I survived my first night. It was difficult. The sleeping schedule here is strict. Every patient must have their lights off by eleven. A nurse even comes by every hour during the night to make sure we are asleep. I only know this because I woke up several times to a flashlight shining in my face. They weren't even shy about it.

What the night nurses didn't know was that my roommate, David, and I stayed up until nearly two in the morning. I can't put into words how nervous I was to have a roommate. Everything about sharing a room with another person made me uncomfortable. However, everything about David made me feel the opposite. We both laid in our beds in the pitch dark and told each other so much. I felt a connection to him that I had never felt with anyone before. Part of me never believed I would meet another boy who suffered from an eating disorder. The best part of our conversation was when we were waiting for the night nurse to enter our room while we pretended to be asleep. We burst into tears of laughter whenever she left.

"Is she gone?" I whispered just loud enough so David could

hear me. The door was shut, but light still peered in through the hallway. David laughed.

"I think so," he whispered back. "I wish she would take that flashlight and shove it up her ass."

We both started laughing. That, itself, was one of the greatest feelings in the world. David and I had only just met, but we were talking and joking with each other like friends at a middle school sleepover.

"This is all so crazy," I said to him. "I mean, what do they think we're doing in here? Is it really necessary to check on us so often?"

"I told you, Chris. I've been here a few times. You wouldn't believe the things people do," David replied. I heard him turn over and lay on his back.

"Like what?"

"Most of the time, it was just exercise. Finding any possible way to burn a calorie or two. Sit-ups, jogging, jumping jacks—anything that doesn't make the floor creak too much," David paused a moment and laughed. "Besides that, you got the real freaks."

"Were you one of those people?"

David sat up in his bed. "What—the kind of person to have sex in a hospital?" We immediately burst into laughter. I looked over at him and put my hand over my mouth to keep myself from making too much noise. *Do people really do that in here?*

"I mean, you wouldn't be able to tell if someone had been knocked up," David continued. "Those meals they give us make us all look at least six months pregnant."

We laughed again until there was a pause.

"David, I'm not ready for this," I said out loud. I looked for more words to say, but nothing came out of my mouth.

"I don't think anyone truly is," David slowly responded, "but don't worry. We are all in this together. And we have each other."

His words comforted me.

"And besides—when you leave this place, you could just lose

all the weight over again," David said as he turned over in his bed.

I didn't respond.

At that moment, our door creaked open again. A light shined into our room, signaling the return of the night nurse doing another round. When she left, David and I finally dozed off.

I was officially woken up today at 5:30 in the morning when a nurse came in to check my vitals. From there, I walked across the hall to an office where I had to undress, put on a robe, wait in line behind the other patients, and get weighed in. This will be my daily routine for as long as I am here. Wait, I forgot the best part—I was forced to use the bathroom attached to the office before I was weighed. And yes, the toilet was checked. I think I may have weighed a little less than yesterday, but I wasn't told. I did not drink anything with my dinner last night. I was so afraid to fill up my cup with water because, apparently, doing that too much can be considered an eating-disordered behavior. Besides, I didn't even know where the water fountain was until David showed me.

I then took a shower in the most awful shower I have ever been in. It was in a room by itself near the nurse's station. It was literally just a room with a shower. The room was so small I could barely move to wash myself. Clumps of hair and gum clogged the drain so badly there was an inch of water pooling at my feet. It was a good thing I brought sandals with me. Thank you, mom.

Today for breakfast, I had vanilla yogurt, a blueberry muffin, coffee, and some chunks of pineapple.

Mornings were always my favorite time of the day. They were perfect for body checking. I'd use my hands as measuring tape and make sure that no area of my body was taking up more space than it did the day prior. I'm going to try my hardest not to do anything like that in here, but I'm sure it'll be hard.

Right after breakfast, any students on the unit have an hour to meet with tutors and get some schoolwork done. I was told that my school had been contacted and would be sending out work as soon as they had the chance. I must be putting my guidance office through hell. It almost makes me laugh. My counselor was never the nicest to me, so I don't mind. I do not have any assignments yet, so one of the tutors told me to either read a book or write, which is what I am doing now. I wish I could go to my room and take a nap. That is the only thing I'd like to do besides go home.

9:45 AM

Still in school. There are about fifteen minutes left.

One of the older patients just came in and sat down at the computer in the way back of the room. I would not have even seen it if I wasn't told it was there. It is only supposed to be used by patients without a laptop for mandatory school assignments, but she totally just checked her email. What does she have to lose? This is the same patient who kept glaring at me last night at dinner. I think she is leaving today.

Word travels fast around this little unit. As one patient leaves, another is rumored to come in. Maybe it is the girl I met in the parking lot elevator yesterday. We exchanged a few glances, and I could tell just by the way she was acting that she was there for the same reason as me. Her shoulders were slumped, and her eyes felt dim. Ironically enough, we went through the whole evaluation process together but split up when I was brought to the unit and she was not. I wonder what happened to her.

I have my first group psychotherapy session very soon. It's actually my first group therapy session I will be a part of at all. Am I supposed to know what that entails? The daily schedule I was given yesterday is enough to make even the brightest person's head spin. What does psychotherapy even mean? Am I spelling it correctly?

11:05 AM

I am guessing each psychotherapy session will be different, considering there is no actual structure to the group. In other words, if something is on your mind, you say it. Other patients may chime in and offer advice, and the doctor or nurse proctoring the meeting usually stays out of it unless minutes go by without any sharing. I was way too nervous to say anything just yet. I was told that I needed to change that and learn to express myself better. I bet I will be hearing that an awful lot here.

David started the conversation by opening up a bit about his sexuality. It is something he has struggled with for most of his life, and he linked many of his current issues around food to the insecurities he has dealt with for a long time. Being gay, he said he always felt pressured to look a certain way and fit a certain mold. He shared his hope that society will soon become inclusive to all members of the gay community, not just the ones who fit a physical stereotype. I felt the urge to chime in, but I was too afraid. My face would've turned bright red.

Another patient opened up about how miserable she felt about herself after catching her husband sleeping with another woman. It was ultimately the reason why she ended up here. She spent the entirety of the group in tears.

Other than that, I didn't learn much about the other patients. Most of them kept quiet or only spoke a few words when called upon. Much of the hour was spent listening to some of the newer patients, like me, describe how they are adjusting to life on the unit and how challenging the meals have been. I'd be lying if I said I didn't almost doze off a couple of times.

Afterward, I was given a few minutes to chat with my assigned doctor. His name is Burton. Well, that is his last name, at least. Everybody just calls him Burton. He reminds me of my doctor at home, Dr. Fischer, but a lot older. He is tall, wore gray slacks just long enough to cover his ankles and a long, almost grim smile from ear to ear. Okay, he doesn't remind me of Dr. Fischer at all. Any doctor other than Dr. Stonavich is a win in my book, though.

We met in the same room that I was weighed in this morning. I hardly noticed because I was half asleep. I was much more awake now. I sat across from him as he made himself comfortable in his chair, crossing his legs and adjusting his glasses. He spent a few moments looking over some papers before talking to me. It's an uncomfortable feeling I've experienced several times in the past 24 hours—having judgments made about you right in front of your eyes.

"Chris, the good news is that your blood tests from yesterday came back clear," Burton said with a slight flair in his voice. "That's unusual for someone like you. Everything looks good. No problems there."

"Oh, okay," was all I could mutter. I didn't know how to receive his comments.

"You weighed in at—" Burton paused a moment before reading, "the same you weighed in at yesterday. You're not gaining much weight here, Chris," he told me with a sigh.

I thought he was being sarcastic at first.

"It's only my first full day here," I said with a pretend chuckle. Maybe that was just his sense of humor.

"Still, we like to see some improvement in your physical state," he replied, looking down again at his notes. "We'd really like to see you start to gain some weight. Where your weight is now," Burton said, looking at me, "...is dangerously low. Especially for a boy your size."

My size?

"I'll be monitoring your weight carefully, Chris. We'll take it day by day," he said. Burton uncrossed his legs and leaned his arms onto his knees. "I just want you to remember the impact that every action you make from here on out has on your body. Your body is weak, and it will soon begin trying to rebuild itself."

"I know."

"And now that we have begun the refeeding process, your metabolism is going to go haywire. If it were up to me, I'd have you lying in bed all day!" Burton laughed.

Honestly, that didn't sound like the worst thing in the world.

2:50 PM

I only have ten minutes until my first Relapse Prevention group, so I will make this quick. I just met with my therapist, Connor, for the first time. He is no Cori, but nevertheless, he is very nice. He's young, probably in his thirties, and has short, curly, brown hair. I hate myself for saying what I am about to say: he is pretty cute. *Did I just admit that I find my therapist cute?* He introduced himself to me as I was lying in bed after lunch. He even gave me the option of staying there throughout our session, but I figured that wouldn't give the best first impression. I eventually sat up, and we began talking. I believe there are three or four therapists here on the unit, but I am glad I was assigned to Connor. The other ones I've seen walking around don't seem as friendly.

I suppose the first meeting with your therapist is almost guaranteed to be the most difficult. I wish I could have just pressed play on a movie and let Connor watch the last few years of my life unfold without having to address it verbally. My meeting with Cori was more eating disorder and treatment focused. This meeting with Connor more so set the tone for how therapy here is going to go. Instead of repeating my disordered thoughts and explaining how I coped with them in the past, he said we would dig to the root of the problem: why those thoughts happen in the first place. He noted our sessions are meant to be tough, and if I hated him after every single one, it would mean they were working. However, we kept it minimal for today. I opened up to him about Oliver, my not-so-ex-boyfriend, and how everything in my life kind of spiraled after *that* whole experience. I am not sure he understood anything I was saying. I always get tense when I bring up my sexuality. I try so hard not to make it a big deal, but I can tell it is something I will have to revisit.

Excluding weekends, I will be seeing Connor every day. I think we will get along, though I am sure some of our sessions are bound to make my head explode. I'm looking forward to what we will talk about in the future. Today purely felt like an introduction to the introduction.

Connor also ran Art Therapy today. The entire unit met in the multipurpose room, and our theme for the day was forgiveness. Our assignment was to create a piece of art that symbolized whatever was on our minds when we thought about forgiveness. One girl drew a sunflower, with each petal collaged with different words. A different patient drew a picture of her mother and shared that she hopes her family will forgive the years and years of pain that her eating disorder had caused. I sat for a while before drawing even a single line on my paper. I eventually decided on a large, green alien face that took up almost the entire page. David thought it was the stupidest thing he had ever seen. Oliver had a thing for aliens.

My stomach is in so much pain right now. My lunch was the biggest lunch any human has ever eaten. Silly me chose the tofu stir fry, thinking it would be light and airy, considering the entire meal counted as only two vegetables on my meal plan. I feel like I ate an entire garden—soil and all. Along with that, I was served a blueberry yogurt and more pineapple. I do not think I will ever eat pineapple again in the future. Things taste so much worse when being shoved down your throat.

4:05 PM

Is it seriously four o'clock already? Some group sessions go by so much quicker than others. One day soon, I'll have to go over all the different ones we have throughout the day. There are so many, but they do rotate. We don't have every single one every single day. We just wrapped up Relapse Prevention. We talked about our mission statements—? Yeah, I don't know, either. I tuned out about halfway through. My only mission is to gain enough weight to get myself out of here as quickly as possible.

6:25 PM

Dinner is complete! It was not so bad. However, grilled cheese does not sit too well with a third bowl of pineapple. Halfway through our meal, we were all introduced to two new patients. The girl, Jodi, looks to be about my age and reminds me a lot of my sister. Her black hair is chopped below her shoulders, and she looks like someone you'd meet strolling down an artsy street in lower Manhattan. The boy, Emmanuel, reminds me of somebody I'd see on one of those old western television shows my father watches. The bowl-cut hairstyle did the trick. I think he is around my age, too. Neither of them spoke or completed their meal.

10:20 PM

I forgot to mention that I also met with my nutritionist, Stacy, for the first time today. She has short, blonde hair and wears large, oval-shaped glasses. She looks like a character from some Disney movie, but I cannot put my finger on who. I'm getting Edna from *The Incredibles* vibes. Rumor has it she used to be a patient here a few years back. I sort of got the feeling just by talking with her. Either that or she just naturally knew all the right questions to ask.

"Was there a set time in the day that you believed you should stop eating?"

"Around six o'clock," I gulped. Actually, it was four o'clock. I read on the Internet once that after that time, your body begins to shut down for the day and gets prepared to go to sleep.

"Let me guess," Stacy said with a smile, "you read that on the Internet somewhere."

I nodded.

"Your body is constantly burning calories, Chris. Even when you are sleeping," she told me. "Anything that tells you otherwise is complete nonsense."

What I liked about Stacy was that she was very soft-spoken. She seemed compassionate and empathetic. She looked like she knew what I was about to say before I said it myself. It's what I liked about Stacy that also made me increasingly uncomfortable.

"Let's talk about what you *do* eat," Stacy began. "Many people have what we call safe foods and fear foods. They're pretty self-explanatory. Safe foods are food items you eat reasonably normally. Fear foods, for whatever reason, are quite the opposite," she said while looking around the room and making motions with her hands. "Fear foods aren't necessarily bad foods. Perhaps, you associate the food item with a particular memory that triggers some type of negative feeling for you, and if you eat the food, you feel like it is the end of the world," she said, expanding her hands around her head to mimic an explosion.

"I kind of feel that way for all food," I said. I couldn't think of any specifics.

"Yeah, that's what some people say at first. It could be difficult to recognize these foods in the beginning," Stacy said. "Are you vegetarian? Vegan? I didn't notice much meat on your menus."

"I'm vegetarian," I said. "Well, I've been eating vegan for the past few weeks, but I don't plan on continuing that in here."

"You know, many people with eating disorders use veganism as a way to disguise their disordered eating," she said with a sly grin on her face.

"Yeah, that's why I'm not doing that anymore," I told her, "but I want to remain a vegetarian."

"Why is that?"

"I don't really like the taste of meat," I told her. "I never did. I haven't eaten meat since I was eleven, I think."

"Are you sure?" Stacy smiled again. My eyes began to burn.

"I mean, my sister is a vegetarian, so I was kind of inspired by her to make the leap," I said. "But no, I never much liked the taste."

Stacy let out a sigh and took a moment before answering me.

"Well, that's fine. I'm sure we will dive deeper into that topic another time," she said. "You will have to be okay with the fact that your meals will appear larger than everyone else's. You'll have to eat more to match the caloric density of meat products."

"That's fine."

I was nearly sweating after that conversation. Finally, Stacy was curious to know what my ultimate goal weight had been. I told her, though I wasn't sure it was even possible given my age and height. Stacy laughed, which translated in my mind as, "*Of course* it was possible, but you were too much of a failure to obtain it."

Stacy ended our session by letting me know that my caloric intake would increase soon.

Inpatient Grou[p]

	Monday	Tuesday	Wednesday	Th[ursday]
6:30-7:30am	Morning Care	Morning Care	Morning Care	Mornin[g]
7:30-8:30am	Breakfast	Breakfast	Breakfast	Breakfa[st]
8:30-10:00am	Free Time\School	Free Time\School	Free Time\School	Free Ti[me]
10:00-11:00am	Psychotherapy	Psychotherapy	Psychotherapy	Psycho[therapy]
11:00-11:30am	Free Time\Snack	Free Time\Snack	Free Time\Snack	Free Ti[me]
11:30-12:30pm	Meal Planning	Nutrition	Meal Planning	Nutritio[n]
12:30-1:30pm	Lunch	Lunch	Lunch	Lunch
1:30-2:30pm	Journaling	Nursing ED	Art Therapy	OT
2:30-3:00pm	Free Time	Free Time	Free Time	Free Ti[me]
3:00-4:00pm	Relapse Prev.	OT	Relapse Prevention	Body I[mage]
4:00-5:30pm	Free Time\Snack	Free Time\Snack	Free Time\Snack	Free Ti[me]
5:30-6:30pm	Dinner	Dinner	Dinner	Dinner
6:30-7:00pm	Goals	Meal Processing	Wrap up	Meal Pr[ocessing]
7:00-8:30pm	Visitation	Visitation	Visitation/Multi Fam	Visitatio[n]
8:30-9:00pm	Free Time	Free Time	Multi Family	Free Ti[me]
9:00-10:00pm	Snack\Meds	Snack\Meds	Snack\Meds	Snack\M[eds]
10:00-11:00pm	Free Time	Free Time	Free Time	Free Ti[me]
11:00pm	Bedtime	Bedtime	Bedtime	Bedtime
12:00am				

p Schedule

ursday	Friday	Saturday	Sunday
g Care	Morning Care	Morning Care	Morning Care
ıst	Breakfast	Breakfast	Breakfast
ne\School	Free Time\School	Community Meeting	Meal Processing
therapy	Psychotherapy	Nursing Education	Nursing Education
ne\Snack	Free Time\Snack	Free Time\Snack	Free Time\Snack
n	Meal Planning	Free Time	Free Time
	Lunch	Lunch	Lunch
	Recreation	Free Time	Free Time
ne	Free Time	Visitation 2pm	Visitation 2pm
age	Meditation 3-3:30	Free Time\Visitation	Free Time\Visitation
ne\Snack	Free Time\Snack	Visitation 5pm	Visitation 5pm
	Dinner	Dinner	Dinner
ocessing	Wrap up	Free Time	Free Time
on	Visitation	Visitation	Visitation
ne	Free Time	Wrap-up	Wrap-up
Meds	Snack\Meds	Snack\Meds	Snack\Meds
ne	Free Time	Free Time	Free Time
e	Bedtime	Free Time	Bedtime
	Bedtime	Bedtime	

Thursday, January 30, 2014
DAY 3 OF RECOVERY

6:30 AM

I am happy to report that for the first time while being here, I slept very well. With that being said, I am still tired. Trying to recover from an eating disorder will do that to you. I have a long day ahead of me, but I am feeling optimistic. I do not have much of a reason to be. I just sat on the toilet for a good twenty minutes, and still—nothing. My legs started to feel tingly after sitting there for so long. I almost fell on my face while standing up.

9:55 AM

This morning's breakfast sucked. Did you know that eating dry cereal is considered a disordered eating behavior? The nurse in the room demanded I empty my carton of milk into my cornflakes. But, get this—all I had was chocolate milk! Now, if eating soggy, chocolate milk-filled cornflakes is not considered an odd eating behavior, I am not quite sure what is. Why should it matter whether I eat the cereal dry or wet? As long as I eat it, who cares? Just one week ago, I wouldn't have even fathomed the idea of eating a single spoonful.

I am only on my third day here, and I am already getting sick and tired of this place. Maybe I'm just ticked off about the cereal, but still. Some of the patients here are getting on my nerves. It constantly feels like each patient is trying to one-up each other. Maybe it is all in my head, but it just feels like a giant competition. Who will not complete their meals today? Who will sit in their chair at breakfast with their legs scrunched up to their chest to appear the smallest? Who will cry today during psychotherapy? Who will resist recovery the most? It's tiring.

10:15 AM

To make matters worse, I just met with Burton. He alerted me that the calorie increase Stacy warned me about yesterday begins today. I am now up another 250 calories. The only way I can seem to cope with such a number is if I make a promise to myself that I will lose every single pound I gain in this place the minute I get discharged. I will finally get to my goal weight. I know I will. I have to.

It was easy for me to say I wanted to recover when I wasn't being force-fed mountains of calories. Now that I am here, I don't want to be here. Instead of constantly contradicting myself, I'll leave it to the simple fact that I don't know what I want anymore.

I had to choose what to add to my meal plan to compensate for my increase. I am trying to stay away from those awful supplemental drinks for as long as I can, so I added a slice of carrot cake to my dinner. I've never had carrot cake before. I'll probably save it for snack time tonight.

I am sure the nurses and doctors here have seen and dealt with everything. Sometimes, I wonder what has been the most ludicrous behavior that a patient has done under their care. I would love to find a way to exercise here. Perhaps I can jog in the bathroom or do some squats in the shower. If I had my room to myself, it'd turn into a gym the moment the lights get turned off. That is, of course, granted that the camera located in the upper corner of our room does not have night vision.

11:10 AM

A patient by the name of Amanda is abruptly leaving today after lunch. She and a few nurses have been on the phone with her insurance company since the end of breakfast. They're refusing to pay for any of her treatment going forward, and she must go home immediately. Hearing that blew my mind, but it is apparently all too common. How crazy is it that some random person in an office somewhere gets to decide when someone is "recovered" enough to be discharged? What exactly are the qualifications? I doubt Amanda, or even any of the doctors here, knows the answer to that.

The new boy, Emmanuel, has come in my room to visit me a few times in the past couple hours. Half of the time, he doesn't even say a word. He walks in, takes a seat next to me on my bed, and just sits there. Sometimes, that is all one needs. I like the company, too. Emmanuel is a lot different than David. He is a lot quieter. You can tell there are a lot of things on his mind. I also don't think this is his first time in treatment for his eating disorder. He told me there had never been another boy on the unit at the same time as him before, and he didn't know how to feel this time when walking onto the unit as the third boy. I'll admit that I was just as surprised.

4:05 PM

Connor gave me an assignment today. He told me to create a timeline of my eating disorder. He wants me to try and pinpoint when I think it first developed and think about what was happening during that time. For me, it is quite simple. Years of bullying throughout middle school will definitely wear down your confidence, and it was then that I unknowingly began restricting what I ate. Doing so wouldn't make me feel good. It felt awful. Yet, anything was better than facing what I was going through head-on. All the names and slurs that were thrown my way couldn't touch me as long as my eating disorder was by my side. Nobody seemed to notice anyway.

My earliest memories of childhood contain some form of bullying in one way or another. It was something that followed me everywhere. Whatever situation I was in, I was a target. It didn't matter if I was at school, an extracurricular activity, or even walking around town. Kids would call me names, throw things at the back of my head during class, spread rumors about me—you name it. Early on, I learned how to make myself the least present wherever I was, and I practically memorized the layout of my elementary school so I knew where to hide and take shortcuts when I felt afraid. My favorite spot was the library. During lunch, I'd sneak off down the hall, through the heavy wooden doors, and into the library. The room was typically pitch black during that time. There were enough aisles of books that one could go unnoticed even if a teacher walked by.

Another one of my favorite hiding spots was the balcony seating area above the gymnasium. I attended a Catholic school, and the rules there were strict. Nobody was ever allowed up on the balcony, even during gym class. It was practically forbidden. There were shelves of trophies, an abandoned snack stand that looked like it hadn't been used since the 1950s, and a single row of blue bleachers that always managed to smell like they were newly painted. Spoiler alert: they weren't.

Middle school was no better. One day, during recess in the seventh grade, a group of boys walked over to where I was sitting. They stood over me, pulled down their pants, and leaned over so each of their crotches was inches away from my face. I looked up and saw a boy that I had once considered a friend now partaking in the very actions he used to defend me against. They danced and laughed until they were finally scared off by a nearby teacher.

Another time, a mass text message was sent to several kids in my class from this one boy about me. The message claimed that I was a "gay faggot who liked it up the butt," along with a list of popular male celebrities with whom I'd want to have sex. The most hurtful part was having kids that I called friends responding to the message with laughter. The message itself was actually sent from my good friend Anthony's phone, but it was signed by someone else. I didn't know what hurt more: the words themselves or the fact that Anthony was now friends with one of my bullies. I remember rushing to show my mom, who then brought them in for my principal to see. When I confronted Anthony about the text message the next day, he laughed and told me it was only a joke.

There were days I felt so scared to attend school that I'd purposely make myself sick or hurt myself so I wouldn't have to go. I became comfortable with the prospect of not having many friends my age. Many adults seemed to like me.

From an early age, I learned that kids were afraid of what they did not know. Any difference from what they were taught as "normal" ignites harsh judgment only thwarted by education, open-mindedness, and tolerance. I didn't grow up as myself. I didn't wear what I wanted to wear. I never played with the toys I wished to. I didn't know a way to express myself without the fear of being judged or bullied by my peers. I grew up conditioning myself to be like those around me, even if that meant casting away any premonition of who I thought I was. That never worked out the way that I would've liked either. The world around me soon caught on to the fact that I was different, and it rarely let me forget.

My eating disorder was there for me when it felt like nobody else was. It provided a shield—a numbness that disabled me from feeling anything but the thoughts of my disorder. I'd become so distracted by how many calories I was eating that the bullying no longer affected me. It was still there, but it hurt less.

Connor also wants me to think and write about one thing I like about myself, excluding my hair and my eyes. That's an answer I'm sure he and every therapist here have heard quite often. I began going down the line of every part of my body that could be a possible choice. My arms? *Too long.* My legs? *Too wide.* My hips? *Uneven and disgusting.* The worst part of all that? Each one of those will only become worse as the days go on.

I chose to write about my height. I figured that it's the only thing that shouldn't change throughout my time here. It is actually something I am very insecure about. Any comment about my height was always followed by a comment about my weight. They both became something I ultimately grew to loathe. However, the part I may leave out to Connor is that it took my eating disorder for me to finally find some comfort in my height. The taller I became, the more distributed my weight became. That held especially valuable whenever I punched my numbers into those silly body mass index calculators you can find on the Internet. My eating disorder sure got a kick out of those.

<u>*8:35 PM*</u>

The only thing that made this day worthwhile was the visit from my mom this afternoon. My mom is my everything, and I truly believe she wants me to recover. I know she wants me to recover. I know she is doing everything she can to better understand what I'm going through.

"You take all the time you need to get through this," she always tells me. "And I will be by your side throughout every minute of it."

I miss her so much. I miss my home so much. I miss my bed so much. All I want to do is go home.

On the bright side, my mom brought me two things from

home. I am sure both could have gotten her into a lot of trouble if she had been caught. The first thing she brought me is one of my favorite stuffed animals that I have had since I was seven years old. His name is Buddy, and he is a brown and white spotted dog. I like to say he is a rescue animal because I purchased him for fifteen cents at a flea market that my grandma's church once held. I was stunned when I learned patients weren't allowed to have any stuffed animals on the unit. Apparently, patients in the past have stuffed them with pills, drugs, and razors. Others would rip them open in the middle of the night and stuff them with food they snuck away from their meals.

The second thing my mom brought me was my cell phone. Under no circumstance is any patient on the unit allowed to have their phone. Visitors aren't even supposed to bring their own on the unit. It is probably one of the strictest rules they have around here.

The Internet is full of triggering things. On almost any social media website, you can find thousands of posts detailing the most effective ways to starve yourself, along with tips on how to divert your appetite and hide disordered behaviors from your family. There are also blogs dedicated to uploading pictures of thin people and chat rooms where you can talk to others who will hold you accountable for every single thing you eat. There are more people running these sites than you'd think, and most disguise their disorder as a lifestyle or a choice. It is sad, disturbing, and fascinating all at the same time. I never became too invested in a community like that. I posted a few triggering photos on my Tumblr account here and there, but I didn't keep up with it as much as my eating disorder would have liked me to. The mere thought of another person being affected by the words I wrote or the photos I took of my body made me hate myself even more. I kept those things to myself.

I didn't ask my mom to bring me my phone to look at any of that. I wanted to check if any of my friends from school had been trying to get in touch with me. Turns out, a lot of them had. Half of the numbers I don't even recognize. A lot of the messages are asking where I am. I know if I told one person where I was, the whole school would find out in a matter of minutes. That is something I am not prepared for.

Friday, January 31, 2014
DAY 4 OF RECOVERY

8:35 AM

Back in the real world, Fridays were always a good thing. They meant you were one day away from the weekend. You could finally rest after making it through the week. Here, the days are the same. If it weren't for the daily doctor visits and constant group meetings throughout the day, I could see myself completely losing track of time.

Today is the first day I have received homework from my school. It feels good getting back into the routine of something familiar. I often find myself imagining my guidance counselor scavenging around my school, looking for work to send me. I do not think she is allowed to tell any of my teachers where I am, but I wonder if she has.

I am confident that the highlight of my day will be the shower I took this morning. There are two showers on the unit, and the one I used today is so much nicer than the one I used my first couple of days. Not only is it cleaner, but the water pressure is better, and there is even an extra room attached that seems almost perfect for exercising. I jogged for a few moments once I got dressed. It was exhilarating. The feeling of my calves burning was something I grew to love. I got worried someone might be able to hear me, but I didn't care. I couldn't stop.

    I jogged and jogged until a sudden wave of sadness rushed over me. My feet clenched. I stopped jogging and looked at the ground in front of me. I thought about all of the patients before me that had been in the same room and how many of them must've gone mad, praying they would not get caught trying to burn a few extra calories. My heart felt heavy. I wanted to comfort that imaginary person and tell them that it was okay, but then I remembered that person was me. I quickly got my things together and walked back to my room.

    If I am lucky, today I will be taken off of Fall Risk! There are three different "phases" at Cherry Oak. They determine your status and certain privileges you receive. For example, if you are on Phase Three, you are allowed two fifteen-minute supervised walks around the entire hospital each day. Each patient begins on Phase One and typically will only stay there for one day. I am waiting for my Phase Three clearance. However, for that to happen, I must be taken off of Fall Risk, though I'm not really sure what it means. I think I have to gain a certain amount of weight, but I could be wrong. David, Emmanuel, and even Jodi are already on Phase Three.

    The number of patients here has declined. Both Liz and the Breatharian I met on my first day were moved to the general psychiatric ward, and a few others seemingly disappeared overnight. I am beginning to adjust to life around here being that there is only a handful of us. I feel like we are beginning to feel like a family.

    I have opened up much more to David in the past few days, continuing our nightly routine of staying up late and chatting in the dark. I told him more about my life back home and found out that he, too, faces some struggles in his family. His mother is very overprotective, and he probably spent a good half-hour explaining the types of church services he and his family attend. It is interesting how each person here has a story that is so drastically different, but we have all been led to the same place. Funny how that works.

"She is super strict with me," David said about his mother. "She watches what I eat, how I dress, and practically what I do every day. Did I tell you that I'm homeschooled?"

"No, I don't think you ever mentioned that," I said.

"Yeah. Have been since I was a kid," he said. "It makes it hard to meet people. Most of my friends are from my church."

"Are you close with them?"

"Yeah. Well, they're all I really have," David replied. He put his head down and began to pick at his fingernails.

"Do they know you're gay?" I asked.

"N-no," he stuttered. "At least, I don't think so."

We locked eyes for a moment and smiled at each other. When I first met David, I got the impression that he was already out. Now that I know more about him, I see why that isn't the case.

"Does anybody in your family know?" I asked.

David shook his head and chuckled.

"Do you know what my mom would do if she found out her only son was gay? I don't think I'd have a place to sleep," he said.

"Has she ever said anything like that to you before?"

"Not exactly," he said, "but she proclaims that all homosexuals are God's test of humanity. Only the ones who seek God and change their ways are worthy of eternal peace," David said in a mocking tone.

"What about the ones who don't?"

"Oh, they just burn in hell."

David slowly looked over at me. His mouth twitched, and he started to laugh. I laughed, too.

"Oh, my God. David," I looked over at him once we had calmed down. "That really fucking sucks. I'm sorry you have to deal with that every day of your life."

He shrugged.

"I'm used to it. I just can't wait to get older and do whatever the fuck I want. Did you know she doesn't even let me wear skinny jeans? She says they're too feminine," David said, rolling his eyes. He looked down at the pants he was wearing. They were a pair of basic denim jeans that looked to be about three sizes too big.

"These make me look so fucking big," he said.

"I struggle finding pants that fit me well, too," I said. "They're either too short, too long, or too baggy...I typically end up buying women's pants for the fit."

"My mom would never allow me to buy women's clothing."

I stood from my bed and walked over to my small dresser where I kept most of my clothes. I reached my hand into the bottom of the second drawer and pulled out a pair of my favorite black skinny jeans.

"Here," I said to David, handing him the pair of pants.

A smile glazed upon David's face.

"You're giving me a pair of your pants? Are you sure?"

"Of course," I said. "They're all yours. I have another pair just like them. I don't need two."

"My mom won't even know they're women's!"

"That's right!"

"Thank you, Chris," David said to me in a softer tone. He stood up, unfolded the pants, and pulled them over his legs.

"They look great," I said, smiling at him.

David ran over to me and gave me a big hug. We aren't allowed to have any personal contact with anyone here, but the hug felt nice. It was something neither of us had felt in a while.

<u>*10:15 AM*</u>

I am already dreaming of the day that I'm granted my first pass. Passes can run for either four or seven hours, and we are obligated to have at least one meal out on our own. It's supposed to test how we will react to food outside of a hospital setting. I suspect it may take a while for me to get one, but it is definitely a motivator for me. Ashley's sweet-sixteen birthday party is on February 15, and being able to attend that would be unreal. I know Burton would be concerned about the amount of physical activity I would do there, but trust me, I am not the dancing type. Seeing my friends for a few hours would be great, even if I just sat at a table eating as much cake as I physically could and praying that my weight doesn't go down.

11:10 AM

Earlier, Stacy told me another calorie increase would kick in today. I wanted to prove to her that I was not afraid of any of the items on the menu, so I let her choose what to add. An hour later, I found out that she had given me more cereal. Seriously? How many boxes of granola could a boy eat? I already had one with breakfast, and I don't think I ordered any milk for dinner. I am going to have to add it to my lunch so I can eat it with my chocolate milk again.

I had the opportunity to talk to the new girl, Jodi, this morning. She stayed in the multipurpose room after breakfast and sat by herself, away from me, David, Emmanuel, and the rest of us. I walked over to her and introduced myself. It was a short conversation, but possibly one of the strangest I've had since coming here. Here's how it went:

"Where do you go to school?" I asked her, trying to make conversation. She took a moment to reply.

"Uh, Stewart Lane Academy." She looked at me with green, bulging eyes.

No way, I thought to myself. I know that place. I mean, I don't know *much* about it, but I know it. Both my sister's best friend and her current boyfriend attend school there. It's more of an alternative school. I think they incorporate group therapy sessions into their school days, but I could be wrong. Whatever the case, it doesn't have the best reputation. I asked Jodi if she recognized the name of my sister's friend or boyfriend. She lit up.

"Oh my God, your sister is Ava?" she asked, practically jumping out of her chair. She leaned over to tell me how commonly my sister is brought up in random conversations among the students. She was practically a celebrity there. Jodi also told me some of the crazy things my sister's boyfriend had done there.

"One time," she started laughing, "he became so angry, he stormed out of the classroom and slammed the door so hard that the clock fell off the wall. The glass shattered into a billion pieces. I thought he was going to knock out our teacher!"

Yup, that sounded about right.

"Another time," she continued, "he got caught having sex with a girl in the backseat of his Jeep. Well, you know, *allegedly*."

"Oh, my God. That's crazy," I said without giving much emotion. I pretended to be shocked. *If only Jodi knew I heard that story about a thousand times before.*

From that conversation on, I knew Jodi would become a good friend of mine. It was like we'd known each other for years, and in a strange way, we did.

1:35 PM

After lunch, Jodi helped me fill out a few of my menus for the next couple of days. They are becoming increasingly harder to complete, given how high my caloric intake is now. It comforted me to know that Jodi was on the same number as I was. Like many situations in life, doing things with others makes them a hell of a lot easier. With her by my side during lunch, I finally had the nerve to participate in actual conversation. David let the table know that he would be discharged early next week as long as he kept gaining weight at a steady pace. God, I am so jealous. I'm not sure he's ready, though. In private, I know he struggles. In groups, he seems almost confident. All of the nurses adore him, and many of the patients confide in him—myself included. He talks a big game about his recovery. I hope he can walk the walk.

2:50 PM

Let's switch gears for a minute. *Oliver.* My therapist wants me to write a letter to Oliver. I want to vomit, but I shouldn't be surprised. He is arguably what consumes my mind almost every second of every day, and each session I have with Connor almost always involves him. I just can't imagine writing a letter to him. I have had to hold back everything I have wanted to say to him for so long. If he stood in front of me right now, I wouldn't be able to say a word. I wouldn't even be able to look at him.

The good thing about Connor is that he is very easy to talk to. He is also very open-minded. I have never opened up to an older straight male about my sexuality, but it feels safe with him. It's something I've never felt with another man before. Then again, who knows? Connor probably laughs at me in his car his whole way home.

4:00 PM

I want to take some time and write about the different types of group therapy we have throughout the week. Each takes place in the multipurpose room, and different nurses, doctors, and therapists proctor each one. I've only been here for a few days, so I haven't sat in on every kind there is. I'm sure the names of them will tell you enough.

The first group we have each morning is **Psychotherapy.** No topics are off-limits during psychotherapy—except, of course, those containing specific names of food items, numbers pertaining to one's weight or caloric intake, or certain disordered eating behaviors. For a group that is supposed to promote vulnerability and openness, there is quite a list of things we aren't allowed to discuss. Most of the time, we go around the table and share whatever is on our minds. It can be about upcoming family meetings, doctor visits, relationship issues—you name it. You can cry. You can get angry. You can shout every curse word you know at the top of your lungs if you feel up to it. The floor is yours. However, I have yet to actually speak during psychotherapy since I've been here. This afternoon was the first time I said more than one word during a meal. Hopefully, that will change soon. I suppose it will come with time.

Possibly the second most important group we have is **Meal Planning.** During each session, patients are given about three days' worth of menus to fill out for their upcoming meals. As I mentioned before, the amount of food one chooses depends on the caloric intake they are currently assigned. Once the menus are completed and checked by your dietitian, you are then required to jot them down in something we call a Food Journal. The purpose of a Food Journal is to keep track of what you have been eating so you can recognize any patterns or common pairings. For example, you should shy away from ordering the same dinner two days in a row. You must also be cognizant of any food combinations that may be seen as strange or ill-intentioned. It seems pretty subjective, I know. You'd be surprised by what ordering a salad and a piece of chocolate mousse cake looks like in the eyes of your dietitian.

Not all groups are as serious. **Art Therapy** and **Occupational Therapy** are my two favorites. Typically, an outside nurse from the hospital joins us with overflowing carts of crafts and supplies. The entire multipurpose room becomes transformed into our own personal A.C. Moore. Some days the groups have structure, and some days they don't. I guess it depends on the vibe in the room or what topic is currently being discussed on the unit. The main purpose of these groups is to create a distraction to get our minds off of our eating disorders. It is interesting to see where everybody's mind goes when they are given a small prompt or instruction. Mine almost always turns to Oliver.

Every night, thirty minutes after dinner, we have either **Wrap Up** or **Meal Processing.** Interestingly enough, Meal Processing is the only time we are ever allowed to name or talk about specific foods. I'm not sure how I feel about that. Part of me believes that shying away from those topics won't really help. My relationship with food is what got me into this mess to begin with. Restricting conversation about it seems discouraging.

A few of the less common groups we have are **Nutrition**, **Relapse Prevention**, **Journaling**, **Recreation**, **Meditation**, and **Nursing ED.** We have about one or two each per week. Oh, and I can't forget about **BDD**, which stands for Body Dysmorphic Disorder. It's almost a consensus among everybody here that BDD is the least favored group. The one thing that is possibly more difficult than opening up about your eating disorder is talking about how fucking disgusting your body is. Talking about your body is almost scarier than talking about anything else because, well, *everybody can see it*. It's not like the eating disorder voices in your head or the sometimes-subconscious behaviors you do during a meal. Your body is just...*there*. It is there for anybody to judge.

Anyway, during Meditation today, we received a new patient. Her name is Casey. She walked into the multipurpose room halfway through the group session and darted for the back of the room. Her hair was pulled in a tight ponytail, and she wore a baggy white t-shirt and a pair of gray sweatpants that practically swallowed her. I couldn't take my eyes off of her. I have never seen anyone in my life who is so thin.

My disorder looked at her with envy. *If only I could look like that. Every single problem in my life would go away.* Those were the words my eating disorder looped in my head.

Looking at Casey again, the rest of my body felt differently. I no longer felt that jealousy I had a moment before. It was like I suddenly saw her for who she was. She has a family. She has a life.

I'm sure she has a job and has friends. I could only imagine what was going through her mind at that moment. I suddenly felt every ounce of her pain. Her world was now mine. Pushing aside whatever life she'd lived before stepping foot onto the unit, we were now one. It was like that with the other patients, too, but some you felt connected to more than others. I wanted her to get better.

On the bright side, Burton remeasured my height. He clocked me in three inches shorter than what he previously had, which meant my discharge weight is now a lot lower than what it was. Burton seemed almost excited to tell me. I didn't react nearly as gleefully as I wanted to. It felt like he was testing me.

8:35 PM

I just got off the phone with Ashley. We had a great talk. She filled me in on everything going on at school, her boy problems—which seemed way more entertaining to hear about now—and what a few of my classmates had been saying about me. A couple of people think I got the flu. Others swear I'm taking some lavish vacation and won't be back until the summer.

"You didn't tell anybody, did you?" I asked her.

"Chris, of course not!" she exclaimed. "I would, like, never do that to you. Ever. This is your story," she paused for a moment, "and it is up to you when you want people to find out."

"Part of me doesn't want anyone to find out," I said. "I mean, why should they?"

"Yeah, I mean, well, I certainly won't say anything," she said.

"I know you won't," I said.

I wished we could have talked for longer. We spent over an hour on the phone, and it was such a nice escape from my life here in the hospital. It consists of the same things every single day. I really miss Ashley, and I cannot wait to see her once I get out of here. She has opened up to me in the past about how she, too, has struggled with eating, which makes her all the more understanding of what I am currently going through.

All in all, today was a success. For one, I am so hungry right now. That's a first. I could probably eat an entire pizza. I haven't felt hunger in so long. I got so used to the feeling that it eventually went away, and the absence of that feeling became something I almost celebrated. Hunger cues aren't something the average person thinks about, but for me, feeling them means I am doing something right.

I also talked during Wrap Up for the first time. It took place after dinner, and luckily for me, Connor was the one in charge of it. He knows me best, so I felt comfortable sharing my thoughts about how I am adjusting to life around here. Other patients on the unit who I have never even spoken to before told me they saw a change in my attitude, too. Let's see how long it lasts.

Oliver

SUMMER OF 2013 (7 MONTHS BEFORE TREATMENT)

Oliver was a dream—a warm, delicate, ethereal dream. The more I looked at him, the more certain I was that he wasn't real. He was like an illusion. I felt myself living on a cloud. From the moment I woke up to the second I fell asleep, Oliver was on my mind. It never ended.

Oliver was a mystery—a dark, concealed, puzzling mystery. The night he first messaged me, I wasn't sure he even went to my school. My friends didn't know who he was, and I had surely never seen him. All I knew was that one night in the summer of 2013, the most angelic boy I had ever seen left his number on one of my Instagram posts, along with an invite to his birthday party, which was a couple of months away.

I had just finished my freshman year at Our Lady of Peace High School in northern New Jersey. The student population had to be less than 300, which was barely enough to fill the gymnasium. For me, it was the perfect size. I had toured various schools during the eighth grade, yet Our Lady of Peace had been my favorite. It was small enough that you were able to develop a personal connection with your teachers but still big enough that you were able to find places to hide from them if you ever dared to skip a class.

What made the school particularly special was that I had entered it without knowing a soul. Nobody from my middle school had chosen to go to Our Lady of Peace, and that in and of itself was enough to get me excited. Essentially, I would be starting my life over. Nobody knew me. Nobody knew how previously bullied I was. Nobody had any prejudgments about the way I presented myself. Nobody even knew my name. Driving to my first day of high school, I imagined completely reinventing and presenting myself in a way that wouldn't be anchored down by who I used to be. I wanted to rid myself of that victim narrative and enjoy what was left of my childhood the way that I wanted. Personally, I think I did a pretty good job.

For starters, I made friends. And I made a lot of them. I'll admit, it wasn't easy for me at first. I ate lunch in a bathroom stall for about a week and became red in the face whenever anyone tried talking to me. I knew that wasn't the way I wanted to live for the next four years. So, day by day, I challenged myself to let my guard down just enough where I'd come home and be proud of how my day went. Even the smallest interaction with one of my classmates made me feel like I had won.

It could've been as simple as giving a girl a compliment on her shoes or walking down the main hall of the school with my chin high in the air, passing the cliques of jocks and cheerleaders that I once felt threatened by. Those were the moments that made me feel like I was becoming a more confident version of myself.

As time went on, I found my people. Though it may sound cliché, I did so by being myself. I think people were drawn to that. I had accepted who I was, and the urge to conform to how I thought other kids my age wanted me to act no longer influenced my actions. The things I was bullied for back in middle school were now my best-selling points. It seemed like every girl I met wanted their own feminine guy best friend, and I was happy to provide that accessory if that meant I didn't have to sit at lunch or run the mile during gym class alone. Looking back many years later, I can't say whether or not the friendships I made at Our Lady of Peace were real or purely material. At the time, I did not care. I went from having a negative number of friends to my social media following quadrupling overnight. Every weekend, I attended a new friend's quinceanera or sweet-sixteen party. I finally knew what it felt like to have friends. I was beginning to fit in and find my place among hundreds of teenagers only seeking to do the same.

What changed the most was my mentality. I felt like a brand-new person. I refused to allow myself to be the target of any bully, and I learned that giving no reaction was the most effective and powerful kind. It was tough to comprehend at first, but over time, I noticed that it had worked. I'd occasionally find myself in situations where the old me would've reacted differently. For example, there was this kid a couple of years older than me. Whenever I'd walk past him in the hallways or the stairwell, he'd pretend to sneeze and spit directly on me. Once I noticed the obvious pattern, I offered him a tissue the next time I saw him.

Despite the growth I experienced throughout my freshman year of high school, it was the following summer that my growth was put to the test.

- HEY, *it's chris.*

I waited a few minutes before hitting send. Those minutes felt like hours. Texting a friend or family member is one thing. Texting an impossibly attractive stranger you may or may not have seen walking down the hallway in between classes who just invited you to his house for a birthday party on Instagram is another. I stared down at my phone until it lit up with a response.

- *hi. sorry. i didn't mean to put you on the spot. you're welcome to come to my party if you'd like. you don't have to. you probably won't know anyone there, but it'll just be a few of us. i'll be there. i want you to come.*

I had a thousand questions. I had never even been invited to a high school party before, but I had to play it cool. Inside, I was freaking out.

- *that's alright. i'll see if i can go.*
- *nice.*
- *one question—have we ever met before? i'm just a little curious why you messaged me.*
- *can i be honest?*
- *of course*
- *i've wanted to have sex with you since the moment i saw you.*

I threw my phone across my room. The time for playing it cool was over. I couldn't decide if I wanted to vomit or dunk my phone in a bucket of holy water. Why would anyone think it was okay to message someone that? I was barely a sophomore in high school. The only sexual experience I had was making out with my arm in the fourth grade to see how it'd feel. I never talked to a boy like *that* before. I wasn't even sure that I *liked* boys the same way that I liked girls. I hadn't even had my first kiss yet.

- *oh. lol.*
- *don't worry—i've only had sex with three guys. it'd be just as special for me as it would be for you. i don't just have sex with random guys.*

I almost choked. Oliver's confidence was uncanny. Was I meant to be impressed by anything he told me? Part of me couldn't comprehend the conversation we were having. Part of me didn't want to. I always pictured being in my first relationship by the time I was forty. Having sex was nowhere on my radar. Was this type of communication normal for kids my age?

I decided that if my relationship with Oliver would be anything more than over the phone, I'd have to be honest.

- *uh, thanks.... i really don't have any experience in that department.*
- *have you ever been with a guy before?*
- *no.*
- *have you ever hooked up with a guy before?*
- *no.*
- *have you even had your first kiss yet?*
- *no.*
- *would you like to?*
- *i guess so...one day.*
- *come to my party and we can do whatever you want.*
- *sounds tempting. lol.*
- *what would you wear?*
- *what do you mean?*
- *clothing wise—what would you wear to my party?*

I thought it was a strange question.

- *not sure. i bought some new white doc martens the other day. i think they'll go well with a pair of black skinny jeans. i still don't even know if i can go...*
- *i'd like to dress you if you'd let me.*
- *what would you dress me in?*

A few moments later, Oliver sent me an image of an outfit sprawled out on his bed. It was the ugliest thing I had ever seen—a t-shirt with a huge lion's face on it, a pair of black slacks, silver, blinged-out shoes that looked like they were either purchased at Party City or a high-end fashion store for $3,000, and a black pair of boxers. I couldn't imagine myself in something so not my style.

- *nice.*
- *you don't like it.*
- *i do!*
- *you don't.*
- *the shirt wouldn't be my first choice...or the shoes...but I can try it on.*
- *prove it.*

- *i'll wear it!*
- *prove it. do you send pics?*
- *what kind of pics?*
- *i want to see you naked.*
- *sorry. i am not really comfortable with that.*
- *i can go first. do you want to see me naked?*
- *um. i don't know. we just started talking not even thirty minutes ago. i'd then feel obligated to send you pictures and i don't feel comfortable doing that just yet.*
- *you don't have to.*
- *okay.*
- *so?*
- *so what?*
- *so do you want to see me naked?*
- *whatever you want...*
- *is that a yes?*

I blushed and locked my phone for a moment. At least he asked.

OLIVER and I stayed up texting until five in the morning. Our conversation wasn't anything like how it began. He told me about his favorite artists, movies, and places to shop in the city. He told me about his undying love for Madonna and recommended three documentaries about her for me to watch. He told me about his future dream of becoming a music producer and even emailed me a few of his demos. The passion he had for what he loved was unquestionable. Despite giving me several reasons not to, something in me trusted Oliver. I wanted to get to know him more.

Before I knew it, the sun was rising. I heard my parents waking up and the whispers of the sun peeking through my blinds. I threw my phone on my bed as I began to take in all that had just happened. Were Oliver and I now a "thing?" Was I now required to text him every day? Was he going to text me first? I stood up and walked over to the full-length mirror in my room. Every insecurity I thought I had hidden away over the past year suddenly drifted back. I slowly started to undress. I imagined Oliver standing next to me. What would he think about my body? What would he say? Were my legs too long? Were my arms too skinny? What about everything else? I became flushed with embarrassment.

I wasn't ready to have sex. To be blunt, I didn't even know how to do it. Middle school sex talks aren't exactly inclusive of same-sex relationships. I had no idea what went where or what precautions to take beforehand. Was it truly worth it? Was I even interested in guys *like that?* Oliver told me he had lost his virginity when he was twelve. Had I truly lived my life so closed off for the past fifteen years?

Oliver was unlike any person I had ever talked to. I learned a lot about him from our first conversation, but it didn't feel like enough. For starters, I learned that he was into a lot of drugs.

- *acid tabs are my favorite.*

What the hell was an acid tab?

- *can't say i've ever tried one...*
- *would you like to?*
- *not sure... i've never really done anything like that before...*
- *i think you'd like it.*
- *how does it make you feel? like what does it do? lol*
- *you just see everything differently. like your phone screen and keyboard. they become kinda 3D.*
- *oh that's cool!*

Except, I didn't find it cool at all. I found it scary. All my life, I was taught to stay away from drugs. It was a topic commonly discussed at school and church. My parents often prided themselves on never trying one cigarette in their lifetimes. I had every desire to do the same. However, I wanted to impress Oliver, even if that meant having the anxious Catholic schoolboy within me get slaughtered right before my eyes.

- you know when's the best time to do it?
- lol when?
- during sex!! my ex and i would film it and rewatch it because it was so good.
- oh my...lol! sounds fun
- i'd love to take you on your first trip, chris.

My mind began to flood with possible scenarios that would lead to that occurring. Would it be during school before homeroom? At his house? When we hang out? Would Oliver be as interested in me in person as he was through text? I had no way of knowing.

Oliver was also part of a fairly wealthy Italian family. He had an overprotective twin sister he often complained about and parents that didn't seem to mind him being so rebellious. He grew up in a large house just a mile or two outside of New York City, which is where he spent most of his time away from school. It's almost like he lived a double life. Meeting him *in* school, you would have never expected him—the quiet boy who sat alone at lunch—to be the one getting dressed up in Jeremy Scott and Alexander McQueen to go to all the most popular gay bars and clubs in the city. He had a decent following on social media, most of which consisted of older, married men. Oliver would refer to them as his "daddies" and often bragged about how quickly he could make one of them fall for him. I think he did this to make me jealous, but I didn't mind. Any day that Oliver and I talked, no matter the conversation, was a win in my book.

And there were a lot of those days. One conversation led to the next, a day turned into a week, and suddenly, we had been talking for months. My days revolved around him. Every thought in my mind belonged to him. The attraction I felt toward Oliver was intense and very real. I felt like I could tell him absolutely anything and everything, and I did. I told him about what was going on with my sister at the time, and how I felt betrayed by the one person I thought accepted and supported me most. In terms of my sexuality, I explained how I wasn't exactly "out" yet, though I never denied being queer if asked. I assumed everybody already knew, and the concept of coming out seemed dated and unnecessary. I even told Oliver about my past with eating disordered behaviors beginning in middle school and the changes in high school that helped me overcome them.

Oliver responded with a few things I would never forget. First, he told me love can make you do crazy things. It can make you act in a way that those around you would not find familiar. My sister still loved and cared for me, but she was young. All she could see was the perceived love and affection she acquired from her boyfriend. Nothing else frankly mattered. It was my responsibility not to take the distractions that were plaguing her life so personally. She was on her own journey, and it was selfish to look at her burdens as if they were my own.

I wasn't fond of Oliver's response. If he could have lived in my house for just one night, I'm sure he would have been able to understand where I was coming from. Was I wrong for wanting to get involved when I heard my sister getting beat up in the room next to mine? Was that really her battle to fight alone? Was I wrong for wanting to take pictures of the bruises staining my sister's arms and legs, hoping they'd be useful in a court of law one day? What was I supposed to do when I heard my sister tell my mom that she'd kill herself if anyone dared to help her? Those were only a few of the thoughts going on through my head at the time. I felt so helpless.

Second, Oliver didn't like the idea that I was not officially "out" yet. Whenever I mentioned a friend or family member in one of our conversations, he'd ask me if that person knew that I wasn't straight. I felt terrible whenever the answer was no. I never asked, but it seemed to me that Oliver had been openly gay for years. The last thing I wanted was to push him back into the closet. I didn't want him to have to hide who he was. I felt like an amateur compared to him, and I knew I needed to start embracing my sexuality if I wanted my relationship with Oliver to continue.

Third, Oliver didn't have the response one would hope for when you open up to somebody about your past eating-disordered behaviors.

- *did you lose weight when you weren't eating?*
- *yeah, a little. i was like 12 years old. it wasn't really about the weight.*
- *but you lost a bunch of weight?*
- *yeah. a little.*
- *great. no more food for me!*

At the time, it didn't occur to me that Oliver may have also struggled with disordered eating, but whatever the case, Oliver's words were hurtful and dismissive.

I pushed those feelings aside as the day of his party approached. Every aspect of our relationship had been over the phone, and I was anxious to finally be with Oliver in person. I wasn't just anxious. I was downright terrified.

The weekend before his party, my family and I took one of our seasonal trips up to Utica, New York, to visit a few of our older relatives. These trips typically consisted of me, my mom, my aunt, and my grandma, and the trips were extremely family-oriented. We hopped from nursing home to nursing home and cemetery to cemetery while revisiting the places my grandma and her parents grew up. Early on, I made it a priority to not spend much time on these trips with my hands glued to my cell phone, but this time was different. I felt incapable of doing or thinking about anything that didn't have to do with Oliver or his party. Instead of spending time with my ninety-year-old aunt or eating with my family at my grandma's favorite restaurant, Kirby's, I stayed in our small room at the Hampton Inn and talked to Oliver. My family didn't mind much. My mom told me that at my age, she wouldn't even go on trips with her family anymore.

Part of me didn't want that trip to end. I was so nervous about meeting Oliver. I was so nervous about meeting his friends. Most of all, I was nervous about what might possibly happen at his party. The topics of sex, drinking, and drugs were quite common between Oliver and me. I knew all three would be available to me come the day of his party.

As scared as I was, just the idea of attending a high school party was enough for me to feel elated. I had never been invited to something like that—*ever.* Regardless of whatever went on, I was determined to get out of my comfort zone. Oliver often told me that the floor was mine. I was a virgin, I had never taken a sip of alcohol or did any drug, and I had never even kissed a boy before. Whichever of the four I wanted to change the night of his party was up to me.

I felt a little awkward. I didn't want to do half of what he was proposing, but I felt bad saying no. I also worried about sounding desperate, so I often toned down how I felt about him and talked to Oliver with a slight disinterest in my voice. My inexperience showed, and I couldn't help but feel intimidated by Oliver. I felt the need to conform myself to validate Oliver's ideas of who I was, though I didn't exactly know what they were. Oliver didn't know the real me. All he knew was how I presented myself online and over the phone with him. The same could be applied the other way around. That's what made the thought of attending his party so nerve-racking.

The drive over to Oliver's was long. Both my mom and my dad drove me, which was unusual. I wanted it to just be my mom. My dad was never too involved with my personal life, so it felt strange with him in the car. My mom told me she wanted his company to help her with directions, but I didn't believe her. Their son was going to his first-ever high school party at a *boy's* house, and any parent would be crazy not to be a little nosy. I was just upset that I had to sit in the backseat.

My mom, dad, and I couldn't believe our eyes once we pulled up to Oliver's house, or dare I say, Oliver's *mansion.* It was beautiful, and I had to check my phone a few times to confirm we were at the right address. The house was at least three stories high, and it had a staircase from the sidewalk leading to a wrap-around porch. The house itself looked like something from a Disney movie, as if someone took Cinderella's castle and shrunk it down to fit a suburban neighborhood.

I noticed Oliver was waiting for me at the door. I quickly rushed out of the car, waved goodbye to my parents, and ran through the middle of the street into his arms. Hugging him felt like home, like I had just entered the most secure place on the planet. He smelled like a mixture of alcohol, sweat, and expensive cologne. I was in love.

He walked me down to his basement, where about eight of his friends were sitting. I noticed a few familiar faces I recognized from school, but the majority of them were strangers. I took a seat next to a girl I knew from my art class, Bree.

"I didn't know you'd be here!" I said. This girl and I had only talked a few times but were friends on social media. We liked each other's pictures every now and then.

"Same," she said, smiling. "I didn't know you were friends with Oliver."

"We only began talking a few weeks ago," I told her. I looked around and tried to familiarize myself with the room: a coffee table in front of me, a TV set behind me, and a room full of strangers. I knelt on the floor and leaned in closer to talk to Bree.

"Ah, I get it."

"Get what?" I asked.

"He's totally into you," she told me. "He doesn't just invite anyone over to his house."

I laughed and shrugged her comment off.

"I mean, we've been talking a lot. But I don't know much about him, honestly," I said.

"Neither do I," said Bree. "I don't think he has many friends. I'm not quite sure why he invited me," she said, laughing.

"I'm glad he did," I told her. I was noticeably anxious, and chatting with Bree helped calm some of my nerves.

"Don't worry," she said. "I got you."

Bree leaned over and gave me a hug. A moment later, Oliver came over and began pouring drinks. I think they were a mix of Four Loko and whiskey, but I could be wrong.

As Oliver looked away, Bree grabbed my drink and took a big sip of it.

"Drink it slowly," she told me.

In an attempt to impress Oliver, I chugged the rest of the drink down. The entire room burst into laughter. *Oh God, did I do something wrong? Was it possible to drink—wrong?* The strangers around me quickly offered me what they called a "chaser." I had no idea what that was, so I declined. I couldn't believe what I had just done. The only alcohol I had ever tasted was the cheap wine my church fed me as a first-grader receiving communion. My mouth burned. Oliver immediately began pouring me another.

Before I knew it, my mind was gone. Any doubts I had about being at that party completely vanished. Oliver's friends and I began dancing to the music playing and singing along at the top of our lungs. I was completely embarrassing myself, but I was too drunk to care. Everybody at that party became my best friend. Toward the end of the night, we all exchanged phone numbers and snapped pictures together to remember how special the night had been.

What made the night even better was the time I spent with Oliver. He showed me to his bedroom, which was painted dark blue and covered in posters of Marilyn Manson and Courtney Love. He tried to show me some of his music equipment, but it was hard for me to focus. All I could think about was how lucky I was to be there. Oliver was the most beautiful person I had ever seen. He was as tall as I was but slightly more toned and muscular. His hair was dark brown and messy, yet somehow styled to perfection. I could have looked into his hazel eyes for hours. Being around him made me feel so special. After weeks of messaging over the phone, I couldn't believe I was finally with

Oliver in person. Not only that, but I was standing in his bedroom.

We were sitting on his floor when he suddenly leaned over and kissed me. It probably took me a good ten seconds to realize that he *was* kissing me. It felt right and wrong at the same time. After a few moments, both of us stood up. Oliver threw me against his wall, started touching me, and all I wanted to do was forget the party and rip off our clothes. My thoughts were quickly interrupted by Oliver's sister storming through the door. *Uh, oh.*

"Oliver, really?" she snarked with a disgusted look on her face.

"Sorry," he replied and turned back toward me in a huff. "We'll finish this another time." He walked out.

I looked over at his sister.

"Sorry," I said with a squeamish smile. I began walking to the door when she grabbed my arm.

"Be careful," she said. "He does this a lot."

She smirked and walked out of the room.

He does this a lot. What was that supposed to mean? The alcohol running through my body was strong enough for me not to care.

DESPITE ITS AWKWARD MOMENTS, the days following Oliver's party were fine. I found myself constantly replaying the time I spent with Oliver over and over in my mind. All I wanted was to be around him. He made me feel untouchable. He made me feel free. There was something about him that allowed me to forget everything else that was happening in my life. Everything else disappeared. I became numb to every feeling. That was especially useful when it came to what my family was going through in regards to my sister.

Oliver was my *person*. Whatever was going on with my family or in our home, talking to Oliver distracted me enough to remove me from any situation. He provided a way out. The terrible things my sister was going through didn't affect me as long as I was talking to Oliver. The constant shouting between my sister and my parents didn't affect me as long as I could run back to my room and text Oliver. I think that's one of the reasons why I became so attached to him. He entered my life at one of the worst possible moments.

Spending time with Oliver also taught me a lot about my sexuality. He took me into the city a few times and brought me to some of his favorite gay hangout spots and shops. It was something entirely new for me. While I was uncomfortable most of the time, I saw an entire community of people who were just like me yet living authentically and unapologetically. I witnessed how others in my community embraced the things about themselves that society deemed odd or strange, taking power in the art of being different. And with that, nobody was truly different. The sight of rainbow flags on every street corner made me feel like I belonged. I didn't need to "come out" or seek approval from anyone for who I was. Walking around New York City with Oliver was enough for me.

One of our most memorable times together was when he took me to a haunted house attraction in the city. It was located right in the middle of Times Square. We took the train in from New Jersey then walked less than a mile to the pop-up. I swear it was called Times Scare or something cheesy like that. Holding hands, we paraded around the site, laughing and overdramatically reacting to the things around us. In one room, a man dressed as a zombie chased us around with a real chainsaw, coming so close to us that I thought for a second one of us was going to get cut. We clung to each other's side like we wouldn't make it out of there alive. It was our first real "date," so it felt like we were still getting to know each other in person.

Oliver introduced me to a world where I felt accepted. I no longer felt left behind by a society that had done little to prepare a kid like me to enter the world. It was exhilarating. My perspective on the world changed, in addition to the way I viewed myself. I gained a sort of confidence that I had never had before. I was ready to embrace who I was, and I felt that nobody could stop me.

That was, of course, except Oliver himself.

Saturday, February 1, 2014
DAY 5 OF RECOVERY

8:55 AM

My body is changing. My hip bones are now more difficult to feel with my hands, and my stomach is nowhere as toned as it was just last week. It barely seems real. I feel like I'll blink and everything will return to how it used to be. I always thought of my body as a work of art. Not that I admired it all that much, but it was something I put hours and days and months into perfecting. Something so scary about going into treatment was erasing all that hard work. What was it all for? What was the point?

Despite these thoughts, I would like to believe I am still making strides toward recovery. For example: this morning, I tried scrambled eggs for the first time. Yes, you read that correctly. Eggs have always been something I steered away from as a child. They were always shoved in my face. Growing up, the only thing I would hear out of some of my family members' mouths—some of whom I only saw twice a year—was that I needed to start eating eggs.

"You need more meat," my little grandmother would say in

her Polish accent. "You need more meat on your bones. Too skinny! You need to eat more eggs!"

Naturally, I tried to stay away from eggs as much as possible.

Last night, David and I had another one of our talks. We had just got back to our room from Wrap Up and were settling in for the night. This talk, however, was a little different.

"Can I be honest about something?" he asked me. He sat pretzel-legged on his bed and peered over at me.

"Yeah, of course!"

"I don't want to trigger you."

"Considering I just ate the most rancid slice of pizza along with a carton of chocolate milk for dinner, I don't think anything can," I said with a laugh. I looked over at David, and his head was lowered to his chest.

"When I first saw you," he paused, "on your first day, I was just—speechless."

"What do you mean?"

"You're skinny, Chris. Like, *skinny* skinny. You're all I ever wanted to be."

I looked over at David as he began to cry. Hearing those words only a week ago would have made my entire day. Hearing them now only makes me uncomfortable. I wish I could strip away all meaning from that word. That's all it is: a word. It is a word that has the ability to manipulate and distress any bit of confidence you may have had. I never thought I looked skinny. Any mirror I looked into seemed to agree with me. My legs were too big. My chest was too big. Everything was *too big*. I couldn't comprehend David telling me I was skinny. I didn't know how to respond.

"Oh," I muttered.

The rest of the night was slow. David pranced around in the new black pants I gave him, often checking his reflection in our room's window. We talked a little about our favorite artists, discovering that we both shared a love for Miley Cyrus and her newest record *Bangerz*.

"I feel like we have been friends for years," I told him right before we headed to bed. David smiled.

"I really like the idea of that," he said, shutting off the lights in our room.

David also told me that he was happy that I did not sleep with Oliver. I am happy about that, too.

11:05 AM

Today, everybody on the unit was given a job to do, almost like a chore. In theory, this was a reasonable request, but we get scolded whenever we make any unnecessary movement that can remotely be considered exercise. We are not even allowed to stand for more than a few minutes, and here we are cleaning the entire unit. My job is to wipe down the table before every meal. It's not a bad job considering the other options. David has to clean the microwave three times a day (which, by the way, we are only allowed to use once per meal), Emmanuel's job is to dust the windowsill in the multi-purpose room, and Jodi's is to write motivational quotes each day on the dry erase board. I doubt these jobs will last more than a week.

My mom called a bit ago to warn me that my grandma and aunt will be coming with her to visit me tonight. I am a little nervous. We are all very close, but sometimes it's those people you're closest to that you have the hardest time opening up to. My aunt has a habit of being overprotective and happy all the time, which is not an attitude too appreciated around here. My grandma sometimes fails to filter the words that come out of her mouth. No, this isn't the grandmother who is obsessed with eggs. She's on my dad's side; the one who wants to visit me is on my mom's. But, still, when dealing with eating disorders, it is so easy to say something triggering or inappropriate to someone without even knowing it. I'm not worried about myself. It's David and my other friends on the unit I am concerned about. I hope nothing stupid is said. At the same time, I cannot expect perfection. I'll give my family a few passes.

There are some patients here that I have not seen get one visitor. I get at least one every night. I am thankful for having the support, but some days, it just feels like too much. Some days, all I want to be is left alone. I don't know how to tell that to my family.

In other news, I have found that listening to music has helped me better connect my feelings for Oliver. It is all too relatable. I suppose I should give this letter that Connor wants me to write to him a whirl.

10:15 PM

Despite my nerves going wild in anticipation of my visit with my aunt and grandma, I got through dinner without any problems. The visit was a bit awkward. No one exactly knew what to say at first. I spent most of the time explaining what my daily schedule looks like and introducing them to some of my friends here on the unit. I could tell they were just as surprised to see two other boys on the unit as I was. They seemed genuinely interested in taking the time to listen to all I had to say, and I think they tried to understand everything as best as they could.

Once they left, I joined Jodi, David, Emmanuel, Casey, and a few others in the multipurpose room. They were playing Hedbanz—a game where one person picks a card with a word on it, puts the card on their forehead, faces the other players, and asks questions to determine their word. I sat a few seats away and watched until I finally gathered up the courage to ask if I could play. They said yes, and I think I laughed more tonight than I ever have in my entire life. A nurse even came in to tell us to quiet down and go back to our rooms. She probably thought our laughs were burning too many calories.

Tonight made me feel a lot more bonded with everybody here, and I can feel the dynamic changing in a lot of our attitudes. I haven't gotten a chance to talk one-on-one with Casey, but I can tell she is warming up. Recovery is hard, but doing it with others makes it just slightly easier.

Sunday, February 2, 2014
DAY 6 OF RECOVERY

8:50 AM

Breakfast today was pretty slow. I have been thinking a lot about Oliver since I woke up, and it is difficult to explain my thoughts about him. They change almost every day. I refused to participate in any of the silly table games we typically play every meal. I said that I was too tired to focus on something other than completing my meal.

I should learn how to keep my emotions off my sleeve. The nurse in the room also asked me what was wrong. I told her my therapy sessions have been challenging lately, which wasn't a complete lie. She told me that we would have a group therapy session later dedicated solely to sitting in the dark and focusing on our breathing. Any other day that would've sounded terribly boring, but today, it sounds perfect.

My dad called to let me know that my uncle—his brother— would like to visit me. It doesn't make much sense. I am not close to him, and it is not like we see each other often enough to miss one another. He lives a few houses down the street from ours, but it is normal not to see him for months. It's strange. I typically only see him on holidays. He doesn't even send me birthday cards anymore. Part of me thinks my dad is forcing him to come because nobody on his side of the family has visited me. Another part of me thinks my uncle is just being nosy. Whatever the case is, I am going to reject his visitation.

"I understand," my dad told me. "I'll let him know you're not up to having visitors just yet."

"Yeah. I don't know," I said. I wasn't nervous about any backlash from my dad about saying no. He didn't seem too phased.

10:45 AM

I feel like every ounce of happiness and motivation I garnered over the past few days left my body in a flash. I have this knot in my stomach that will not go away. I just feel like I don't know who I am anymore. Everything is changing and it's all too fast.

Something that no one seems to be talking about here is the loss of identity you feel beginning recovery. We're told that our eating disorders do not define us. They are not our identity. They're only a part of us, and it's up to us to change that. Yet, for years, it *has* been my identity. My perception of the world, who I was, and life itself was defined by my eating disorder. It was the only thing I had. I wasn't proud of it. It wasn't a pride thing. It was a blanket. It removed the parts of my life I wished would disappear. It was numbing. It was the most obscure way of coping with things out of my control. I'd be lying if I said I wasn't going to miss it.

This afternoon, our Nutrition group was all about bowel movements. We were given the once-in-a-lifetime opportunity to listen to the most horrendous and vile stories the nurses had to share about previous patients. I am not sure if the stories were meant to scare us or not, but let's just say that every patient on the unit now has a new appreciation for their—uh—*intact anuses*. According to one nurse, there once was this patient who was so malnourished that her entire anus basically fell out. It didn't just fall out once. It became a reoccurring thing. The nurses described it as if it was no big deal, and she would just have to pop it back in whenever it decided to get some air. She would even do it during meals. I am not quite sure about the science or anatomy regarding that, nor do I wish to know. The patient eventually lost all control of her bowels and would shit herself multiple times a day without even noticing. It took weeks to return to normal.

Anyway, today has been a strange day. It feels like a major setback from how well I felt I was doing yesterday. I hope I snap out of it quickly. I would hate for it to seem as if I was seeking attention from anyone. I can't help but think I am forcing these negative feelings upon myself. In my defense, I suppose that is what an eating disorder will do to you. All I want to do right now is listen to sad songs, further contemplate every conversation and experience I had with Oliver, and cry over the fact that I am not home. I miss my home so much. I miss my mom, my dad, my sister, my bed—my life. I just want it all back.

4:00 PM

Time in here either goes by incredibly fast or unfathomably slow. We have had so much free time today. In my case, that means a lot of time to question and overthink. If only doing so burned calories, I would have hit my goal weight by now.

David is currently on a pass. His mother arrived a little while ago, and we were all anxiously waiting to get a glimpse of her. He talks about her a lot during group. For his pass, he told me he would be going to the nearby mall in search of some ankle-high boots, similar to the ones I wear around the unit. Mine are technically women's shoes. Considering how conservative his mother seems, I doubt he'll have any luck strolling through the women's department.

7:10 PM

I was called to the nurse's station after dinner. As I walked toward the front of the unit, I recognized the scent that haunted me just a little under an hour ago: my lasagna. It was terrible. It was cold, mushy, and uncooked. I was proud of myself for finishing it until I saw my plate on one of the nurse's desks. I almost gagged at the sight of it.

A nurse pointed to my plate and told me I had not completed my meal. I looked at the leftover sauce that was on the plate and almost laughed. What did she expect me to do? Lick it clean? I could've sworn she was joking until two other nurses came over. I was stunned. I worked so hard to finish that lasagna, and there was a possibility of it not even counting.

Before any of the nurses thought about marking my meal incomplete, I asked for a fork. They refused to give me a fork. They had already all been sent down to the cafeteria. I then noticed a pack of saltine crackers sitting on one of the nurse's desks, so I asked if I could use one of them to finish the sauce on the plate. Again, they refused. Eating an extra saltine cracker went over my provided meal plan. I paused for a second, brought the plate to my face, and, yes, I licked it clean. Not one of my proudest moments. At least I didn't get an incomplete.

Monday, February 3, 2014
DAY 7 OF RECOVERY

9:20 AM

I awoke this morning to at least a foot of snow outside my window. Our unit oversees parts of the hospital's roof, and I spent at least an hour this morning watching the sky. I would give anything to be able to go outside and run through the snow. I cannot tell you how tempting it is to try to open my window every night and escape. The roof is right outside my window, and I would be able to walk right onto it. Could you imagine? Where would I go? What would I do? Would I even make it past the parking lot?

Connor is out today, so I met with a different therapist this morning. I am not sure how effective it is to talk with a therapist who only just met you, so the session was quick. She did not have much to say to me either.

"Is there anything else you wish to talk to me about?" The therapist sat across from me with her legs crossed and hands gripping her clipboard. She hadn't looked at it once during the session.

"I suppose that's it," I said. I just finished telling her a fake story about the vice principal of my high school catching me throwing up my lunch in the bathroom. I don't think she believed me.

The only memorable thing to come from our conversation was her saying that I would have my first family meeting either tomorrow or the day afterward. That means that my mom and dad will sit in on a therapy session between Connor and me, and we can discuss anything I wish. That should be terrifying. How do I prepare for that?

11:20 AM

Burton just informed me that my calorie intake has been increased again because I have stayed the same weight since my second day here. My jaw dropped to the floor when I heard those words come from his mouth. I figured he was lying to me. I have put in so much work—not to mention calories—into myself over the past few days. I have nothing to show for it. *I seriously haven't gained anything? Not even one ounce?* Connor would argue that the real change happens mentally, which is true. It would be nice to see myself inching towards my goal weight for discharge, though. The only way I will and can be discharged is if I gain the weight that I need to. I still have such a long way to go. I hope I start gaining weight soon. I can see myself being stuck here for months.

5:00 PM

This evening, I made the bold decision to call one of my best friends, Arielle. Despite her being one of the loudest and most obnoxious people I know, she has been there for me since the beginning of high school. We clicked almost instantly. She's one of those people who is sort of friends with everybody. I would feel like a fool to skip out on her support during this time in my life.

"Hello?" she spoke into the phone, seeming a bit confused.

I'd be confused, too, if a strange number from a hospital in the middle of New Jersey was calling me, but I was so happy she answered on the first ring.

"Arielle! Hi! It's Chris!"

She screamed. "No way! How are you doing? Where are you? Everyone at school is talking about you. Nobody knows where you are. I think Ashley does, but she refuses to budge. Oh, my gosh. It's really you! I have been worried sick about you! Wait until everyone in our class finds out I talked to you. Your name has been on everyone's lips since the day you left! Hello? Are you still there?"

At that moment, I knew I made a mistake by calling her. However, part of me did not care about her or anyone else knowing where I was. It was bound to come out eventually. With some hesitation, I decided to tell Arielle exactly where I was and why.

"I'm actually in the hospital," I told her.

"God! Are you okay?" she responded before I could continue.

"Yeah. Well, no. It's, um, for my eating disorder," I gulped. The moments after you tell someone that you have an eating disorder are some of the most terrifying and vulnerable moments I have ever experienced.

"Aww, Chris!" she yelled. "So, they make you, like, eat more?"

I rolled my eyes. *Yes. Are you kidding me?* I wanted to tell her just how much I am forced to eat here, but I did not want to reaffirm her idea that eating disorders are all about food and not wanting to eat. So, for the next ten minutes, I attempted to describe to her my daily schedule, and besides eating and getting physically healthy, treatment is mainly focused on becoming mentally healthy.

"You know, you don't have to do things like that, Chris!" Arielle told me with a slice of empathy in her voice. "You don't have to starve yourself. You are perfect!"

Yikes. If only it were that easy.

"Yeah, I mean, it's a lot more than just that."

"Oh, yeah. Like, throwing up, too. Right?"

I sighed.

"Yeah. It's just a lot."

We chatted for a few more minutes until I told Arielle that I had to go. I can only take her in small doses.

8:50 PM

My relationship with David is—weird. Every night I feel us getting closer. I'd be lying if I said I didn't have feelings for him. I'd be lying if I said I didn't think he felt the same way. It's strange. At times, all I want to do is walk over to his bed and lay with him. I want to kiss him and hug him and just forget about everything else in the world. Our late-night conversations are one of the few things keeping me sane around here. This evening, we spent about an hour prank-calling each other's friends, which was very fun. I attempted to call his cousin, but I hung up as soon as an older woman—I am assuming his mother—picked up the phone. I am bad at prank-calling. I was so embarrassed. David called another one of my friends from school who actually believed it was me. I had to grab the phone from him before he said anything too embarrassing.

It's almost like there's a switch with David. The minute he brings up anything recovery-related, I lose all interest in talking with him. It all sounds so fabricated, and sometimes, I feel like he talks to me like I am stupid. He pretends that he has everything in his recovery figured out but will be the first to body check his legs in front of our window after a meal or complain about his meal plan. It's a little hypocritical.

"Chris, these pants make me look so fucking fat," he told me while squeezing the extra fabric behind his thighs. They were the same pair of pants I had only given him the other day. I kind of miss them.

"They look great on you."

"Oh, shut up. You're just saying that."

And don't even get me started on Oliver. I suppose it is my fault for constantly bringing him up. I had to convince David that prank-calling Oliver would be a terrible idea. David seemed set on the thought of doing so. I can sense his annoyance with me growing every time I bring him up.

Yet, David was eager to share with me the fact that he was not a virgin. According to him, he met some guy on a gay dating website, met up with him, and had sex. Boom. Just like that. I pretended to be interested in his story, but only half of me believed him. As someone who only this past year has had any experience with a guy, it was astonishing to hear. David reassured me, once again, that not having sex with Oliver was the right thing to do. I swear he thinks he's a life coach or something.

Tuesday, February 4, 2014
DAY 8 OF RECOVERY

11:10 AM

Breakfast this morning killed me. All I was given was a scrambled egg and a stale piece of bread, but I just couldn't do it. I woke up feeling full, which isn't an excuse you can use around here. It doesn't matter if you're full. It doesn't matter if you don't feel like eating. It doesn't even matter if you aren't a fan of a certain food. If you don't finish something, for whatever reason, that is a direct sign of your eating disorder controlling you. Well, in the nurses' eyes, that is.

I could see some issues with that, though not directly for myself. I received my first "incomplete" since I got here. I'm okay with it, though, because I knew I physically couldn't eat anymore. Others, however, may feel differently. Binge eating isn't something I have direct experience with, and I don't mean eating five sticks of celery when you're only supposed to eat two and calling that a "binge." I mean *real* binge eating. I have learned a lot about it during groups and talking with others. It's tricky in an environment we are in, where we are almost adopting a "completionist" mindset and only doing so to abide by the rules that we have been given. Everybody here is about "normal eating" and learning to listen to your body enough to eat whenever you want and how much you want.

This morning, I also had my first "treatment team" meeting. Now that I have been here for exactly a week, my doctor, therapist, and nutritionist wanted to touch base with me—all at the same time. They wanted to go over my progress thus far and understand how I am adjusting to life in recovery. We all met in Burton's office. I sat in a chair in the middle of the room while Burton, Connor, and Stacy stood over me like hawks. It was intimidating.

I think Connor saw how uncomfortable I was because he was the first to speak. He said that he's been pleased with how our sessions have been going. I've been open with him about many of the struggles I am facing, and I don't hold back my thoughts when it comes to my family and the other things that we talk about. I'm glad he stopped there. I didn't need Burton or Stacy to know anything further about my pathetic relationship with Oliver or my fear of my body changing.

Connor did say that I was too quiet during meals and during groups, which is something Burton and Stacy unanimously agreed on. They told me I need to begin expressing my thoughts more openly with the other patients and become more "socially aggressive" in groups. I feel like I have been working a lot on speaking more confidently during groups, so I was disappointed to hear that.

Another thing my entire team is hung up on is my vegetarianism. I have been a vegetarian since I was eleven years old. I don't know how many times I will have to tell my team that it has nothing to do with my eating disorder. They don't want to hear it. They want me to challenge myself. It'd be easy for them to shove a steak down my throat if they wanted to. They want *me* to *want* it. It seems like Stacy and Connor are so focused on fixing things that have absolutely nothing to do with my eating disorder, yet the moment I disagree with something they have to say, I am the one in denial. It's the most frustrating thing. I cannot win.

As if I am not in a bad enough mood already, I have to get ready for my first family meeting.

4:15 PM

Based on my poor history of public speaking, I had expected myself to completely freeze in front of my parents. However, I am happy to report that the family meeting went alright. It started off a little strange, though. I sat on my bed and waited for Connor to come and find me. Once he did, he led me to a small room that was practically right next to mine. I had never even noticed it before. The door was always closed. As I entered, the presence of my parents was overwhelming. The air was cold and awkward. They sat at a table next to each other with two empty seats across. That would be where Connor and I sat. I am so thankful that Connor was there to somewhat monitor the meeting, as he gave me the confidence I needed to speak up. I saw my parents often. My mom visited me almost every night. However, this time it was different. This time, it was serious.

After a few minor introductions from Connor, we began the meeting by discussing the poor feelings I have toward my sister and her boyfriend. For almost a year now, the two of them have changed the dynamic of our home, and I never felt like my mom or dad did anything to stop it. The constant arguing. The loud sex. The threats and abuse. It affected me, my mom, and my dad equally, but no one ever talked about it. It was almost like an unspoken rule in our house. I want that to end.

We finished the meeting by briefly discussing the grudges I hold against some of my family members for their odd, uh, obsessions with my weight and what I eat. I suspect we will talk about this more as time goes on, as I do believe such talk had a large effect on the development of my eating disorder. I felt bad bringing certain things up in front of my father, but I am glad I did. Many of the family members in question are on his side. I do not remember ever being so raw and open in front of him. It felt good. I am proud of how the meeting went, and part of me is looking forward to the next.

Once the meeting was finished, I walked back to my room. What started as a calm evening shifted once our unit was interrupted by the sounds of hard-heeled shoes and voices on a walkie-talkie. I swear I heard a few dog barks, too. I ran to the multipurpose room and saw a young girl standing sheepishly in the hallway surrounded by guards. She looked no more than fourteen years old. Her name was Britney, and rumors began spreading about her from that moment on. Jodi heard that she was taken from her parents because they neglected her illness. Casey heard she was a serial hospital hopper who got kicked out of her other treatment centers for mistreating the nurses. David just thinks she looks evil. I do not know who she is, nor am I too anxious to find out. If there's one thing that's certain about this place, it is that you never know what is going to come through its doors.

8:45 PM

I was surprised tonight with a visit from my sister. It was great to see her. She is almost five months pregnant, and her belly has gotten so big! I was so excited to hear about everything happening back home, but I could not help but feel sad. The months when my sister is pregnant just so happen to be the same months I am in treatment. Like, *seriously*? The universe works in mysterious ways, and I am not a fan. The only place I wish to be right now is home. I should be planning the baby shower and helping to transform my sister's room into a beautiful, pink nursery. Actually, I think they decided on lavender. Yet, here I am. I hate myself for being so selfish.

Dinner was quite eventful today. We got another two new patients on the unit. One of them looks exactly like the actress

Taissa Farmiga. I think I will just call her that from now on. She looks to be around my age. She is stunning and has the most perfect shade of blonde hair. I sat next to her for her first meal, which maybe was not my greatest idea. She did not touch one piece of her food. I tried to be friendly and show her some support, but she just could not pick up that fork.

Britney, the one who came in with the guards, completed every last morsel of her food. She sat at the head of the table and jumped in on every conversation she could. She'd laugh at jokes from across the table and offer compliments to those around her like she was playing Regina George from *Mean Girls*.

What the fuck? For a second there, I thought someone had let my friend Arielle on the unit. However, I am in no place to judge. She definitely knows her way around these programs. Her therapist will never label her as "quiet" or "isolating." She will never have a feeding tube shoved up her nose by her doctor. She has it all figured out. *The sooner you complete your meals, the sooner you gain weight. The sooner you gain weight, the sooner you are discharged. The sooner you are discharged, the quicker you can return to living your old, disordered life.* Obviously, this is not the frame of mind one should have in treatment, but it is hard not to think of it every once in a while. At times, I find my disorder convincing me that once I get discharged, I will lose every ounce of weight that I gained here. It is difficult not to use those thoughts as motivation to get through this. Hopefully, my mentality will change throughout the next few weeks.

Delores is the name of the other new patient. She looks about sixty years old, though she could be older. I am not even sure she knows why she is here. According to her, she does not have an eating disorder, but is only severely underweight. She told me she doesn't even know what the word anorexia means, and she was stunned to hear a doctor diagnose her with it. Our unit currently consists of mostly younger adults and teenagers, so I am nervous that Delores will not connect well with any of us. I hope to prove myself wrong and get to know her.

It's crazy to think that almost everybody on the unit has been admitted after me. I have only been here for a week, but not many people know that. It's strange having that role. As difficult as it was, it was nice to sit next to Taissa for her first meal. I am feeling more comfortable communicating with the new patients and helping them adjust to life around here. Again, that is a role I certainly never thought that I would take.

Wednesday, February 5, 2014
DAY 9 OF RECOVERY

9:20 AM

I have some good news and some bad news. The good news is that my breakfast this morning went down very well. Jodi told me that ordering a cup of apple juice fulfills a "fruit" requirement on my meal plan, which I had no idea about. I guess I never saw it on the menu.

The bad news is that I lost half a pound since yesterday. I know it is not much, but it is difficult to hear after you feel like you have eaten your entire weight the evening before. It is disappointing, but it opened my eyes to just how hard my body is working to rebuild itself. Despite my incomplete from yesterday, I ate almost 2,000 calories and *still* managed to lose weight. Burton told me I would be taken off Fall Risk once I hit a specific weight. I have not seen anyone on the unit stay on Fall Risk for as long as I have. Most are only on it for a day or two. It makes me a little angry.

11:00 AM

I have more bad news. Well, depending on how you look at

it, it could be taken as good news. I am still deciding. Stacy bumped my calorie intake up another 200. As if that was not enough, Stacy finished our meeting by informing me that in order for me to gain a substantial amount of weight, my calorie intake will eventually have to be over more than double what it is right now.

2:50 PM

David is getting discharged tomorrow. I am so relieved. I will finally have my own room, which is something I have wanted since my first day. The only thing I see getting in the way of my private room is if Emmanuel moves in. He is currently in a room by himself, which I am sure he enjoys. It would make sense to put us together, but I guess it depends on how much space they have on the unit.

4:15 PM

As if I needed another reason to countdown the hours until David's discharge, he told me that my weight loss from this morning was not a big deal. That comment really upset me. I had to stop myself from crying, and I called my mom as soon as he left our room. Sure, losing half a pound is not the end of the world, but it means that I am not going in the right direction. As loud as my eating disorder is, I know deep down that gaining weight is inevitable. It's the only thing that's going to save my life. It just hurts when you have finally come to that realization, you are greeted with a negative on the scale. I wish someone else understood my frustration.

Anyway, enough about David. Let me introduce you to Stephanie. She is another new girl on the unit, yet she is far from *new*. I have already heard her bragging about the multiple treatment centers she has gone through. She even mentioned one out in Los Angeles that a bunch of celebrities have gone through. Apparently, she roomed with one of them. If nothing else will motivate me to recover, it is seeing these patients that wear the number of hospitals they have been to as a badge of honor that will finally get me there.

The first thing that anybody with an eating disorder will tell you about is how competitive they are. It can be as subconscious as sharing how many treatment centers you have gone to. The average person may not recognize it, but I guarantee everybody on this unit can. It is the eating disorder's way of asserting itself as the most powerful and untouchable thing in the room. Everybody else is simply not sick enough.

I must admit, though, that Stephanie has the best knees I have seen. You barely even notice them. They blend in perfectly with the rest of her legs, which are the same width from calf to the uppermost part of her thigh. The capri-length leggings she wore to group showed them off perfectly. Now that I think of it, I didn't think we were even allowed to show skin. Are we even allowed to wear shorts or capris? It's a dumb rule, honestly. It's not like they have to worry about anybody walking around shirtless or in a bikini. Then again, I wouldn't put it past a few people here.

Take me, for example. I hate my body. I hate my arms. I hate my legs. I hate my chest. I hate my face. I hate everything about my body. However, I'd also be the first person to wear skin-tight black skinny jeans with the hopes of somebody commenting on my legs. My social media pages are filled with pictures of my body—pictures that I strategically took where parts of my body, like my ribs or my waist, appeared particularly smaller. And don't forget about the thousands of "pro-anorexia" blogs that can write a book on how much they hate their body and then post ten different pictures of it from every angle. If we hate our bodies so much, why do we show them off? Why do we feel the need to hide our bodies underneath baggy sweaters and sweatpants one day, then strip everything off for the Internet the next? It's strange, and it makes little sense. I imagine how confusing it will be to explain my body dysmorphia to my parents.

Anyway, Stephanie does not seem to care about any of the rules. Even if there weren't any rules regarding clothing, it is more of an etiquette issue.

7:45 PM

Due to the weather, tonight's family event was canceled. Cherry Oak didn't want anybody taking the risk of driving in a foot of snow to attend. Every patient's parents and relatives were invited to come on the unit and have a structured chat with all of the other patients and parents. The hope was that it would help them to gain a better understanding of what an eating disorder is and how they can help. I was looking forward to it. I believe my parents can definitely learn a thing or two about eating disorders. I think it would have helped them to see other people who suffer from them and perhaps realize that they are a lot more common than they may think. Oh, well. I'll have to wait until next time.

Instead of having the family event, we had a makeshift group therapy session that required us to create a collage from magazine clippings of words that described either our eating disorder or our actual self. I had to laugh while flipping through the pages of the magazines. Almost every page had something already cut from it. Pages of diet pill advertisements were torn out, in addition to pictures of food and peoples' bodies. I have to say, this place does a decent job of getting rid of anything that could be even remotely triggering for someone. I am not sure how that prepares us for the real world, but I understand.

10:45 PM

I had my first extra today! Each night, if you complete all three of your meals for the day, each patient has the option to select an extra snack from the unit's pantry. This may include some yogurt, a piece of fruit, or even a cup of ice cream. I had always been hesitant to order an extra. The whole concept is sort of convoluted. I decided to have a slice of carrot cake. I did this to score some points with the nurses, but it felt good having the choice of whether or not to eat something.

    David is almost finished packing. I'm going to go help him.

Thursday, February 6, 2014
DAY 10 OF RECOVERY

9:00 AM

It was easy for me to wake up this morning. Today, I will finally be given my own room. Ah, freedom. I almost forgot what it felt like. There will be no more David taking up all of our allotted bathroom time in between groups. There will be no more awkward clothing changes or someone keeping me up until the early morning. I won't have to continue pretending to care about the things he tells me. I am trying to decide what I will do tonight to celebrate David's departure. Should I blast Miley Cyrus on my iPod shuffle and have a dance party in my underwear? That would burn too many calories. And besides, my iPod is still being examined by the nurses to make sure everything I have on it is appropriate. Whatever. I'm not sure what exactly I'd be hiding in an iPod Nano. I still have time to decide, but I am looking forward to having my mom come and visit me tonight. Finally, we can play our board games together and talk without the wandering ears of David listening in. I figured that it was common courtesy to leave the room if the other patient had a visitor, but David didn't think the same way.

For breakfast, I challenged myself to eat the same meal that I hadn't completed a few days ago—a scrambled egg and a bun. It was nerve-wracking having it sit in front of me. The smell of the egg made me gag, and the bun looked just as dry as before. Thoughts were racing through my head. Despite the pressure I was feeling from my disorder to have another incomplete, I am happy to announce that I ate every last bite. It wasn't easy by any means. Yet, each bite became easier than the last. I peered over at others' plates and saw each one nearly clean.

If they could do it, why couldn't I?

I am hoping that these last few completed meals will have pushed my weight back up. The nurses at the table even complimented me on how well I did. I think they are starting to trust me more. I do not notice them studying how I pick up food with my fork anymore or how long I stand in line waiting to use the microwave. I understand certain things must be monitored to an extent, like bite sizes and leg tapping at the table, but it feels great to have a level of trust between us. I hope it is not all in my head. During meals, I try my hardest not to give them any reason to write me up. Sometimes, I think that I may look suspicious of eating too normally. Again, probably all in my head. It is challenging for me to put a brave face on during meals, but at this point, I refuse to let any of the staff here see me break. Even if I have to run to my room after a meal to cry about something, nobody has to know.

2:15 PM

My dreams of having a room to myself have been demolished. My heart sank to the floor once I noticed David's side of the room was being put back together. I knew what it meant. Emmanuel moved in after lunch. Geez. I barely had three hours to myself! It makes sense that they would put us together, though. Space on the unit is getting pretty tight, and it is only logical to room the two boys together. Speaking of rooming the two boys together, do you want to know something odd? Girls are allowed in our rooms and in each other's rooms, but we are not allowed to be in any of their rooms. Britney had a small get-together in her room last night. I heard everyone laughing from all the way down the hall. David was busy packing, and Emmanuel and I were stuck by ourselves. We tried to make the most of it, but we didn't do much besides sit and chat.

Without David here, I found more confidence to speak during psychotherapy. The whole group was interested in learning about my life back home, but there were too many things I couldn't go into specifics with regarding my sister and her boyfriend. There is a certain etiquette during groups on how to talk and what to talk about. For example, I can't talk about the messages I received from her boyfriend calling me a faggot online. I can't talk about how I could hear her boyfriend making himself throw up after every meal he has in our house. I can't talk about the arguing, the screaming, the threats—any of it. I can't talk about it here. It seems like I can't talk about it anywhere. Ever since my sister's boyfriend moved in, my family and I have lived under the guidelines of *never* talking about *anything* that goes on in our house. It seems like a denial thing. Don't acknowledge it, and it doesn't exist.

<u>*2:50 PM*</u>

My meeting with Connor this afternoon was good. We focused more on my family, especially my grandmother, and how her comments about my weight ignited disordered thoughts in my brain from a very young age. Connor wants to bring this up again during our next family meeting, which I am a little hesitant to do. He thinks I have to learn to be more aggressive and demanding of what I want and expect from my family back home, which I agree with to an extent. The last thing I want to be is any kind of a burden to my parents, and I feel like I have already put them through so much by just being here. It is such an awful feeling, but Connor says I have to get over it. That is the thing I like about Connor—he says the things that I need to hear. I am beginning to really enjoy and look forward to talking to him. Too bad he is married and totally straight.

4:03 PM

I am back in my room after our group session on body image. Ah, everyone's favorite. Our assignment was to go around the table and name one positive thing we liked about our body and one thing we didn't like. The second part was certainly easier. I said that my style was the thing I liked most about myself. *That* was certainly not the answer they were looking for. Jodi began crying when it was her time to speak. She had no idea what to say. The majority of us said that we were insecure about our entire bodies. Only some patients were brave enough to give specifics. Upon listening to each person speak, I began compiling a list of my own.

What I Hate Most About My Body

- my face
- my skin
- how my eyebrows are uneven
- how big my forehead is
- how long my neck is
- how much my Adam's apple protrudes out from my neck
- how my collarbones are not as visible as I would like
- how long my torso is
- how thick my upper arms are
- the freckles on my arms
- how ugly my hands are
- how disproportionate my hands are to my arms
- my hips
- how my hips are the reason I can't fit in a size 00
- how my left hip bone is higher than my right one

- how long my legs are
- how big my legs are
- how the width of my thighs does not match my calves
- how big my calves are
- how ugly my feet are
- ~~basically everything~~

7:00 PM

I feel like I am going to explode. Someone is going to have to hose my guts from off the walls. I do not remember ever eating as large of a meal as the one I just did. I immediately ran to my room afterward to lie on my bed and hope it all stayed down. My dinner consisted of two pieces of the greasiest pizza I had ever laid my eyes on, some carrots, grapes, a carton of chocolate milk, a chocolate Boost drink, and lastly, a small cup of chocolate ice cream. I would be surprised if I didn't turn into a piece of chocolate by tonight.

The only thing that made the meal bearable was sitting with Jodi and Casey. We tend to sit together during almost every meal and group session. We sit at the very end of the table with me in the middle and the two of them at my sides. It has been a long time since I've met people who are so real and down-to-earth, and I hope that we only get closer as the days go on. Conversation comes so easily with them, and we could not stop laughing over the sounds of our carrots crunching in our mouths. Whatever happens while I am here, at least I have a few friends to make it slightly easier. I feel like I have known both Jodi and Casey for so long, and we have already talked about meeting up once this is all over.

9:55 PM

Tonight, Jodi, Casey, and I met in the multipurpose room to

order an extra. I had to laugh listening to us—three anorexics—willingly ask a nurse for another piece of food.

"What the fuck is wrong with us?" Jodi said once we sat down in our usual spots.

"Too much," Casey said under her breath. The three of us burst out laughing.

I ordered some strawberry yogurt, and Jodi and Casey both chose an orange. The unit is a different place at night. Half of the patients go to sleep early, and the doctors and therapists are gone for the day. My friends and I had the whole multipurpose room to ourselves. We spent a few hours watching television until we got on the subject of the other patients.

"I don't know about that Stephanie," Casey said. She curled up her legs on her chair and stared at the table. "She gives me the creeps."

"Have you noticed how much water she drinks?" I asked. "I barely drank anything my first day here. David had to show me to the water fountain. I didn't even know it was there."

"She walks around a lot, too," Jodi said.

"If I stood for even one minute longer than I should, I would be knocked back down to Phase One," I joked.

Jodi and Casey agreed.

Ava

There's no way to anticipate someone you love becoming a victim of domestic violence. It's a startling realization, one that leaves you grappling with the stark truth in the midst of unfathomable pain. The disbelief can seem almost palpable. Similarly to eating disorders, domestic violence knows no boundaries—it doesn't discriminate based on age, relationships, or the strength of familial ties.

The upcoming pages delve into the story of my mostly normal upbringing and its abrupt transformation within a matter of days. Yet, I wasn't the victim here, nor was my mom or dad. The events of the six months leading up to my entry into treatment marked the darkest period of my life, but the shadow they cast on my sister's life was far more profound.

Did my parents or I ever do anything to stop the progression of such a violent, abusive relationship? We tried, but the short answer is no. Anyone who has witnessed the complexities of such a situation understands the paralyzing helplessness that accompanies it.

What follows is my side of the story—a testament to the love I have for my sister and the unyielding hope that one day, things will change, and she will reclaim her voice.

ON THIN ICE

My household consisted of me, my mom, my dad, and my sister. The four of us lived on the top floor of a two-family home in northern New Jersey. My parents swore it was only a starter home for them after they got married. My sister, Ava, was born in 1994, and I followed a few years later in 1998. The gap between my sister and me allowed for a unique camaraderie to blossom between us. I still respected and sought her opinion from an early age, but we were also still able to run around the house and pretend to be characters from *The Series of Unfortunate Events* together. I was always stuck being Klaus.

Growing up, my family life was far from perfect. Beyond the mismatched painted walls and the clutter that found its way into every nook, our home exuded a warmth that transcended material imperfections. We did not have a white picket fence surrounding our house, but a rustic-looking, paint-chipping wooden one that fell apart more and more every year. We did not have a pet golden retriever who enjoyed running around our large, spacious backyard, but a hamster named Oreo who my mom used to wake my sister and me up in the morning by letting him crawl on our faces. We did not have the money to go on grand, international vacations abroad each summer, but enough money to take road trips up to Vermont where we hiked the largest peaks in the Northeast each autumn.

My sister and I grew up attending private, Catholic schools. We attended church fairly regularly and became altar servers as soon as we were old enough. I'll admit it wasn't the most fun thing in the world. I'd pretend to be sick half the time so I wouldn't have to go. My parents weren't wildly religious or anything. It was just part of our day-to-day lives. We didn't know of anything else but waking up on Sunday morning and dragging ourselves to mass. My dad would make up for it by buying us either Subway or Quiznos sandwiches once it was finished.

My sister and I had fairly generic childhoods. We'd make

plans to stay up all night on Christmas Eve together in hopes of getting an early peek at the tree, only to fall asleep just before midnight. We found ourselves overly invested in the *Harry Potter* series, so much so that the two of us (and my mom) cried while reading the final chapters of the last book. We enjoyed the same hobbies—dancing, drawing, and putting together cheerleading routines with our dolls and stuffed animals.

However, the older we became, the more difficult going to school became for both of us. My sister constantly found herself stuck in the middle of toxic friend groups while I struggled to keep any friends whatsoever. By the time I reached middle school, I knew I wasn't like other kids my age. My clothes were different, the way I styled my hair was different—everything about how I acted and presented myself differed from any kid I knew. I didn't understand what being gay was. I didn't even know what that meant. Yet, it was a label that was thrown at me the second my differences became more apparent. I sucked at sports, and the few friends I had were girls. I wore dress shirts and bowties on dress-down days while the other boys wore sweatpants and a t-shirt. I became that kid everyone pointed and laughed at whenever the religion teacher brought up homosexuality. Some kids I thought were my friends left me as soon as their own reputation suffered by being seen with me. I didn't feel safe going to school anymore. Nothing about me fit in.

I CAN STILL REMEMBER the day I told my best friend that I was bisexual. It was in the spring of 2011. I was in seventh grade, and my friend and I had been obsessed with the television show *Glee* since it first aired. My friend had transferred schools a few months prior, and the only time we would see each other was over a brief video chat after every episode came out. She, too, had a long history of bullying at our school, and it was ultimately the reason why she transferred. It was heartbreaking to see her leave, but a big part of me wished she'd taken me with her.

Our favorite character on the show was Kurt Hummel. Played by Chris Colfer, he was the preppy gay boy of the group who struggled to fit in because of his sexuality. Watching him, I felt like I knew him, and he knew me. I felt visible. I felt validated. If Kurt Hummel could learn to accept and be himself, why couldn't I?

"I want to tell you something," my friend said to me about halfway through the episode, "and you may hate me for it."

"What is it?" I asked.

"No, seriously," she looked away from her computer. "If you never want to speak to me again after this, I won't blame you."

She squirmed further and further away from her camera until she was practically on the opposite side of the couch she had been.

"I'm bisexual," she told me. A tear ran down her cheek as she looked up at me, terrified of how I'd respond. I kept quiet for a moment until I answered the only way I could've at the time.

"So am I," I whispered just loud enough so she could hear.

Neither one of us said a word to each other after that. We turned our heads back to our televisions and watched the remaining minutes of *Glee*.

AS MY SISTER and I grew older, she was the first one to show me what it meant to truly be yourself. Entering high school, she began experimenting with various hairstyles, hair colors, and alternative ways of dressing. She'd tease her short, black-dyed hair one day and clip in pink and blue extensions from Hot Topic the next. Her collection of band t-shirts grew exponentially, mostly because she attended concerts at the local School of Rock every weekend. Her music taste began to change from whatever was on the radio or sung on *American Idol* to the latest alternative artists of the time, like Blood on The Dance Floor, The Millionaires, and Black Veil Brides.

Over time, my sister became an online "scene kid" sensation. She grew a following on MySpace and Facebook, and she found an entirely new group of friends she would visit almost every day at the nearby mall. They called themselves "mall rats," or maybe that's what others called them. They'd spend practically every day there, and my mom and I were always the ones to drop her off as soon as she came home from school and pick her up when the mall closed at 10 pm. It was strange, to say the least. But that's where she felt comfortable, and that is all that mattered.

My sister inspired me. Being a young, queer kid, it was easy for me to latch onto any acts of bravery or acceptance. Though my parents were supportive of me (and I am eternally grateful for that), I wasn't comfortable talking about my identity with them. Frankly, I wasn't comfortable talking to my sister about it, either. The difference was that she understood me, and I understood her. There needn't be any further explaining or "coming out" to one another. We were both just strange, untraditional kids who leaned on each other while we struggled to find our places in the world.

Unfortunately, as time went on, I felt my relationship with my sister begin to drift. Once my sister entered high school, she found herself getting involved with bigger groups of friends and experiencing new relationships with boys almost monthly. I'm in no position to judge, but they weren't exactly the kinds of boys you'd want to see your sister with. One of her more serious boyfriends throughout high school was a self-proclaimed Nazi. He wore and gave my sister swastika necklaces for each of their anniversaries and kept a copy of *Mein Kampf* in his locker. Him and I didn't get along very much.

The day my sister ended that relationship, my mom and I were over the moon. The psychological damage it had done to my sister was intense, and we had been encouraging her to break up with him for three years. My sister was now about to graduate from high school, and she had her entire life within view. She planned to move to New York City—her favorite spot in the world—and pursue a career in makeup artistry. She enjoyed experimenting with broad colors and making somewhat questionable decisions when it came to how she would draw on her eyebrows. She had even applied and been accepted to a couple of art schools and random colleges in the area if something ever thwarted her city plans.

ONE OF MY sister's best friends throughout high school was anorexic. Once she received treatment, she transferred to a school that specialized in teaching students who required additional resources that weren't available in other schools. This was the same school that Jodi attended. In between classes, the students had therapy sessions and group meetings where they would work on the hardships they were facing. The teachers were trained to be both educators and social workers. My sister's friend would constantly tell her stories about one boy in particular. He'd throw things during class, punch and destroy the walls, have sex with girls in the backseat of his Jeep, and get into physical altercations with teachers and other students. Just a week before my sister's high school graduation, this boy became my sister's new boyfriend.

Without knowing any of his history, my sister's new boyfriend seemed too good to be true. He would shower my sister with expensive gifts every time he took her out. One day she would be given a $300 watch, and the next, she'd be greeted at the door with a luscious bouquet of roses with a personalized note. It was something new every day, and my sister was over the moon.

I didn't think my sister was ready for a new relationship so soon after breaking up with the Nazi, but she seemed happy. She and her new boyfriend went out practically every night and visited the most popular clubs and bars around northern New Jersey. They'd spend weekends at the beach and eat at well-known Italian restaurants in the area. Every night, my sister would be dropped off home with the sounds of house music blaring from his car. It was as loud and obnoxious as you can imagine, yet a smile would be plastered across my sister's face as soon as she walked through our front door. He wasn't the kind of boy I thought my sister would ever be attracted to, and she didn't necessarily seem like his type either. It was strange, but I trusted my sister, and I wanted her to be happy.

Every so often, the boyfriend would sleep at our house. He was going through some troubling times with his family, and my parents had little to no choice but to allow him to stay the night whenever it was necessary.

One night turned into two. Two nights turned into a week. Before any of us knew it, he was living in our house full-time.

Neither of my parents intended for it to happen. It just—sort of—*happened*. He had been officially kicked out of his house by his mother, and my sister was very good at persuading my parents into allowing much of anything. An innocent threat was sometimes all it took. She'd bring up the option of her and her boyfriend sleeping in his Jeep at a nearby park, and that was all the convincing my parents needed, even if it meant letting a stranger live in and have full access to our home.

My sister and her boyfriend weren't shy in making their presence in our house known. It was overwhelming at times. They'd play really loud music throughout the day and they'd be up until 3 am ordering pizza and lounging together on the small two-person sofa in our living room.

There were a number of behaviors that became normal in our home once we began sharing a living space with the two of them. They'd spend hours in our bathroom every morning and every night, so much so that my parents and I considered creating a schedule for when each person in the house was allowed use of the bathroom. We had strangers walking in and out of our house daily without any explanation of who or what they were there for. My sister was also super open about the number of times they'd have sex throughout the day. It was as if she forgot how small our house was. We already knew.

The two of them constantly argued over the silliest things. My room was next to my sister's, so I'd always be the first to hear. The sound of my sister crying became a perpetual background noise to my everyday life. The stories she'd tell my mom and me about the things that angered her boyfriend left us dumbfounded. He'd always have a problem with the way my mom or I said hello to him—it was never kind or welcoming enough. He constantly complained about the food we had in the house, the way that my sister dressed and the music that she listened to, and whether or not his Jeep—which my sister pled with me to compliment at least once a week—had a prime parking spot in our driveway. My parents were often left to park in the street.

It took my family and me only a few weeks to notice that the tension between the two of them was escalating, but whenever my mom tried to talk to my sister about it, my sister grew ice cold. If I had a dollar for every time my sister told my mom not to get involved in her relationship, I'd be a millionaire. Except, my sister didn't simply *ask* or *tell* my mom. She would manipulate, name-call, and use threats to make sure my mom would regret *ever* doing or saying anything that had the potential to interfere in her relationship. There were times I truly believed my sister was going to get physical with our mom. I'd have 911 pre-dialed on my cell phone, ready to call if it was necessary. To this day, I can never look at my sister the same way I once had. The words she used against our mom were so vile. However, it is difficult to blame my sister for her actions, given the environment she, herself, was in.

One time, my sister walked through our front door in tears while her boyfriend was waiting in the car. She was crying uncontrollably and shouted for my mom from the foyer. I was in the living room only a few feet away when I heard my sister ask my mom if she'd agree to have a threesome with her and her boyfriend. It was one of the few times I can remember my mom telling my sister "no." My sister pulled out her phone, stepped outside, and returned a few moments later. She then asked if our mom would agree to send her boyfriend some explicit pictures if she wouldn't agree to have sex with him.

"Ava, no. Absolutely not," my mom replied in a disgusted tone.

My sister was fuming.

"Are you fucking kidding me? This is going to be so bad, mom. You don't even know. How could you not do this for me? God. I have the worst fucking parents in the entire fucking world. I hate you. I hate you so much. I might as well just slit my wrists right fucking now."

To rehash the months living with both my sister and her boyfriend is ultimately too painful. After just a week of him living with us, everything about my sister changed. One day, her boyfriend took three empty garbage bags to her room, and within minutes, my sister's band posters, Hot Topic wardrobe, and funky hair extensions—everything that made my sister *my sister*—was out on the curb. She stopped coloring her hair black, started eating meat (after being vegetarian for over six years), began shopping at stores like Guess and True Religion, and only referred to me as "Chris," not one of the silly nicknames she had used for me for years.

She became almost untouchable. No one could talk to her or address her without her boyfriend being directly by her side. Every comment or request, no matter how small, had to go through him first. It was as if her life wasn't her own anymore, and all anyone could do was sit back and watch it become altered by circumstances beyond anyone's control.

I'll never forget the first day I saw my sister's arms and legs painted with bruises. There were so many of them. She stood slightly over five feet tall outside of her room, crying almost every night, desperately trying to cover her arms and legs with heavy, oversized clothing. Some of the bruises were big. Some were small. None of them came as a surprise to my family or me. As the weeks went on, the arguments heard throughout our small home only grew more intense. I began banging at the walls of my room every time they started fighting, in case they cared to know that the entire house was listening. The screams and cries of my sister were sounds that became all too familiar, but it was the forced perception that everything was normal that was saddest of all.

Friday, February 7, 2014
DAY 11 OF RECOVERY

9:20 AM

There is only one patient that has been here longer than I have. Her name is Dandy, and she is unlike the other patients here. I think she is in her forties, but from the way she looks, you'd think she is almost eighty. She lives in a wheelchair hooked up to multiple IVs and feeding tubes, pumping her with all sorts of fluids and medicine. She eats every meal by herself at the head of the table and barely talks to anyone. She completes every single one of her meals but never seems to gain a single ounce of weight. She is the only one who I have seen chug down three Boost Plus drinks in one sitting. She does it every single day—sometimes multiple times a day. In summary, she is the absolute sickest-looking person I have ever seen, and I do not know how she is alive. Today, in psychotherapy, she shared her story.

We were all shocked to learn how overweight she had been her entire life. As she got older and had her first son, she decided to undergo gastric bypass surgery. However, the surgery went extremely wrong. Forgive me for not knowing the proper medical terminology, but her stomach apparently shrunk to a size so small that she wasn't allowed to eat anything for months. She lost more than half of her body weight and has lived at Cherry Oak ever since. Her son is now nineteen years old.

The unit was quiet after Dandy spoke. It was the first time many of us heard her speak.

12:25 PM

I was called outside to get my blood drawn during Meal Planning today. I know I sound dramatic, but it truly ruined my day. I hate needles, but the worst part is that blue rubber band they tie around your arm. Just thinking about it makes me cringe. The nurse who drew my blood was nice. I've seen her a few times around the unit, but we've never talked much before. I think she's a night nurse. She tried to distract me by asking what movies I had seen lately. Did she forget we were in a hospital? I am not sure what answer she was expecting. It's not as if I have been to the movie theater recently. Regardless, I am now anxiously awaiting the results of my lab tests. The blood test will show how my body is reacting to the nutrients in the food I have been eating. I hope my results come back clear. I don't need anything else to worry about.

On top of that, my calorie intake was bumped up again. My meal plan is being increased every two fucking days. I honestly don't know how I am still functioning. Eating even a tenth of that at home would have sent me over the edge. Maybe if I stop completing my meals more frequently, it'll send a message to my dietitian that she is giving me way too much food. However, doing that would probably make me lose weight, and I would end up being here longer. In other words, I have no choice.

1:35 PM

Salads used to be my best friend, but having to scoop out every remaining drop of dressing from the bottom of the bowl every time I eat one has changed my mind about them. I cannot tell you how many times I have been called into the nurses' backroom to either lick my yogurt carton or salad bowl clean or suck on the straw of my milk until I am swallowing nothing but air. I think I have learned my lesson by now. Today during lunch, I was sure not to leave a single morsel of my salad remaining. Jodi and Casey noticed the overdramatic show I was putting on and could not stop laughing.

It's difficult to say whether or not I believe Cherry Oak's policies will help me develop more "normal" eating habits. What is "normal" anyway? The concept seems foreign to me. My old "normal" was never eating. My new "normal" is licking my plates clean like a dog. And all of this is for what—to prepare us to eat in more social and vulnerable places? I'd laugh, but I think French dressing would come spewing from my nose.

7:00 PM

As strange as it sounds, my confidence has grown in the weeks that I have been here. Before entering treatment, I would isolate myself and avoid communicating with others as much as possible. At school, I would skip lunch to spend an hour in a bathroom stall listening to the new Lorde album, timing each song perfectly with how much longer I had to hide until my English class started. I would go to bed at eight o'clock just to be alone and not be tempted to eat anything else for the rest of the night. Now, I find myself hanging out in the multipurpose room, constantly wishing Jodi or Casey would come in so we can talk and be together. Before, the nurses and I feared that I would be spending a lot of my free time in my room. They even contemplated limiting the number of novels my mom brought in for me to read and the amount of time I'd be allowed to work on my homework outside of school time, but now, I only go to my room to sleep. I feel like a completely different person. I wonder if being around other people with eating disorders has made me more comfortable since we all understand what we're going through, at least to a certain extent. My confidence will most likely diminish the moment I have to re-enter the real world, but we will conquer that task when the time comes.

8:40 PM

My mom just left after a short visit. We did not talk about anything too serious. It was a nice change. She filled me in on the events happening at my high school for Catholic School's Week. The events are nothing major, only a few themed dress-down days and pep rallies. They are a nice change of schedule, though, and classes are always shortened. I am a tad disappointed that I am missing out on the activities this year, but I am relieved at the same time. Faking school spirit has never been on the list of things I enjoyed doing, and my friends would always gravitate toward kids who were louder and more outgoing than I was; therefore, I would be left alone, spending the time staring at the clock on the wall waiting for dismissal to come around.

Making friends has always been difficult for me. Keeping them has been even harder. Maybe it is because any friend I ever had either bullied me behind my back or took advantage of me. Maybe it is that I'm scared of becoming too attached to someone. I don't miss my friends from school very much. Ashley may be the only exception, but I'm not so sure. I hate to throw my friends under the bus like that, but most of them are the fakest people I know. I always felt like a backup friend to them, a second choice when there was no one else for them to talk to, and when I was finally spoken to, I never felt good enough. I constantly battled being myself versus being the person I thought my friends wanted me to be.

Being in an environment like the eating disorder unit of a mental hospital, you don't have to worry about silly things like that. Throughout the day, you are constantly sharing your deepest and darkest insecurities with rooms full of strangers. You don't get judged as harshly by them because everyone is as screwed up as you are. Any connections you make with people are real because they see the true, raw version of you.

I think everyone could benefit from something like this.

9:00 PM

Yogurt is easily becoming my favorite snack to have at night. I have ordered it as an extra for the past couple days, and now I can hardly go a day without it. Oh, gosh. Is this my eating disorder talking? Am I developing a new ritual: eating yogurt every night? These are the things I have never thought about before coming here. It just seems like anything you say or do involving food around here will be twisted to your disadvantage. Can I please just enjoy my yogurt in peace? I am a victim of my own paranoid mind.

On a lighter note, I think eating something extra at night is helping me gain weight. I know that my calorie intake will be increased shortly, so as long as I do well with eating an extra at night, I should be prepared for any upcoming calorie increase. I am not quite sure what it means for my recovery and mental state, but I am currently doing everything I can not to lose weight. Silly, everyday things, such as standing and walking, have such heightened physical effects on someone whose metabolism is cranking faster than a speeding bullet. I am always conscious of whatever my body is doing, and I try my hardest to move as little as possible. I am even breaking my habit of nervously tapping my foot whenever I am sitting.

Before coming to Cherry Oak, I was terrified of gaining weight. Now, I am horrified at the idea of losing weight. I am not sure if that is me talking or just my strong desire to get discharged from this place as soon as possible. Whatever the case may be, I am running with it.

11:15 PM

    I had the best evening tonight with Casey. We spent hours after dinner in the multipurpose room working on a puzzle of New York City while we talked and opened up to each other about the most random things. We talked about things we aren't allowed to talk about on the unit. Of course, we were alone, careful not to let anyone hear what we were chatting about.

    Casey told me the weight which she had been upon being admitted. It was incredibly low. I couldn't tell if there was a sense of pride or disappointment in her tone. She continued to look down at the puzzle, her bony fingers grazing each piece in front of her. I didn't know how to respond. I was startled, jealous, and thankful at the same time—thankful that she's in here with me getting the help she needs. The thought of anything else made me want to cry.

    "Wow," was all that I could mutter out. "My lowest weight sounds like a joke compared to that."

    Casey laughed.

    "I'm also about a foot-and-a-half shorter than you," she said to me. "And you're a guy. We're built a little differently."

    "Do you know that girls used to tell me that they wished they had a body like mine?" I began laughing, remembering how happy those comments made me. Something about having a more feminine physique was attractive to me. It meant that I was smaller, more petite. I remembered one comment in particular that a girl left on one of my Instagram pictures where I was wearing skinny jeans. She said that she couldn't believe that I—a boy—had better legs than her.

    "Now, that's just weird," Casey chuckled.

    We stood around our puzzle and admired how it looked. There were only about twenty pieces left. They were all part of the sky, which is naturally the most difficult part of any puzzle. The city skyline looked beautiful, and it was something I missed. The possibility of being free enough to walk around somewhere like New York City again felt like a dream. It seemed so far away.

"Look!" Casey said, pointing down to a billboard that was plastered against one of the buildings on the puzzle. It was of a slim woman in a bikini. I couldn't tell what the billboard was for, but it looked like it was for a new line of swimwear or a Victoria's Secret advertisement. The woman on the billboard was tall and had long, blonde hair that appeared to be caught up in some wind. "It's you!"

"Shut up!" We both burst out laughing.

"You two better not be having too much fun in here," a nurse said as she peeked her head into the room. "It's getting late."

"Yeah. We're going to bed now," Casey replied.

Once the nurse left, Casey and I decided to delicately move our almost finished puzzle to a nearby table that wasn't being used.

"I don't know how I got here."

Casey's tone became dull.

"What do you mean?" I asked.

"I don't know how I got this bad," she said. "After my mom died last year, it's like I became a new person." Casey's head was down as she continued playing with the leftover pieces of the puzzle. She moved and spoke slowly, carefully choosing her words.

"I'm sorry to hear about your mom," I told her. I already knew about the passing of her mom based on what she has shared during groups, but I never got the opportunity to talk to her about it one-on-one. "Losing a parent must be the hardest thing in the world."

"Yeah. Look where I am now," Casey said. "I never meant for all this to happen. I lost control."

We continued chatting for a few moments before we parted ways. I walked back to my room with my mind replaying every word Casey spoke. *Her weight was so low.* I am not sure I could have gotten down to it without literally dying. I sure would have liked to try.

What stuck with me the most was what Casey said at the end. Eating disorders are all about control. Who has it? You or the disorder? I'm not sure what I believe these days.

Anyway, to top this whole day off, I fear that I have lost my favorite Bic pen. I need to mourn.

Saturday, February 8, 2014
DAY 12 OF RECOVERY

8:50 AM

It's Saturday again. It feels like just yesterday that I was saying the same thing. Doesn't time fly when you're having fun? Maybe I haven't lost all hope in this place. Today, I hope to spend most of my time finishing up my Spanish homework and working on a new puzzle with Casey. That would be nice.

Our schedules on the weekends are always screwed up. Over half of the doctors and therapists do not come in, meaning the amount of group therapy sessions we have is basically cut in half. I used to love weekends for this reason alone, but now that I am making friends and opening up more, I look forward to being around people and connecting with them. However, it is nice to have a couple of days after a long week to refresh and ready your mind for what is to come. People on the outside cannot even fathom how difficult it is to get out of bed every day around here.

Plus, I am happy to report that my Bic pen has been found. Casey had it the whole time. I am so relieved. I have this habit of forming deep connections with inanimate objects at times.

1:20 PM

I think today's lunch holds the record for the most "incompletes" I have seen since I have been here. Neither Jodi, Casey, or Emmanuel finished their meals. Something must have been off, or perhaps it was a full moon last night. That is just not something I would have expected from any of them, especially Emmanuel. He is supposed to be leaving on a pass in a few hours, and not finishing a meal the day of risks that opportunity. He did not complete his meal last night, either. If I didn't know any better, I'd think he doesn't want to go on his pass. Maybe he is afraid to have a couple of meals outside of our safe environment here. Maybe he isn't sure how he will do. I could understand that. Still, I would not jeopardize any chance I had at getting out of here for a few hours, even if that meant taking food journals to the nearby Panera Bread to keep track of each thing I put into my mouth. I'd be curious to find out just how fatty or full of starches their macaroni & cheese is. When I say that I'm curious, what I mean is that I'm downright petrified. Alright, I am actually curious, though.

4:00 PM

I just woke up from a terrible nightmare. First of all, a nurse from the outpatient program down the hall woke me up because she thought I was stretching. Has she ever seen someone take a nap before? She looked stunned. Almost a second later, another nurse from my unit came rushing into my room and lifted my body into a sitting position. She accused me of stretching, too. I practically went blue in the face trying to explain to her that I wasn't. I don't think she believed me.

Now that I think about it, I am glad I was woken up. I dreamed that it was the middle of March, and I was still here in the hospital. I was missing the Ellie Goulding concert that I have been looking forward to since I bought the tickets last year.

Anyone who knows me knows that Ellie Goulding is the absolute love of my life. Her music, that is. It has gotten me through the worst of times. If I ever had a terrible day, I knew that I could go to my bedroom, make it pitch dark, and play her records until everything I felt went away. Last year, she finally announced that she would be going on tour *and* coming to New York City. I purchased the tickets the minute they went on sale during my history class, and it has been the only thing getting me through these last few weeks. If I am not out of here in time for that concert, I am not sure what I will do.

6:20 PM

Dinner was a tad disturbing tonight. Here's the thing—salad dressings count as two fats on our meal plans, so you would have to be dumb not to use that to your advantage. To order dressing, you must order a garden salad on the side, which, unfortunately, does not fulfill any part of the meal plan requirements. Still, the fats from the packets of dressing make the dreadful chewing of hospital lettuce worth it. For a reason unbeknownst to me, I had three packets of French dressing on my tray during dinner, but I only saw one. I finished my salad as I normally would, and I swear my heart skipped a beat when I laid eyes on the two remaining packets of dressing under my napkin.

My hands began to sweat. *What should I do? Should I grab them and hide them in the sleeves of my sweater? In my socks?* I didn't want the nurses to think that I left them uneaten on purpose. I just truly hadn't seen them. *Perhaps I can somehow slide them off my plate and onto the floor. From there, I could kick them, so they'd appear under someone else's chair. Then again, a simple peek at the orders from today would tell the nurses who had three packets of salad dressing with their meal.*

"Complete," I heard Britney shout from across the table. It was time to go around the table and let the nurses know whether we completed our meals or not. *Shit.*

Before I could decide what to do, I ripped open those two packets of French dressing as if my life depended on it and swallowed them whole. I do not even know how I did it, and I can't think about it too much without having the urge to vomit. Leaving that dressing uneaten on the tray was just not worth getting an "incomplete" for the day, even if it meant having the feeling of drinking salad dressing ingrained in my memory forever.

"Complete," I said shyly. The room applauded. The nurse in the room wrote down whatever she had to on her clipboard to indicate that I had completed. Little did she know that I had a salad dressing smoothie sitting in my tummy.

10:45 PM

Word on the street is that Stephanie got busted doing some jumping jacks in her room. What's worse is that Delores, her roommate, was in the room with her the whole time. I could not imagine so blatantly disregarding another person's triggers or feelings like that. Even if I had the urge to, which I do almost every night, I'd never do anything like that in front of Emmanuel, and I expect the same from him. Delores said that she told a few nurses what she saw, but nothing has been done about it yet. It must be difficult to room with Stephanie. The mere presence of her can trigger someone out of their mind.

Then again, I shouldn't be so harsh. Eating disorders are competitive by nature, and frankly, I'm jealous. I'm jealous that a person a few doors down from me had enough nerve to exercise in a place like this. Actually, I'm not sure nerve is what it takes. It's clear Stephanie is struggling.

11:30 PM

I don't mind having a roommate anymore. Emmanuel and I have become pretty good friends, and he is very easy to talk to.

He's the kind of person who you never really know what is going through his head, but you just roll with it. He's also very awkward. He doesn't say much, but when he does, you know he wants to say more. He makes this strangely endearing face before he speaks, like he is planning every word that wants to come out of his mouth.

It is similar to the face I make when I know I am about to stutter, which is happening more often than I'd care to admit. I went to speech therapy for most of my childhood, and my stutter seems to come and go. I notice it be more prevalent whenever I'm nervous or talking with someone new, which makes sense of why it is becoming a bigger issue at the moment. It's embarrassing, and I'm so tired of thinking I have it under control when I don't. I have been dealing with it for so long. I'm not sure if it's easier for me to imagine a life for myself without my eating disorder or without my stutter.

Sunday, February 9, 2014
DAY 13 OF RECOVERY

<u>8:50 AM</u>

I woke up tired. All I wanted to do was go back to sleep, rest my head down on my cardboard pillow (which felt strangely comforting when I first woke up), and drift away. I do not remember the last time I woke up at five o'clock in the morning on a weekend. After we get our vitals checked, sometimes it is easier just to stay awake. The unit is typically pretty quiet, and everyone is still asleep. The only sounds you hear are the different color codes being announced from the speakers in the hall and the occasional footsteps of the morning nurses making their hourly rounds. It's way different than the mostly terrifying environment of the unit during the day. I like it.

Things began to rustle up on the unit once word got out that Stephanie apparently took a two-hour shower in the middle of the night. I was told the showers get unlocked around five in the morning once each patient finishes with their vitals and weigh-ins, so I don't know how Stephanie found her way into the stall. To make matters worse, she was also caught exercising. The nurses here are skilled at monitoring the lights and shadows that appear under the doors adjacent to the flooring; therefore, any movements in our bathrooms and shower stalls can somewhat be detected. I don't know how she can be trusted to take a shower on her own ever again. One girl said that she thinks Stephanie's shower privileges will be taken away. For the sake of every patient here, I hope that isn't true. Another guessed that she will be assigned a personal nurse to follow her around wherever she goes to ensure no extra movement is being done. That sounds like a more realistic solution.

1:25 PM

Note to self: cottage cheese is the single worst food to ever exist on the entire planet. Do not order it ever again. I'm not even sure why cottage cheese is a thing. Who in their right mind truly believes it tastes good? I give myself props for trying it, though. Once the mealtime nurse saw me struggling to keep it down, she suggested I mix it in with my pineapple. I wished that helped, but it made it worse. I finished all I could without having the urge to rip out each taste bud from my tongue, but I knew the bowl would not be empty enough to be counted as complete. The nurse noticed, stood up, and walked over to me.

"Is this your first time trying cottage cheese?" the nurse whispered to me.

"It is," I told her. "I don't think I'll be having it again, but I'm glad I tried it."

She gave me a wink and took the bowl with the remaining cottage cheese off of my tray.

"Good job," she said as she walked away. I couldn't believe it.

This nurse's name is Junko. She is the sweetest person on the entire unit, and this is not the first time she has been lenient with me. She was the nurse who drew my blood the other day, and she asks me how I am doing every time we pass each other on the unit. I think what I like the most about her is that she looks like and reminds me of my favorite teacher from middle school, Mrs. Shawl. They almost look the same, too. Junko has short and curly, light-brown hair and thin, rectangular glasses. I always breathe a big sigh of relief whenever she is present on the unit. She isn't here every day, but I wish she were.

When leaving the table after lunch, Junko patted me on the back and told me how proud she was of me for trying to complete something that I visibly did not want to. It feels good when certain things like that are recognized. Because mental illnesses are *mental,* it can sometimes be difficult for outsiders to see your progress. Speaking to Junko always makes me feel validated and warm.

On the other hand, I am going to have to talk to Stacy regarding this whole cottage cheese fiasco. If I remember correctly, I ordered it three more times this week. At this point, I would rather drink four more packets of French dressing.

6:25 PM

It looks like another snow day today. Good thing I don't have to shovel! And the best part is that nobody here expects me to.

Jodi saved me a seat next to her at dinner. I noticed Stephanie almost took it when I walked in. She gave me a strange look as I sat down and moved to the opposite side of the table. Neither Jodi or I meant it to be malicious. I've sat next to Jodi almost every day for every meal, and being with her makes me comfortable. In my eyes, anything I have to do to complete a meal is worth it—even if that means further distancing myself from Stephanie. She didn't say a word the entire meal.

7:30 PM

I just got off the phone with my mom. My sister's room is almost completely transformed into a part-time nursery. They have almost finished painting the room after deciding on a lavender, periwinkle color. I think that's too dark. Maybe it's a good thing I am not there to help. I feel like I'd be too annoying.

During visiting hours today, it felt like a Britney family reunion. I met every single one of her relatives, including her three younger sisters, parents, and a couple of others that I lost track of. I could have sworn we had a four-visitor-per-night limit. I have learned to like Britney, despite her ability to make you feel like the most inferior piece of garbage with a single glare. I was fascinated by her family. I can see where she gets her attitude and independence. Her mom is super thin and looks like someone who would ask for a manager at a retail shop after her expired coupon rang up incorrectly. My mom saw her and actually thought that *she* was a patient, not Britney. Her sisters were blinged-out head to toe in designer shoes and jewelry. Having them on the unit felt intimidating, though I'm sure that's only my insecurity speaking. I think that in many ways, Britney is a representation of several things I want to be: confident, thin, seemingly wealthy, etc. I don't know. Maybe I'm just a jealous brat.

8:40 PM

Someone put Toy Story 3 on in the multipurpose room. Are they trying to make me cry? I swear the ending gets me every time. I do miss some of my stuffed animals from home. I sleep with a bunch every night, and my heart broke when I learned I couldn't bring them to the unit.

I am waiting for Jodi and Casey to put on their pajamas and come back to the multipurpose room so we can finish our game of cards. All three of us ordered an extra, which should be here in a few minutes. It saddens me to imagine life on the unit without them. I wonder who will be the next to leave. Maybe Jodi? Emmanuel? He has been doing pretty well recently. Then again, so has Britney. It's hard to tell. I have never felt more comfortable around people than I have here, and I hope that newfound ability of mine isn't lost once I get discharged from this place. I know I don't have to worry about that for a while.

Monday, February 10, 2014
DAY 14 OF RECOVERY

9:50 AM

My worst class in school is Spanish. I cannot remember the last time I got over 60 percent on an assignment. The only reason I scored *that* high was because I would jot down every exam answer in my English-to-Spanish dictionary that we were allowed to use during class. That, and writing algebraic formulas on the back of my calculator, are the only reasons I'm even passing my sophomore year. I am sure you could guess how excited I was to be sent a stack of worksheets from my Spanish teacher. I panicked for a bit, only then realizing that I would have to basically teach myself whatever it was that was written on the worksheets. The good news is that there is a Spanish tutor here who has given me every answer to my homework so far. Needless to say, I have had a pretty good morning.

1:40 PM

One thing I cannot stand about my meetings with Connor is how he seems to be studying me every minute of our fifty-minute session. He reminds me a lot of my dad. Whether it be mentioning how my legs are crossed, what my hands are doing, or how far away on my bed I am sitting from him, he never fails to make me feel self-conscious about literally every part of my body. He talks as if the way I position my body somehow means something—something deeper. We both already know that I am a socially awkward teenager with debilitating anxiety and fear, so what else is there to truly uncover? Connor also reminded me that I have my second family meeting this upcoming Friday. I wonder if this will be the one my sister decides to come to. Boy, I sure hope not.

I have some bad news about Emmanuel. He is having a very difficult time gaining weight. In fact, he told me that he has actually been losing weight. His meal plan is probably the largest of anyone's on the unit, which has caused him to incomplete four meals in a row. If that number increases to five, he will be put on bed rest and only allowed to leave his room for meals and groups. I feel bad for him, and I can't help but be appalled at the amount of food this place is attempting to feed him. His meal plan would be difficult for anyone to finish, let alone someone struggling with anorexia.

8:50 PM

The visit with my mom went well tonight. Throughout my life, she has always been there for me no matter what, and it is amazing to have someone who believes in you on your team. She showed me a graph she obtained from Dr. Fischer, my pediatrician from back home, that showed my annual weight compared to other boys my height and age. It was clear that I had *always* been underweight and within the lesser 25 percent.

My mom seemed pretty convinced that the goal weight Cherry Oak had provided for me was too high, and I should not be obligated to reach it to be discharged. I tried convincing her that my past weight doesn't matter, and I have been taught that Cherry Oak cannot legally let me go without a doctor's approval if I am still under my goal weight. We both seemed equally as uncomfortable about that idea, so she actually agreed to sign a forty-eight notice after I gain a bit more weight and feel comfortable leaving. Basically, a forty-eight notice is a form you sign giving a forty-eight-hour warning that you have decided to leave the hospital against a doctor's approval. In other words, if anything were to happen to you after leaving, the hospital isn't responsible. I'm still a minor, so either my mom or my dad would have to sign it for me.

"That's just not who I am," I said to my mom, referencing the idea of me being in a larger body. My body had become a part of my identity, and it wasn't a part that I was ready to remove.

It made me happy to know that my mom believed in me so much she trusted my ability to say when I was ready to be discharged. It also made me happy to know she was willing to sign that forty-eight. My dad, on the other hand, may be a bit more difficult to convince. Being a psychologist and all, I'm sure he'd have some thoughts on whether I was capable of making the right decisions for myself. It is *my* mental health that is on the line, and *I* was the one who desperately wanted to receive treatment in the first place. If I feel like I am ready, why should someone get in the way of that?

On the other hand, it upsets me to know that all that is keeping me here—or anyone, really—is a goal weight. The first thing any doctor or therapist will tell you about eating disorders is that they are mental illnesses, yet sometimes, it feels like all anyone cares about is the physicality of it. Just because someone hits their goal weight does not mean that they are mentally recovered enough to go out on their own. I'm sure this will not be my case, as I suspect that I will be far along in my mental recovery by the time I gain the weight I need to leave this place. Still, I wish one's mental state played a larger role in determining how well someone was doing in recovery. My weight has been pretty stagnant for the past few days, yet I feel like I have taken strides in my recovery and my perception of a healthy life. Does that count for anything? That seems to be a major misconception that many have about eating disorders, that they're all about looks and how skinny you are. Recovery is mental, and a person's weight or body type cannot determine the severity of their eating disorder.

All anyone sees here are numbers on a scale. *That* is the number that defines how much you have progressed in your recovery. *That* is the number that determines whether you are sick enough in the eyes of society. *That* is the number people look at to reassure themselves that you are healthy. What about every "normal-sized" person? What happens to them? What happens when they need help, only to be mocked and turned away by a system riddled with stigma? There are so many stereotypes about eating disorders. *They are all about food. They are all about weight. Only white, teenage girls can have eating disorders. You have to have the privilege of being properly diagnosed by a world-renowned doctor even to claim that you have an eating disorder. You have to be so weak that your bones cattle when you walk and your cheekbones plunge out of your face to be taken seriously.*

Fuck that. That needs to change.

Tuesday, February 11, 2014
DAY 15 OF RECOVERY

<u>8:50 AM</u>

Do you ever feel the need to get dressed up real nice just to prove that you still have—I don't know—*it?* I felt like doing that this morning. I decided to crank out my favorite blue button-down shirt and gray cardigan from Urban Outfitters, along with a pair of black skinny jeans and boots. Maybe I am trying to convince myself that my appearance does not have to suffer once I gain more weight. Maybe I am subconsciously attempting to prove something to the other patients here. But, *what?* It felt good to dress up, but I became nervous once I thought about the other patients and staff perceiving the way that I looked.

The only full-body glance I've gotten of myself is from my reflection in the window of my room. It's right beside my bed, and if I stand far enough away from it at the perfect time of day, I can see myself. I can see my legs. I can see my hips. I can see my thighs. I can see every part of my body that I have loathed for so long. They now appear almost distant, like I don't know them anymore.

11:05 AM

Psychotherapy was emotional today. Jodi shared that she might be discharged later this week. She has reached her goal weight, and her treatment team believes she is prepared to leave. She looked frightened.

Toward the end of psychotherapy, Jodi was called out of the room by a nurse. She returned a few moments later, sobbing, quickly handed Casey a note, then left again. Casey read it and nudged it over to me.

> **My grandmother had two aneurysms.**
> **I have to leave to say goodbye.**
> **Be back soon - maybe.**
> **-Jodi**

Great. That's exactly what she needed right now.

I am anxiously waiting to meet with Burton today. If I am not up at least a pound or two, I will have no chance of getting a pass for this weekend, which is Ashley's sweet sixteen birthday party. Would Burton even let me go? I hope he knows, just based on my personality type, that I am not one to dance or do anything crazy at parties. Knowing me, I would be so paranoid about losing weight that I would spend the entire time stuffing my face with cake and mediocre buffet entrees. Picturing myself doing so is making me laugh. My friends and classmates would have no idea who I was.

1:20 PM

It was strange not having Jodi next to me during lunch. I wonder how she is doing. I hope she comes back soon so we can all shower her with support.

Jodi certainly missed out on a funny lunch, though. We had a nurse I had never met before supervising our meal, and none of the patients could stop laughing at how awful her face looked. She looked like she had about ten syringes of Botox injected into her face right before the meal, and I swear her expression did not change the entire hour. Lucky for me, I had the privilege of sitting next to her at the head of the table. I found it quite amusing watching her watch us eat our weight in greasy lasagna and protein shakes, when it looked like she, herself, had not eaten in days. I hope she is not going to be a regular around here. I didn't even catch her name. It was so uncomfortable.

2:40 PM

We had a different group session today called Nursing Ed. Based on the name itself, one would think it would have something to do with, I don't know, *nursing eating disorders*. The more scientific and technical side of recovering from an eating disorder? No. All we did was create Valentine's Day break-up cards to "Ed." It was actually pretty funny. We were given pink and red construction paper and markers and told to have fun. I opted for some black paper to make mine a bit edgier.

It's strange to think about your eating disorder as an actual person—someone you were friends with, someone you were almost in a relationship with. However, it actually makes a lot of sense. Comparing it to an abusive relationship is surprisingly liberating. You know your eating disorder so well, and oftentimes, it's the one thing in your life that is constant. Everything becomes about your eating disorder. It is always there to put in its two cents, persuading you in the direction of its benefit. Life becomes so devalued that your sense of being, along with your feelings and attitudes toward others, becomes altered. It felt great writing that letter. I kept mine short and sweet. It went along the lines of this:

Dear Ed,
You do not own me anymore.
Your power and control over me are gone.
It's over. Fuck you.

That wasn't the only breakup that happened on the unit today. Dandy is finally off of her feeding tube! I don't think she is hooked up to her IV anymore, either. I am so happy for her.

7:00 PM

I can hardly write. My entire body feels like it may combust at any moment. Not only that, but I feel about five months pregnant. Maybe six. I think it is safe to say that I just ate the largest dinner of my life. Have I said that before? I probably have. This time, I mean it. I would have been fine finishing my two slices of pizza if it weren't for the two cartons of whole milk, the individually wrapped chunk of carrot cake, and the three sides of fruit that were waiting for me afterward. It would have been easy to give into my disorder and ignore my need for this many calories and nutrients, but I know I'd only be hurting myself if I did that.

During dinner, a slice of Casey's honeydew flew from her fork and onto the floor. I am not sure how it happened, but a chunk of green melon flying through the air struck me as one of the funniest things I had ever seen. It landed right by my foot. Casey and I stared at it for a good five minutes with no idea what to do. No one else knew what we were laughing at, and we didn't want to mention what happened in fear of Casey being blamed for possibly "purposely" letting her food drop to the floor. I ended up kicking the honeydew further under the table with the hope that it would appear next to someone else. I hope the cameras in the room didn't catch that. If they did, boy, I'd be in trouble.

10:25 PM

If I don't weigh more by tomorrow, I'll be so upset. All I want to do is gain weight. I have such a far way to go, and I do not know what else I could do to put the weight on faster. I shared my frustration with my mom, who agreed to sneak in some of my favorite candy and snacks from home. And yes, believe it or not, no patient here is allowed to eat anything more or anything less than what is specified on their meal plan. In my case—my *anorexic* case—I find it funny that I am not allowed to eat anything besides what is on my menu, especially if I am actually hungry and *want* to eat! However, there are many types of eating disorders, and I suppose it would be difficult for the staff to monitor who has what eating disorder or who can eat extra outside food and who cannot.

My mom brought two pink cake pops from the nearby Starbucks, along with about six bags of gummy bears and a ton of other crap. I am so excited. I hope I can finish it all tonight. That way, I will definitely have gained some weight by the morning. I hid all the food in my school backpack that is to the left of my bed beside the wall.

Before I go to bed every night, I stop and think about how lucky I am to have the people in my life that I do. I don't think anyone else's mother would defy doctor's orders and sneak in candy to their kid. I'm sure many wouldn't agree that it's the right thing to do, but I don't care. Something like this would have terrified me just a few weeks ago. Here I am, today, anxiously looking forward to locking myself in my bathroom and stuffing my face with candy in hopes of every calorie sticking to my body like glue.

I am also very lucky to have found people here that don't make me want to scream into my pillow and hide in my room. I know I have said it about ten thousand times before, but Casey is just incredible. It feels like we have been friends forever, even though it has only been two weeks. She agreed, and she said that she loves me. I don't know what I would do without her. Just her presence alone lifts my mood by about 200 percent. I wake up in the morning excited for the day just because it means I can see her and sit next to her for breakfast. I hope she knows how much our friendship means to me.

Wednesday, February 12, 2014
DAY 16 OF RECOVERY

<u>9:35 AM</u>

OH MY GOD! I think I just got the greatest news of my life. I am finally on Phase Three! I am so happy I could cry. The benefits of being on Phase Three may not seem too impressive, but I am now entitled to two fifteen-minute walks around and outside the hospital. I am also *that* much closer to my eventual discharge. Burton called me to his office after breakfast, and he was very impressed with my weight gain, which is almost a two-pound difference from yesterday. *How did that happen?* Something must have been off with the scale, but I am not complaining. It also might've been the hundreds of calories of candy I ate last night in my bathroom at two o'clock in the morning, but Burton doesn't need to know about that.

As happy as I am, I'm not entirely pleased with the news I received. Before this morning, I believed that being on Phase Three automatically made me a candidate for a day pass outside of the unit. I'd be able to eat with my parents, go shopping at the nearby mall, and maybe even see a movie. I was wrong—very wrong. In order for me to get a pass, I must weigh at least 75 percent of what a "normal weight" is for a boy my age and height. In other words, I am still nine pounds away from getting a pass. I'm going to talk about it with Connor. I would do anything for an hour away from this place.

10:15 AM

I was so distracted by the events this morning that I forgot to mention what I woke up to. To keep it brief, well, my *briefs* pitched quite the tent under my sheets. Do you like my creativity in making that sound as PG as possible? I can only hope that nobody ever reads this journal. In my defense, I haven't gotten a boner in weeks—maybe months. Not even in the mornings. For a teenage boy, that's a pretty long time. Part of me wants to ask Emmanuel if his *stuff* hasn't been working as it should, or maybe I should ask Connor. It's no question that there is certainly not enough information out there about males with eating disorders, much less the side effects one may encounter, such as erectile dysfunction. Thankfully for me, that issue has seemed to work itself out.

If there is one thing I learned while being here, it is that eating disorders affect *every* part of a person's body. Your body is not designed to survive an eating disorder. It can only do so much with what you give back to it.

11:20 AM

If someone looked at me right now, they'd probably see smoke coming from my ears. I am so upset. There's another therapist on the unit. Her name is Barbara. I have only had a few conversations with her, but she has got to be the most unpleasant woman I have ever met. One time, she was over ten minutes late to proctor a group and scolded *me* for being late because I ran to fill up my cup of water and coincidentally walked back in the room at the same time she entered it. She thought I was late, too. She embarrassed me in front of everybody. I understand therapists are meant to push their clients, but she takes it too far.

Every patient was equally confused when Barbara came into the multipurpose room today to moderate psychotherapy. She never proctors psychotherapy. I certainly knew that I wouldn't be jumping out of my seat to share my thoughts unless I was specifically called on, which is exactly what she did.

I hesitantly shared my thoughts for the day, feeling frustrated by my doctor's inability to give me a clear answer on whether I would be able to get a pass to Ashley's sweet sixteen party. It seemed silly bringing this up since going to a party was practically the last thing on anyone else's mind, but this has been something that I have been holding onto for weeks, and it has been one of my biggest motivators thus far to gain weight and progress. If there was *any* opportunity that I could go to that party and see my friends, I would take it.

"I can tell you right now that's not happening," Barbara spat, glaring at me from across the table.

I think I blinked a good twenty times in a row. I didn't know what else to do with my face. Every person in the room was staring at me, waiting for a response. I told her that Burton said it was still a possibility, but she shot that down with the same snarky tone.

The thing is, I knew all along I wouldn't be able to go to the party. I knew I wouldn't be medically cleared in time. I knew I wouldn't be granted a pass. However, nobody ever told me that. It was always, "we'll see," or "maybe," or "let's see if you gain the weight in time." False hope is the worst thing anyone can give. Barbara cut straight to the chase without any remorse. I could not stop crying. I felt so hopeless.

I want you to know that I know how stupid and trivial this all sounds. But it still sucked. A sweet sixteen party is the last thing I should be worried about. *A sweet sixteen party? Really?* It wasn't even about that. It wasn't even about Ashley. I was just hoping to feel like a normal teenager again for one night.

1:20 PM

I have calmed down since my psychotherapy fiasco. Maybe it is best that I don't go to the party. Maybe it's for the better. Everything happens for a reason, and I hope to call Ashley tonight to tell her just how hard I fought to be able to go. I am absolutely powerless in this situation.

I felt the same way during lunch. I was still so upset. It would have been so easy for me to just not complete my meal. If I ever had a good excuse to do so, today would've be the day. As I sat in front of my meal, I thought to myself: "Am I really going to punish myself for something that I have no control over?" I wasn't going to let someone, let alone Barbara, cause me to incomplete my meal. I wasn't going to give her that. I sat there and ate every last morsel of my lunch.

2:50 PM

Okay. Maybe I am not completely over what happened this morning. I basically spent my entire hour with Connor complaining about how much of a bitch Barbara is. Bad move. He alluded to the idea that he wants me and Barbara to sit down and talk things over. I'd rather drink a gallon of bleach than do that. I'm not sure what I'd even say to her. He told me he would try to talk to the rest of my treatment team about the possibility of still going on the pass to the party, but it is basically a no-go. I am not going to get my hopes up.

4:03 PM

Is today, like, Let's-Annoy-The-Crap-Out-of-Chris Day? I like Connor, I really do, but why does he find the need to call me out during every single group he runs? Whenever Casey and I make eye contact or smile at each other, he asks me to share what we are talking about. I literally never know what to say to make this guy happy. What do you want from me? All I want to do is go to bed and forget this day ever happened.

The only thing I am looking forward to is my fifteen-minute walk outside of the unit. I wonder where we will even go. Our unit is close to the maternity ward, so maybe we'll go look at some babies. Gross. I hate babies. However, now that I think about it, it may not even happen because I think we are having another one of those multi-family meetings with everyone's parents and family members. I can so picture my dad talking during one of those. If he does, I swear I will walk out of the room faster than anyone could stop me.

10:00 PM

Not to my surprise, my dad did talk during the multi-family meeting, but it was not as bad or awkward as I had expected it to be. Almost everybody's family came, and we all gathered in a large room not connected to the eating disorder unit. I think it was a few floors down, but I couldn't tell exactly how many since we took the elevator. We were not allowed to take the stairs.

There was not much structure to the meeting. Everybody's parents and families were first given a list of "The Do's and Don't's" for talking to someone with an eating disorder. The paper primarily focused on certain dialogue that would be inappropriate to comment on, such as appearance, weight, and calories. Any topic related to food was basically categorized as a "don't." The "do's" were focused on providing love, support, affirmations, and compliments that were not linked to one's appearance. We patients were also encouraged to tell our families how they can be a helpful support system for us when we return home.

My mom sat next to Casey, which I found really cute. I noticed them talking a bit but didn't hear any of their conversation. None of Casey's family showed up. My dad, on the other hand, had the pleasure of sitting next to Stephanie and her father. I was honestly afraid for him. Everyone in the room noticed the look on her face whenever her father opened his mouth, but I could tell he was trying his hardest to understand. It broke my heart a little.

The meeting helped everyone forget about the chaos that erupted at dinner. Long story short, Emmanuel vomited up his *entire* meal. I was sitting across from him when I noticed his face go expressionless.

"I'm going to throw up," he mouthed.

"No, you're not," I whispered back to him. "You're okay."

He wasn't okay.

Emmanuel stood up from his chair and vomited all over the floor. It went absolutely everywhere. Everybody at the table froze. Half of us were jealous of him, and the rest of us were just shocked. I was a mix of the two. We were all told to quickly return to our rooms and never again talk about what we had just seen. It was clear the nurses proctoring the meal had never been trained for what to do in a situation like this. I had to laugh watching them just stare in complete horror at what happened. Emmanuel was immediately placed on bed rest and was told to only get out of bed for therapy and meals. I feel so terrible for him. I could tell the incident wasn't intentional, yet he is being treated like it was. He has been telling me for days that his meal plan was too large. Maybe now his dietitian will listen.

I just want this day to be over. Every person on the unit just wants this day to be over. I think I will go to sleep now. Tomorrow is another day.

Thursday, February 13, 2014
DAY 17 OF RECOVERY

<u>8:50 AM</u>

There are no tutors here today, so I can get away with doing whatever I want during my school hour. I only have a bit more English homework to do, but I'd rather write in my journal. I'm anxious to see if the rest of the staff makes it in today. It has been snowing nonstop for hours, and we apparently already have eight inches on the ground. I would do anything to be outside right now. Hey, maybe I'll be able to go on my walk tonight! We didn't end up going yesterday because of the family meeting. That's something to look forward to, at least.

<u>12:20 PM</u>

My meeting today with Connor went well. He applauded me for how I opened up to him about my sister and how I was feeling about certain situations back home. He told me he had a chat with my parents about my progress and what we have been working on. I suppose the topic of Oliver came up because he mentioned that my parents were not even completely sure I was into guys. That is the biggest joke I have ever heard in my life. I guess my eating disorder wasn't the only thing they were pretty ignorant to.

Being with Oliver made me feel very comfortable with who I am and my sexuality. It was only with him that I openly acknowledged the fact that I *was* different, and he made me feel proud of it. Very rarely have people in my past ever asked me if I was gay or bisexual. Honestly, I thought it was pretty obvious. Since meeting Oliver, I have been very open about my sexuality. Whenever the topic came up amongst friends, I acted and talked like I had been "out" for years. But the thing is, I never actually "came out." I always found the concept so silly and outlandish. Why is it anyone's business? How does the fact that I am attracted to boys affect anyone? It doesn't, and I hate the fact that we are told that *we* are the ones who have to walk on eggshells in society, sorrowfully hoping that the public approves of who we are. I don't need the acceptance of anyone to be who I am. I don't need it, want it, or seek it.

That's why I was taken aback when Connor told me that I should come out to my parents. I have my second family meeting tomorrow, and he said that would be a perfect opportunity to do so. Thinking about it makes me cringe. I don't know how my parents will react when I tell them, but I sure as hell am not looking for some orchestrated, emotional, coming-of-age conversation about who I am.

Connor also wants me to tell my parents the real reasons why I decided to transfer schools last December. I have tried to avoid that topic for a while. It has been hard for me to admit everything that happened—even to myself. The entire experience was absolutely devastating and one of the worse things I have ever put myself through. To be honest, I'm still trying to decipher what went on during that time. It is all such a blur to me. My actions were influenced by so many things, and it is difficult to pinpoint the reasons why.

Here is what I know for certain. Life at home was awful. School was unbearable. Oliver's constant presence around me didn't help and neither did Ava's boyfriend living in our home. I thought transferring schools would alleviate some of the stress in my life. I thought it would bring in something new. Yet, all it did was heighten the unfamiliarity I felt toward myself and my life.

Bringing this up with my family will be tough. It's hard to admit that you were wrong about something.

1:30 PM

I'm not sure how to bring this up, so I'm just going to say it. Casey has a *kid. A whole child.* Somehow, I'm not surprised. As soon as I met her, I knew she had a motherly vibe to her. I think that's why I am so drawn to her. She's warm, kindhearted, and being around her makes me feel safe. Any kid would be lucky to have her as a mom.

Casey didn't tell me much about her daughter, only that she hasn't spoken to her in over a year. She is almost ten years old, which would mean Casey had her when she was about eighteen. I didn't feel comfortable asking about their relationship or who the father was, but she told me she hopes to reach out to her once she gets her life back on track. I am very touched Casey opened up to me about this.

2:30 PM

I have been staring at the clock for what seems like three hours. Why is it that some days here drag on longer than others? Every patient on Phase Three will soon—

2:50 PM

Jodi came into my room when I was writing to let me know we would finally go on our walk! Ugh. It was incredible. Had I seriously taken fresh air for granted? To make matters even better, it was freeeeezing cold. That is my favorite kind of weather. It makes me feel so alive. My hands are still so cold that it's taking me a lot of effort to even write down my current thoughts.

The walk only lasted fifteen minutes, but I savored every second of it. Jodi, Casey, Delores, and I were the only ones eligible to go. We walked through the maternity ward to the nearby elevator, where we went down a few floors to the lobby. From there, we had to go through a weird security checkpoint to proceed any further. The looks we received from some of the visitors and security guards were honestly hilarious, their eyes filled with a mixture of confusion, side-eye, and shock. If only I could read their minds. If only they knew who we were and why we were in the hospital. It really makes you think, doesn't it? It's a strange feeling, realizing that every person you see out in public has just as complex of a life as you do, and we are ignorant about who people are despite the way they present themselves in the moment.

We were only able to go a few steps into the parking garage. We stayed for about ten minutes until we were forced to walk back up to the unit. One thing that made me emotional was walking past the same chairs in the lobby that my parents and I sat in for hours while I waited to be admitted. If only I knew then that my life would never be the same. I am glad it is not.

We are able to go on another walk at 7:30 tonight. Jodi made a Valentine's Day card for one of the tech nurses who typically goes on the evening walk. It should be funny to see how she reacts. Jodi always tells me how pretty she is. Hey, I get it. I'd be lying if I said I wasn't just slightly attracted to Connor the first few days after I met him. Is that weird—being attracted to your therapist? There's probably some sort of study about that.

<u>*4:05 PM*</u>

Every patient was telekinetically plotting the murder of the nurse in charge of our Body Image group today. We were forced to draw what each of us thought our body looked like at three different times in our lives, one of them being how we believed our body looks now. The nurse flat-out said that this exercise was meant to trigger us. At least she was honest. I took advantage of the opportunity to make my body look as horrendous as possible. I am proud of how it turned out. Most everyone threw their masterpiece in the trash once the group was finished, but I decided to keep mine for whenever I needed a laugh.

10:30 PM

Once all our meals were finished and groups were over, my friends and I hung out together in the multipurpose room. Did I just call them my friends? The word only sounds fitting, but I will still need some time to process that. We spent most of the time watching the Winter Olympics that are currently going on, and we went around the table and rated each performance as if we were the ones judging. It was a lot of fun. We played a few board games, too. Taissa is beginning to spend a lot more time with us. I think she feels comfortable around me, Jodi, and Casey. It has taken her a while, but she is coming out of her shell more and more each day. Emmanuel totally has a crush on her.

Friday, February 14, 2014
VALENTINE'S DAY

❧

8:50 AM

It's Valentine's Day! As if that means anything. The hospital air does feel a bit lighter today. I've never had a Valentine. The closest I've gotten to having one was in the third grade. My sister had just gotten her first boyfriend, and I was convinced that I was running out of time to find love. I made a promise to myself that I wouldn't finish third grade without asking a girl out. Spoiler alert—I didn't ask a girl out.

I'm hoping for an easy day today. I have another family meeting with my parents this afternoon which I am feeling a little anxious about. I still haven't decided what I'm going to talk about. Connor and I have conflicting ideas. It's also snowing a ton outside.

12:15 PM

Meal Planning can officially go to hell. I cannot stand it. I had to order a record of *three* Boost Plus drinks for one of my meals to reach the number of calories I needed. I ordered two chocolates and one vanilla. I can already feel the bloating in my stomach.

Connor was in charge of Psychotherapy today—*again*. It was the worst. Half of the group never talks, yet I am the only one he ever calls out for being "too quiet." I had to pull some things out of my ass to get him off of it.

"I struggled during Meal Planning this afternoon."

"I'm having a bad body image day."

"I'm nervous about my family meeting later."

Seriously, do our therapists ever get bored of the things said during these groups? Instead of calling on us when we clearly have nothing to share, how about we create a safe environment where people can share their thoughts and feelings on things when they actually *want* to?

Speaking of my upcoming family meeting, Connor hasn't helped me prepare for shit. He spent our entire one-on-one going on and on about how I am not letting myself open up during groups, and Jodi, Casey, and I have to stop isolating ourselves from the rest of the patients. Seriously, where did that one come from? He worries that we have formed some sort of "clique." Sure, we spend most of our time together, but we're not hurting anybody. On what planet is spending time with people who make you feel comfortable a crime?

Today's meeting with Connor has only made me feel more paranoid about everybody here. Am I doing something wrong? Are they trying to find something to call me out on? I have noticed the nurses watch me more closely during meals. It has even gotten to a point where I mouth "What?" in their direction as if they had addressed me and I failed to hear. Does it seriously have to do with me spending so much time with Casey and Jodi?

1:45 PM

A hobby that a lot of us have picked up in here is bracelet-making. I curse the first person who brought in the rainbow loom kit because it is now all I do in my free time. It's therapeutic. The nurses like it, too. It doesn't require much effort, only the moving and tying of one-inch rubber bands across a board with pegs. Casey has been showing me how to create a lot of different patterns. It's funny; we are currently in Recreation, a group where we can basically do anything that distracts us from our eating disorders, and everyone has their rubber bands and kits spread out all over the table. We all look like little elves.

Although Recreation is fun, I am looking forward to Meditation later. I think it is scheduled right before my family meeting, so it will give me a good opportunity to clear my head and go over what I want to talk about. I'm still not quite sure about that one. Oliver has been on my mind a lot, and I know that's a topic Connor wants me to introduce to my family. For that reason alone, I don't want to bring him up.

My dad will be there, so I believe it will be a good time to talk more about his mother—my grandma—and the way her words have hurt me ever since I was young. Actually, for as long as I can remember. Nothing good ever came out of the few conversations we had.

Anyway, lunch today wasn't the worst. Our placemats were decorated with drawings of hearts and bows, and each of us received a card from the cafeteria staff on our tray. I thought that was pretty funny. Sometimes, I forget that someone is on the other end of our menus actually putting together our order. I wonder what goes through their minds as they receive a pile of filled-out menus from the eating disorder unit to fulfill. I wonder if they are instructed to make our food look especially appetizing, thinking that somehow a pretty plate will encourage us to have a more positive experience when eating food. Perhaps it is the opposite. Make the food look as horrendous as possible to weaken our expectations, so we are pleasantly surprised by actual food in the outside world.

Whatever the case is, I tore off some pieces of the placemat to keep, and I put the card from the cafeteria staff on my bedside table. I'm pretty sure everyone did the same thing.

<u>5:05 PM</u>

I finally got released from prison. And by that, I mean my family meeting. I don't remember my last one being as long as this one. I feel nauseous. Am I sweating? Is my face red? It's over. The meeting is over. You can breathe now, Chris.

To say the meeting was full of emotions (for everyone involved, I might add) would be an understatement. My dad is a very sensitive guy, so I knew the topic of his mother would trigger a lot of feelings from him. My mom, too, gets emotional from seeing everybody else in the room feeling down. Seeing my dad emotional makes me giggle a bit, but seeing my mom in the same light breaks my heart.

The most difficult part of the meeting was, as I expected, bringing up the topic of my grandmother. My parents would be dumb not to recognize that her words and actions have had at least *some* effect on me, but it was never something anyone talked about. I'd occasionally mention it, but nothing ever came from it. It became something that I learned to deal with. Bringing it up during the family meeting with Connor was so freeing. I was nervous in the beginning, but once I got started, I couldn't stop.

I told my parents how upset I was that no one ever stood up for me or told my grandma to stop making comments about the food I ate and my appearance. I would dread every holiday dinner or birthday that our family celebrated for the sole reason of having to see her and wait for which ignorant comment about my weight she'd shout from across the table. How much longer would I have to put on a fake smile whenever I am around her and be expected to accept whatever judgment she had for me that day?

My voice cracked several times while I was talking, but it felt like I just took a ten-ton weight off my back. It felt good. I've never talked to my parents, especially my father, the way I just did. The last thing I want is for them to feel any responsibility for *anything*, but I just always felt like they could do more to protect me. They could be more on my side.

To my comfort, my parents were quite receptive to my comments. And to be honest, I do have a bit of a new perspective on my grandmother. My dad spent some time trying to convince me that she loves and cares about me, but her past—living in Europe and fleeing during World War II—has shaped who she is today. He went on and on. He talked so slow that my mind wandered almost immediately. I didn't hear half of what he was saying. It all sounded the same.

When I do come home, I hope things will be different. My dad told me that he would begin having serious talks with his mother about where I am and what I have been struggling with, in addition to giving her a list of things not to say to me. Hopefully, I can also change the way I react to certain comments. I mean, that's why I'm here, right?

I did end up bringing up Oliver, too. The conversation wasn't long. I briefly mentioned the toll that our relationship had on me and why I feel so distant from who I was just one year ago. My parents knew who Oliver was, but I don't think it ever occurred to them how close we were. My mom may have had some suspicions, but my dad certainly did not.

"Christopher," my dad began, looking at me with tears in his eyes. "This is the first time you have ever admitted to me that you are gay."

Here we go, I thought. I smiled and looked down. I officially came out to my parents.

The elephant in the room was finally acknowledged. However, the elephant had little to do with me being gay or bisexual or whatever the fuck I was. Who cares? The elephant was Oliver. I just wanted my parents to *know*. Oliver was a chapter in my life nobody knew about.

7:50 PM

The high I felt after the success of the family meeting didn't last long. I went to dinner with tears in my eyes after overthinking about, well, everything. Maybe I have been too harsh on my grandma for the past few years. I thought about the fact that I would probably be in the hospital for my birthday. I mean, how pathetic is that? I also thought about Ashley, how much I miss her and how badly I felt missing *her* birthday. I just feel guilty. So, so guilty. I should be home right now. I should be home helping my mom prep our house for the arrival of my sister's baby. I should be home planning a fun day with my friends for when I turn sixteen. I shouldn't be *here*.

Saturday, February 15, 2014
DAY 19 OF RECOVERY

8:40 AM

Here is some good news: I am mustache-free! Ugh. It feels too good. My mom surprised me last night with a fresh bottle of hair removal cream. I used to use it all the time at home. No one ever taught me how to shave. For obvious reasons, razors are not allowed here. I haven't been able to remove any of my facial hair in weeks. Not that I grow too much, but I was definitely looking like a twelve-year-old boy who hasn't learned that he hit puberty yet. Not a cute look.

Breakfast was fairly large today. I completed my entire meal, and I feel like I could conquer the world. I am looking forward to seeing Burton today. I hope he knows how hard I have tried to gain weight and make some physical progress in my recovery. I hope my numbers validate that.

10:25 AM

Never mind. Burton is not here today. Of course. At least that gives me another day to gain weight. I would love for him to come back to a two-pound weight-gain from me.

Maybe it is a good thing Burton isn't here today because I was then forced to talk to Junko about some trouble I have been having *down there*. I find it much easier to confide in her than anyone else on my treatment team. To put it bluntly, I *have* been going to the bathroom quite regularly, but they're not the most pleasant of visits. I notice a bit of blood in the toilet once I'm finished.

I asked Casey what she would do if her ass began bleeding. She looked terrified. Once she put two and two together, she told me I should certainly tell a nurse. I don't even want to imagine where in this hospital they'd send me if they knew I was bleeding down there. I decided to leave that part out to Junko. That probably wasn't the best decision.

Upon Junko's recommendation, I will start taking a stool softener tomorrow. She told me to keep her updated on the condition of my stools because taking the pill can have the opposite effect once they become normal. They have the potential to catch up with you fairly quickly. That's the last thing I need.

1:20 PM

I thought I would share a quote I heard today during group: "Nothing is impossible. The word itself says, 'I'm possible.'" I don't know who wrote the quote, but it sounds like you'd read it on one of those wooden frames sold at home decor stores. And yet, my eating disorder often convinces me that recovery is not possible. I am too far gone. I am not worthy of a normal, healthy life. It is *impossible* for me to live without this illness. I am beginning to realize that is not the case. Anything and everything is possible, and I have the power to change my life.

3:15 PM

Today has been a good day, so I am not allowing myself to get upset about anything. But, fuck. Right now, Ashley is probably back home getting ready for her sweet-sixteen party. I almost forgot that the party was tonight. I bet she looks incredible.

I am going to read this journal back in a couple of years and wonder why this party meant so much to me. The thing is—it's not about the party. It's about seeing my friends. They were the only ones that were always there for me. Being around them in school made me forget about everything on my mind. Of course, my eating disorder hated that. If there was one thing that could get my mind off of my weight or how many calories were in my school lunch that day, it was my friends. My eating disorder would do anything it could to divert my attention away from my friends and back to the unnerving sensation of an empty stomach. Hell, I even transferred schools because my eating disorder told me to. I mean, how pathetic is that? I think that's why I feel so bonded to Jodi and Casey. Having them around makes me feel like I am home, and I would do *anything* to feel like I am home.

10:00 PM

The night has gone by slowly. Casey and I watched some more of the Olympics to get my mind off of what I was missing back home. I appreciated the attempt. She even made me a few more bracelets from her loom kit.

I think I'll call my mom. She couldn't make it to visitation hours tonight because of the weather. Besides, it's not like I can call Ashley right now.

Cracks in the Ice

FALL 2013

To this day, I have no explanation as to why Oliver stopped talking to me. One day we were planning all the crazy things we'd do once school started back up again—like get drunk in the bathroom before first period and ditch school to take the train into the city—the next, I was being told to never speak to him again.

My mind will shoot in ten different directions if I wonder why. I couldn't bear the idea that something I said or done made Oliver suddenly dislike me. It felt like somebody had thrown a wrench into our relationship, and everything grew ice cold. Our conversations became slimmer and slimmer. The only contact we'd have was initiated by me and would end no better than how it began. It was a classic tale of one person giving eighty percent and the other giving twenty, but it took me a while to notice.

Oliver and I eventually stopped talking completely. The last text I sent him was one of gratitude. I thanked him for exposing me to a side of myself I felt needed to be hidden for so long. I thanked him for introducing me to a world where people like me weren't only accepted but celebrated. I wanted Oliver to know how much he meant to me. He was my entire world. Love is a strong word. I can't say for certain that I loved Oliver, but it was the closest I had ever gotten to it. Those feelings, however, weren't exactly mutual.

Oliver wasn't shy about making his feelings toward me known. He began posting group pictures of us and his friends online with enough of me cropped out just so everyone knew who it was. A few of his friends came up and asked me what had happened between us and laughed when I told them I did not know. I felt like I was missing some ginormous elephant in the room. I did not know how to move on. I didn't even know what went wrong.

Countless nights were spent hypothesizing why Oliver began talking to me in the first place. I didn't want to believe that all he wanted from me was sex. Was that his only goal? It was almost impossible to come to any other conclusion.

Any confidence Oliver brought into my life disappeared. My life felt empty, like a rainstorm pushed away every ounce of joy. Every action I took became painful. I didn't have anyone in my life with whom I could express the way I felt. My friends were too caught up worrying about who was taking who to the homecoming dance later that month, and I did everything I could to avoid talking to my parents about it. Every negative feeling became bottled up in my mind, and I searched every avenue for a way to control my thoughts.

Meanwhile, things at home were only getting more intense. My sister and her boyfriend walked into my room one night bearing news. With hopeful grins plastered across their faces, I was told I was going to become an uncle. I struggled to find words for nearly a minute. My sister's eyes desperately searched for any response.

"Are you serious?" I laughed. "That's crazy."

"We've actually been trying for a while," my sister chirped. "I stopped taking my birth control a few weeks ago. You're the only person who knows."

The boyfriend chimed in. "Are you excited to be an uncle, Chris? There's going to be a little me running around here before you know it. Hopefully, he won't be as crazy as I am," he chuckled. "We were so excited to tell you."

"We were waiting for the perfect time," my sister began again, "but we couldn't keep it a secret for any longer. And I think we want you to be the godfather!"

"Definitely. We love you, bro."

I didn't know how to respond. I stared at my sister, who looked ready to combust if the next words out of my mouth were anything but supportive. Then, I looked to the stranger standing next to her, who had singlehandedly altered any dynamic my family and I had known. I thought I was going to be sick.

"Congratulations, then!" I cheered. I had a choice to make. I couldn't imagine what was going through my sister's mind at the time, but I'm sure the last thing she needed was any type of response from me that'd upset her. It wasn't the idea of a little baby waking me up in the middle of the night that made me weary. I immediately pictured myself staying home from school once in a while to help out with the baby whenever it was needed. It was the fact that my sister's boyfriend now had a permanent, tangible, and living connection to our family. It made my skin crawl. I, however, wasn't about to let that show.

In the following weeks, my sister began making her rounds to our family to tell them about the baby. Though the news was a serious concern to my parents, the only worries they openly expressed were financial. My sister was going to a local cosmetology school at the time, and her boyfriend couldn't keep a job for longer than a week. My parents knew it'd be up to them to financially support the baby, in addition to the living expenses of my sister and her boyfriend, who contributed nothing in the six months he had been living in our house. If it weren't for the help of my aunt—my mother's sister who we'd always joke was the reason my family wasn't living under a bridge—I don't quite know what would have happened.

I quickly found myself in a situation where I felt stranded. The only time I could escape my deranged living situation was when I was in school. It was there where I felt perkier, and my friends never faced any challenge in making me feel welcome. They were all fascinated by my sister. They'd wait by my locker every morning for the latest news in her life. It was amusing. Yet, the presence of Oliver at school was overwhelming. I couldn't bear the idea of seeing him in the hallways, not being able to run up to him, not being able to kiss him. I would have done anything to be able to do just that, but I knew it wasn't for the best.

Mentally, I was lost. The anger and anxiety I felt each day flooded my mind. The only things I felt were anguish and emptiness. I did not know how to proceed in a life where everything important to me suddenly became corrupted by forces out of my control.

And it was in this environment that my eating disorder found its way back into my life.

It was frightening how rapidly my eating disorder prioritized itself. It wasn't something that gradually happened. I remember saying to myself one night: "Okay, I am doing this," and from then on, every calorie I put into my body was counted. I'd challenge myself to see how long I could go without eating after I woke up. My stomach would applaud me more and more the longer I went and would guilt me whenever something didn't go its way. The feeling of anything in my stomach was enough to make me sick, and the only time I liked the way my stomach looked was as soon as I woke up in the morning. I performed checks throughout the day on various parts of my body. I measured my lower arms, biceps, ankles, and, well, just about everything.

My bedroom mirror became full of sticky notes of all the exercises I had to do each night until my legs felt like they'd give out. I'd jog in place, staring at an image of myself that bore almost no resemblance. I referred to that person as Ana. She didn't make herself present all the time, but I saw it in my eyes when she did. I'd sometimes get so scared of Ana that I'd have to turn off all the lights in my room and complete my bedtime exercise routine in the dark.

My body became my personal mixing pot of everything I loathed about myself. I hated the way my thighs looked when I sat down. I hated the size of my arms, the size of my hands and the way they dangled at my side. My shoulders were becoming too broad, and my chest was the most grotesque thing my eyes had ever seen. To help resolve what I thought was wrong with my body, I followed a strict set of rules.

My eating disorder became the center of my life. Every action I took was tainted by its overwhelming goal to control every aspect of my being. It was the only thing that made me feel *anything*. The closer I got to my goal weight, the happier I seemingly became. That happiness was lost the second the scale would read a hundredth of an ounce higher than the time before.

I found it easy to hide my eating disorder from my family. I had been underweight my entire life, so my appearance never drastically changed. My family had always considered me a picky eater, too, so the changes in my eating never stood out. My eating disorder was able to hide in plain sight.

Yet, at this time, I was still reassured that there was nothing wrong with me. In November of 2013, just two months before entering treatment at Cherry Oak, I was rushed to the hospital due to an excruciating pain in my lower abdomen. After a couple of tests and x-rays, it was determined that I had to have my appendix removed as it was nearly ready to burst. In the two days I spent at the hospital for my surgery and recovery, not one doctor said anything about my appearance, my weight, or my food intake. The fact that no doctor mentioned my weight encouraged me to believe that I was doing a good job of hiding my disorder, but it also told me I needed to lose more.

I was out of school for nearly a week after the surgery. I had three small incisions that the doctors made to remove my appendix, and the stitches I was given needed time to dissolve. It was difficult to do anything during that time, so I spent most of my days sleeping and catching up on homework. All I *wanted* to do was get up and do about 200 jumping jacks, even if it meant all three of my incisions busted open. The mental pain was just too much.

Eventually, I was able to return to school. It felt great to be around my friends once again, and they were all anxious to hear about my three-in-the-morning trip to the emergency room. I can't stress enough how much my friends meant to me at the time —Ashley, Ariel, all of them. Without Oliver or a stable and safe living environment at home, my friends were the only ones keeping me grounded and distracted from my eating disorder. And that was the very reason why my eating disorder convinced me that I needed to get away from them as quickly as possible.

One afternoon in early December, just a week after returning from surgery, I sat with my friends at our usual lunch table in the far-right corner of the cafeteria, lowered my voice, and let them in on a secret I had been keeping. I had a habit of making impulsive decisions, and this one may have been the worst one yet.

"I'm transferring schools," I told them, with a fake sadness within my voice. This was a decision I made only a few days ago, one my parents were still in the process of understanding.

"What?!" my friends all exclaimed at once, followed by a series of questions.

"Why so suddenly?"

"You were just out for a week, and now you're leaving again?"

"Is someone bullying you? Is that why you're transferring?"

"Are you moving?"

None of these speculations could have been farther from the truth, and the reason I was about to tell them was just as untrue.

"My sister is pregnant," I began, looking at the shocked faces of my friends. I think they knew where I was going. "The tuition here—it's just too much for my family right now."

"So, you'll be attending a public school?"

"Yes—Elmwood Park Memorial High School. It's less than five minutes away from my house. You guys know the education here sucks," I laughed as my friends all nodded their heads in approval. "I just can't do it anymore. I just can't attend this school anymore. It wastes nearly $10,000 of my parents' money every year, and in just a few months, they'll be struggling to pay for a twenty-dollar packet of diapers. My dad always tells me not to worry about how he and my mom would pay for my education, but how can I not? I just want to help my family out in any way I can."

My friends' reactions were hard to read. Their expressions were bare like they knew I wasn't telling the truth but unable to find the words to question what I was saying. It all happened so quickly that no one, not even myself, knew an appropriate way to react. I was there one day and gone the next.

SAYING goodbye to my friends was one of the hardest things I had ever done. It was especially troubling knowing that I had orchestrated the entire thing. I remember crying in the arms of my friends on my last day, damning the very decisions that led me to the position I then found myself in. I knew I made a mistake. I was completely devastated, but I couldn't let my regret show. There were reasons why I decided to transfer, and I had to remind myself of those every day. By changing schools, separating myself from my friends, and placing myself in a new environment, my eating disorder now had no distractions.

I SPENT two weeks at Elmwood Park Memorial High School. During those fourteen days, I skipped at least ten days' worth of classes. The high school was large, so I didn't struggle to find places to hide. My favorite place to go was a bathroom on the third floor, which was directly between the middle school and high school. It was far enough away from each campus that no students ever ventured out to use it.

From the minute I arrived at school around 7 am to the dismissal bell at 3 pm, I'd sit. I'd give names to the cracks in the wall, count the number of marks on the floor, and see how quickly I could memorize the checkered patterns on the stall door. Nothing else made sense for me to do when the only things I found any comfort in were starving my body and exercising as much as possible to quicken that process. I wanted nothing more than to disappear.

I didn't gain a thing from transferring schools. It was nice to get away from Oliver, but that was the only solace I found. I felt a severe disconnect between who I thought I was and where my life was headed. Each day that passed was another reminder of how empty my life had become.

I RETURNED to my old school in less than a month. It felt like the first step toward reclaiming a life that no longer felt like mine. By then, I had lost so much weight that standing up or walking to class left me dizzy. I knew what I was feeling wasn't normal. I felt it in my brain, in my bones, and in the way my body seemingly betrayed me with every step.

My mind often wandered back to how I felt once I graduated from middle school, a time when the weight of my eating disorder momentarily lifted. All the negative feelings I had toward myself vanished the minute I left the environment that taught me to question and loathe the person I was.

My eating disorder hadn't followed me to high school. The

promise of a clean slate was enough to dull the insecurities that had shadowed me for so long. For the first time, I could breathe —I felt free.

I craved to feel that way again, but I didn't know how. I needed help, and I knew that I couldn't do it alone.

Sunday, February 16, 2014
DAY 20 OF RECOVERY

8:50 AM

I had to save two items from my breakfast for snack time, which is at eleven. I couldn't finish my meal. My mind felt like it weighed 1,000 pounds. So many thoughts were spiraling through my head. Besides missing Ashley's birthday, the fact that I would be missing mine was hitting me hard. I mean, it shouldn't. I cannot remember the last time I did anything significantly fun or interesting for my birthday. There is so much hype and excitement for the day, and once it comes, all you want is for it to be over. Why would this year be any different? For the past couple of years, the most exciting part of my birthday was waiting to count how many messages I received on social media at midnight. The picture collages were always my favorite. Will anyone remember to create one for me this year? Is it sad that this is what is currently on my mind? Absolutely. Someone, please knock some sense into me.

11:00 AM

Once again, Burton is out. Maybe it's because it's the

weekend, but I feel like I have not seen him in forever. Based on how I have been eating the past few days, I'm banking on at least a twenty-pound weight gain by the next time I see him. Okay, maybe five.

My mom is having second thoughts about signing the forty-eight. I think my dad got a little in her head. It makes sense, him being a psychologist and all. I just wish people didn't pretend that they knew what was best for me. I mean, *I* am the one with the eating disorder, aren't I? I suppose it can be difficult to trust the intentions of someone who is just beginning recovery from an eating disorder. You never really know who you are talking to. For all they know, the anorexia in my brain could be the thing persuading me that I am ready to be discharged. Gosh, now I am questioning everything as well.

Maybe my insurance will kick me out before anyone has to make that decision. That seems to be a common occurrence around here—insurance companies suddenly deciding that they have no further obligation to pay for treatment. The idea seems so funny to me. Maybe the hospital is in contact with my insurance company right now, fighting for my right to stay. Maybe my insurance company *is* looking to remove me from treatment. I mean, it's either that or I gain thirty more pounds before I leave this place.

2:35 PM

I realize my life in here has hit a new level of boredom. I am writing to you about my newfound ability to create almost any loom bracelet in the book my mom brought me by memory alone. Never did I think any excitement in my life would depend on this. I wonder if I'll be able to even look at the bracelets I have created once I get out of here. I'll definitely keep them as some strange artifact I'll associate with the beginning of my recovery. I'm sure I'll find a spot for them in the uppermost corner on the top shelf of my closet, never to be touched again.

I feel the same about the clothes I wear here every day. The boots I spend five minutes tying up in the morning, the black skinny jeans I parade in front of my window at night when I can *almost* see a complete reflection of my body—will I ever be able to look at them the same way again, let alone fit in them? Oh gosh, I had not even thought about that yet. I'm going to have to ask my mom to bring in some sweatpants, or else I will be showing up for groups in my underwear.

Thankfully, much of the clothing I brought with me is quite loose. It has become a stereotype that eating-disordered people mainly wear baggy clothing in order to hide themselves, which is true most of the time. Whenever I am having terrible body image days, the first thing I want to do is jump in a sweater three times my size in order to feel smaller. However, most of the time, I find myself squeezing into the tightest clothing possible whenever I go out. I already feel huge, so why would I choose to appear any bigger? Some people may argue and ask why I feel comfortable wearing tight clothing if I hate my body so much. Here is my answer: I don't know. My body dysmorphia makes me feel different things each and every day. Patterns emerge here and there, but I'll commonly wait around in my bed each morning while I wait for my mind to tell me how to feel about my body that day.

Every person who has experienced body dysmorphia will tell you something differently about how it makes them feel. The same goes for eating disorders. I think that's why a strict path to recovery can appear so daunting.

The good thing about being in treatment right now is that everybody understands that, and rules are put into place to ensure a trigger-free environment for every patient here. For example, tight clothing is not allowed. Neither is baggy clothing. It sure does make it difficult to find articles of clothing within the guidelines, though I doubt any specific measurements regarding what is "too small" or "too baggy" exist. I suppose it is up to our discretion. Rules like that are pretty subjective, in my opinion.

Then again, what are we supposed to do once our "normal" clothing begins to fit a little tighter? I, for one, am definitely noticing a pair of my maroon jeans fitting me a bit snugger. It is the worst feeling in the world. Unlike my black jeans, which are almost like a legging-spandex material, I purposely bought these maroon jeans a size bigger to have some extra room in them—to wear whenever I am not going for a tighter look. I never thought my legs would begin to struggle while walking or bending down in them.

To make a long story short: pants are not my friend.

6:20 PM

Please remind me to never order the lasagna from this place again. I felt more and more nauseous with every bite I took. I could have sworn there was some meat in there, too. I feel sick to my stomach.

To distract myself, I decided to call my old friend Camille afterward. I had not talked to her in weeks, maybe months. We have been friends since kindergarten, but our friendship comes and goes in waves. One day, we're telling each other our deepest, darkest secrets, and then we don't talk for a few weeks. It's an odd friendship, but I am thankful to have her in my life. She is one of the funniest people I know, and we are so similar. We listen to all the same music, read the same books, and have the most sarcastic sense of humor. I still remember the day I came out to her. She told me she loved me over and over again, and I knew she truly meant it.

I didn't know what to expect when I called her, but the conversation went surprisingly well. She told me she would like to visit me one day. I am not quite sure how that would work unless my mom brought her along. Knowing her, she'd just burst out laughing the minute she stepped onto the unit. I'd laugh with her.

I have another friend from home who I need to call. Her name is Ivana. We, too, have been great friends since we were little. We went to the same school for eight years and have luckily continued our friendship in high school despite attending different schools. Whereas Camille is quiet and calm (for the most part), Ivana is the complete opposite. She was always *that* girl in school who got in trouble for being too loud all the time. She never paid attention during class but spent her time passing notes to nearby friends and making fun of all our teachers. She was also the girl who, for some reason, learned about sex at a very young age and wouldn't hesitate to make the dirtiest jokes. How she and I became friends is still a mystery to me. In my eyes, no two people could be more unalike.

The reason why I have to call her is because she is supposed to accompany me to the Ellie Goulding concert next month. I have to reassure her that I will make it out of here in time. If not, we must calculate a foolproof escape plan to New York City. Not too much of an ask, no? All I'd have to do would be sneak past the nurse's station, open the doors to the unit, and make a run for the elevator. Maybe the stairs would be faster. I can purchase a hat and a change of clothes from the hospital gift shop before walking by security on my way out. Then, I'd have to find my way to the train station to go home, but we'll think more about that if the time comes.

<u>*11:06 PM*</u>

Damn, I don't think I have ever been this tired in my entire life. My eyelids feel so heavy, and I need sleep. This whole waking-up-at-five-in-the-morning thing is really starting to take a toll on me. I wonder what would happen if I just slept through the day. No one can physically force me to get up, attend groups, eat meals, etc., can they? I mean, the last thing I want is a feeding tube shoved up my nose. Suddenly, I am not that tired anymore.

Casey, Taissa, and I were up late watching more of the Winter Olympics. It is sort of our thing now. We stayed awake in the multipurpose room until one of the nurses told us to head to bed. I am fifteen years old, and I have a bedtime. I feel like a little kid again. A month ago, that would have annoyed the hell out of me. Today, I'm not complaining.

Monday, February 17, 2014
DAY 21 OF RECOVERY

9:35 AM

I am feeling paralyzed. I am unable to focus on anything. My head keeps spinning and spinning, revisiting emotions and feelings I have not experienced in weeks. All I want to do is scream and hide under my covers until the voices in my head level out. It is surreal how one minor happening can completely change the course of your thoughts, actions, and progress for the day. No, I am not talking about my eating disorder. I am talking about stupid, fucking Oliver.

After I got my vitals checked around five, I grabbed my phone from my backpack and ran to the bathroom. That has been my daily routine ever since I convinced my mom to bring it in. Rarely do I actually message anybody or post things. It's tempting, but I don't do it. All I do is take a few moments to reconnect with the outside world. Today, however, I was surprised by a text message from Oliver. It was from one o'clock in the morning.

where are you?

I practically shit my pants when I saw his name on my lock screen. It had not been there for months. I wanted to scream, cry, and laugh all at the same time. I really, really, really liked this boy. After everything that we have gone through and said to each other, I still find myself the same, young, inexperienced person who was completely infatuated with talking to someone like him. A rush of emotions filled my chest, and the world around me went still. I swore time froze at that moment. I just stared and stared at my phone, contemplating what to do next.

I couldn't answer—right? I mean, it had been almost four hours since I got the text, and I am only now reading it. How weird would it be to answer someone at five o'clock in the morning? He had been thinking about me enough to actually *want* to text me. That alone made me want to cry. Maybe he is curious about where I am or how I am doing. Or maybe he was just trying to see where I was so he could tell the whole school. Regardless of what the reason was, I battled the strongest urges in my body and decided not to answer.

God, this fucking sucks. I am probably overthinking this. Maybe he was drunk and does not even remember texting me. Knowing him, that scenario is likely. I could always pretend I didn't receive the text. The thing is, do I even want to talk to him again? Do I want to be hurt by him again? I know those feelings are inevitable, and all I want to do is move on and forget he exists.

My emotions followed me to breakfast, where I struggled to complete my meal. I had a piece of toast, a scrambled egg, some granola cereal, yogurt, a carton of milk, and a Boost drink. If there were to be a day to incomplete, today would've be the day. I was not going to let Oliver have that.

11:55 AM

I got the greatest news from my doctor just now. Because of my recent weight gain, Burton told me we would push for a pass this weekend and possibly look at mid-March for discharge. He did not sound too confident about that last part, but I know I can do it. What it all comes down to is my weight. *I must gain weight.* I will do whatever it takes.

1:40 PM

To say my afternoon has been stressful would be an understatement. Junko pulled me aside this afternoon and asked if something was bothering me. I guess someone noticed my mood during breakfast. I told her about the text message. I did not tell her I *had* my phone on me, just that my mom has my phone and told me about the text. I am not sure I made the right decision. She is bound to tell Connor. Maybe I should tell him first so it doesn't look like I am hiding something.

Speaking of which, I need to call my mom and fill her in on what happened today. I don't believe Connor would call my mom (would he?), but I have to fill her in on the lie. I recognize this could get messy really quickly.

Emmanuel is officially being discharged next week. He told me he hasn't even met his discharge weight, yet he will still be leaving. Well, that goes against just about everything I have been told since I got here. Perhaps it is more complex than he is making it out to be. Maybe his doctors are hiding something from him like he actually *did* hit his goal weight, or his insurance is refusing to pay for any further treatment. Whatever the case is, I am extremely proud of how far he has come. Talking to him, I do not believe he is mentally prepared to leave, but I know he is on the right track. I have faith that he knows what he has to do to progress in his recovery. All I can hope is that he takes the initiative and does just that. Besides, it will be nice to finally have the room to myself.

4:15 PM

It has almost become a daily routine of mine to cry at least once. The worst is when it happens right before a meal.

Everybody looks at you and your big, puffy, purple eyes and studies how you eat with a magnifying glass. They know something is wrong, so they do all they can to use it to their advantage and make it something eating disorder-related. The truth is my emotions have been running wild, and I just miss my home. I expressed those thoughts to Connor this afternoon.

"Well, it's because of *you* that you're here," Connor explained for the millionth time. "*Your* eating disorder is causing you to miss home, miss your family—miss everything. You are missing out on things in your life because of *your* eating disorder. It's up to you to change that. Don't blame anybody but yourself."

I understand what he means, but hearing it doesn't feel great. Connor also doesn't seem to think I will get a pass this weekend. What a motivator he is! I suppose he is only trying to be realistic, but I am so over this whole tough love thing. I hope I can prove him wrong.

9:15 PM

Our multipurpose room has four cameras, one in every corner of the ceiling. Oftentimes, I wonder if they are on even when mealtimes are finished, like during free time.

Today, I learned that they are.

My sister came to visit me tonight and was super excited to show me some of her recent ultrasound pictures. She told me she had them on her phone but was scared to pull them out in fear of getting in trouble by staff. I did not care. I had to see the pictures!

I had been talking about my sister's pregnancy practically every day during group, so my sister and I made our way to the multipurpose room to show everyone the photos. I knew Casey would appreciate seeing them, at least. I didn't hold my sister's phone in front of Casey for more than ten seconds before some nurse came running into the room, demanding my sister take her phone back and put it away. I couldn't believe what happened.

Come on, Cherry Oak. It's not like we see the size of a fetus's leg and get triggered.

On top of that, I was told that the extras I ordered tonight were a "weird combination" and couldn't be given to me. I asked for an orange and a slice of carrot cake. What is so weird about that? Sure, the pairing doesn't sound too conventional, but neither do any of the other combinations I have had here. Chocolate cake and yogurt, an apple with some pound cake—they all sound equally weird to me.

I ended up just going with the carrot cake.

Tuesday, February 18, 2014
DAY 22 OF RECOVERY

<u>8:50 AM</u>

I have officially been in treatment for three weeks. It feels more like three months. Each day is beginning to blend together more and more. If it weren't for the food journals we are required to fill out for each day, I would not remember what I had for dinner last night. I've noticed that the average stay for most patients here is two to four weeks, so I'm pretty sure it is time for me to pack my bags. Sometimes, I do so at night just to feel like I'll be leaving in the morning. Hope truly does breed eternal misery.

I have a meeting with my entire treatment team later on today, so I am hoping something will be brought up regarding my expected length of stay. I sure feel like I am prepared to head on home, but I suppose that's what everybody says. Even just receiving a pass would mean the world to me. All I want is to feel like a normal human being again.

<u>2:40 PM</u>

The meeting did not go as well as I had hoped. Whenever I

feel like I am on the right path, something or someone is always there to force me back into reality. There is absolutely nothing like sitting in the middle of a pale, cold room surrounded by people studying every aspect of your being. The way you sit, where your hands are placed, how many times you blink—it all means something to them. Connor made it very clear that I shouldn't be surprised if I weren't given a pass for at least three more weeks. With that being said, my eligibility for a pass solely depends on my weight, which went down half a pound since yesterday. Three weeks ago, that would have been the best news I could hear. Now, all I want to do is to cry.

It's almost like they want a reaction from me. They want me to cry, beg, look them in the eyes, and try to convince them that there is nothing wrong with me. How am I supposed to react to the news that I am still looking at another month or two in this place? My treatment team agrees that I have made significant strides in improving my mental health, yet my weight is still holding me back.

The truth is, I have never been a "normal" weight in my entire life. I have always been underweight. I have never had the build of an average boy my age, and over time, my lanky body just became a part of who I am. It was never truly an issue growing up, and it certainly never held me back from anything. Sure, I was always a picky eater, but I ate my meals, remained active, and was considered pretty healthy overall.

When I began losing weight due to my eating disorder, no one noticed. It was never brought up or talked about because, well, *no one noticed*. I think that was part of the reason why my parents had trouble wrapping their brains around the fact that their son had an eating disorder and needed help. They never noticed a change in my eating, weight, or behavior. It was never on their radar.

Being in treatment, not only do I have to gain all the weight back that I have lost over the past few months from my eating disorder, but I have to make up the weight for fifteen years' worth of being underweight. I think that is something my treatment team has trouble understanding. I have never been a "normal" weight. I have never been a "healthy" weight. When I am finally discharged from this place, I will look like a completely different person.

Something else my treatment team brought up to me is that they, along with some other patients on the unit, are beginning to view me, Jodi, Casey, and Taissa as a clique. Some have even expressed that we make them uncomfortable. The second I stepped onto this unit, the first thing I was pressured to do was make friends and socialize. I didn't realize I had to do so with every person here.

I am now being instructed to step out of my comfort zone as if it hadn't already been shattered by the everyday weigh-ins in my underwear and the stuffing of my face with thousands of calories worth of food. I also have to shy away from spending time with my friends. What am I supposed to do now during mealtimes, sit next to a new girl who completes a third of her meal by cutting everything into hamster-sized treats? My team argues that by doing so, I will ready myself for eating out in the real world where we have no choice in deciding who we sit next to. We can be faced with an array of challenges, and we have to teach ourselves the proper skill set to deal with them. This made sense to me at first, until I recognized how utterly hypocritical it was. I live on a unit where we are not even allowed to call food by its name for fear of triggering somebody. One time during group, we were given copies of an article about eating disorders and had to take a black marker and color over the word "hamburger." But sure, let's purposefully make Chris uncomfortable during mealtime because eating at a restaurant is nothing like at Cherry Oak.

10:00 PM

My grandma and aunt came to visit me tonight. We played a

few games of Scrabble (which I won), and I gave them some loom bracelets that I made for them. They seemed to really love them.

 This has been a hard day, and I am glad that it is over. I still have a few things to do before I head to bed. Taissa is being discharged tomorrow to the partial hospitalization program down the hall, so I want to write her a little farewell note. Though it is not confirmed, Jodi believes she may be discharged tomorrow, too, so I need to have her letter ready as well. If that's true, tomorrow is going to be a very sad day. Is it selfish that all I want is for Taissa and Jodi to stay in here with me? Probably. And I feel terrible for saying that. I cannot imagine a meal without them.

Wednesday, February 19, 2014
DAY 23 OF RECOVERY

9:15 AM

Just as I imagined, this whole "clique" thing has gotten blown way out of proportion. Walking into breakfast this morning, we were all told that until further notice, seating assignments would be given.

"This will allow you to get to know others on the unit you normally would not have the chance to talk to," the nurses cowardly claimed as if every person in the room didn't know that this was purely a way to switch things up between Casey, Jodi, Taissa, and me. As a result, not a single person spoke throughout the whole meal. If there were ever a meal anyone wanted an excuse not to finish, this would have been it. The thought definitely crossed my mind. *You moved me away from my friends; therefore, I'm not going to eat. Haha!*

Then, I realized that this was exactly what they wanted to see. They *wanted* to see me uncomfortable. They *wanted* to test how I would eat in a different environment. Once that clicked in my mind, I plastered a slight grin on my face and completed my entire meal. I ate two scrambled eggs with the driest English muffin you could imagine. The packet of butter did no justice. I occasionally glanced down the table at Casey and Jodi, and it seemed like they were doing the same thing. I'm proud of them.

11:20 AM

To put it lightly, my friends and I got roasted today during psychotherapy. A new girl opened up our session, proclaiming how "unwelcome" she felt because of the "cliques" she had seen during her first few days here. I am really getting tired of that word. She then mentioned how she had noticed some rules being broken regarding food talk and triggering language. I'll admit that Jodi, Casey, and I *do* spend a good chunk of our free time talking and complaining about whatever we ate that day, which is technically against the rules, but we always tried to do so whenever we had the multipurpose room to ourselves. I mean, who wouldn't? To be blunt, I figured everybody quietly wished that they could talk openly about certain things that we aren't allowed to. I was wrong. Such talk can definitely be a trigger, and I now see why rules like that exist.

Halfway through this girl's speech, Casey broke down crying and left the room. I knew she felt guilty for some of the things that we had said and done in the past, but I couldn't let her take all of the responsibility. As everyone in the room watched Casey leave, I quickly batted my eyes and spoke up.

"I can't let Casey take all the blame for this. We have all equally talked about things that we shouldn't have, and I want to apologize for that. I think it is great that we are getting new faces on the unit to provide us with a fresh perspective."

Taissa chimed in, too. She began explaining how forming friend groups and participating in gossip is an easy distraction away from the reality of being in treatment, to which I agreed. It's easy to get wrapped up in it all. It is just *something* to focus on other than how much you hate your body that day or how many Boost drinks you had to chug.

Jodi didn't say a word.

The rest of the meeting continued with more people sharing how they, too, have felt intimidated by the negativity and "high school mentality" around here. Stephanie even claimed that we laugh at her during various group sessions and meals, which couldn't be farther from the truth.

I left psychotherapy feeling defeated and unkempt. I don't know where Casey and I stand, let alone every other person on the unit. Jodi and Taissa are leaving tonight, meaning Casey truly is all I have left. I hope she will still want to be my friend after this, but I can't blame her if she doesn't. In the meantime, I will put some effort into strengthening my relationships with other people on the unit, including the new girl who called us out. I think I'll make her a bracelet.

5:15 PM

"I don't want to talk about what I know you want to talk about. I know what I did wrong, and it won't happen again. Can we please just not talk about it?" I spat out the second Connor came into my room for our session. I knew it was a long shot, and Connor would definitely want to talk about what happened during psychotherapy, but it was worth a try.

"You know we have to talk about it."

"Well, *you* could talk about it, but I'm not talking about it."

He laughed.

I felt so embarrassed. I am not the kind of person who gossips about people behind their backs and causes drama. I am not a bully. I am here to focus on myself, and my insecurities got in the way. As it turns out, I still have a lot of them.

8:40 PM

There is a void on the unit without Taissa and Jodi. Their parents were here to pick them up right after psychotherapy. Our goodbyes were hard. We spent a few moments remembering all the fun times we had together and how none of us would have been able to survive treatment without the other. I'm not sure what's next in the cards for Jodi, but I should still be able to see Taissa around the hospital. As I mentioned earlier, she will be entering Cherry Oak's partial hospitalization program, which meets in a room directly down the hall from our unit. Sometimes when the doors of our unit are open, we are able to see all the partial hospitalization patients shuffle into their room. It looks like our multipurpose room but smaller, with lockers lined against the wall like a high school gym locker room. We aren't allowed to communicate with any of them, but sometimes I sneak a wave. I've gotten in trouble for doing that a few times. I wonder if that's where I'll be headed once I'm discharged. They only meet for a few hours per day, and I think they only eat one meal together. For me, it would be pretty difficult to come here every day since the drive is a little over an hour away from my house. I'm sure my mom would still drive me.

Casey and I haven't spoken since this morning, and she has been in her room all day. As horrible as I feel, I refuse to spend any more of my energy worrying about what happened. All I can do is move on and try to be a better person. All I want is to focus on my recovery and gain the weight I need to be discharged.

As awful as it sounds, I feel as though that is the only reason why I am still here—to gain weight. I notice I am distancing myself from groups and mealtime conversations. I am over it. I want to go home, and mentally, I feel prepared to do so. If I were home right now, I would trust myself enough to say that I would eat. I would eat what I want and when I want. My mom agrees that she has seen me take tremendous strides towards a healthier mindset and outlook on food. I don't entirely trust her judgment on the issue, but it is nice to hear. I will continue my attempts to convince her to sign a forty-eight for me. If not, I am still looking at a few more weeks, maybe even months, in this place.

My discharge weight is nearly twenty more pounds than what I am right now.

"No one could expect a fifteen-year-old boy to spend any more time in here than what you already have," my mom told me as she looked into my eyes. I could tell she was on my side.

10:00 PM

Apparently, word got out at school that I'm at a hospital, but not exactly for what. Ashley called to let me know. She doesn't know how it happened. I can't think of any explanation either, besides someone—like Ariel—blurting it out. In this day and age, you can't expect anyone to keep anything a secret. Oh, well. It was going to get out eventually.

Walking back into my high school will be tough after this. What will people say? What will people think of me? Will I look *that* different? Will people even notice I am back? At this point, do I even care?

Thursday, February 20, 2014
DAY 24 OF RECOVERY

8:50 AM

The only words spoken today during breakfast were a quiet, "Are you okay?" from Casey. I walked into the multipurpose room this morning to every single seat that Casey and I would sit at taken.

The only seat available for me was the one directly next to the nurse proctoring the meal and a new woman named Lorraine. Lorraine has some of the craziest hair I have seen. I swear some of it got into my food.

Sitting there next to the nurse, it felt like my first day on the unit all over again. Every emotion I felt these past few weeks came flooding back. I felt alone, uncomfortable, and back to square one. I got too confident. This always happens to me.

The only exciting thing about breakfast is that we get to take our meds. During our meal, everyone waits patiently for their name to be called so we may leave the table and walk outside the room to the med cart. It is located right near the front desk. The only thing I am currently taking is a multi-vitamin and the occasional Tylenol.

"We're very sorry, Chris. We don't have a vitamin for you

today. You have been here so long that we had to reorder yours, and they still haven't come in!" the nurse told me, laughing. I faked a smile.

If that interaction didn't add to my desire to go home, something continuously in the back of my mind is the day next month I will be seeing Ellie Goulding live in concert. It's been one of the only things keeping me afloat these past few weeks. There is no way I'm missing it. I don't see how I would. The concert is weeks away, in the middle of March, and I don't see too long of a future for me here at Cherry Oak. I'm beginning to gain weight at a steady pace, and if all else fails, I know my mom wouldn't allow me to miss the show. My eating disorder has taken away so much from me. Seeing Ellie Goulding live will not be one of them.

9:30 AM

There is a chance that my Uncle Paul will come to visit me tonight. I am not sure how I feel about that. He's my mom's brother, and I typically only see him and his wife during the holidays. In the past, he made insensitive comments about my appearance and the food I eat, referring to my vegetarian diet as "bird food." Going to his house for a meal was similar to having a meal with my grandmother—I *knew* comments would be made about my weight, food, and appearance. I *knew* that I'd be leaving the meal feeling terrible. It was expected. It became almost normal.

With that being said, I'm not opposed to seeing some new faces around here. I can't help but wonder if it was his decision to come and visit me or if my mom asked him if he wanted to tag along.

2:35 PM

Yikes. I just got in some trouble. During psychotherapy, a

nurse from the front desk began calling each patient out of the room and wouldn't return for a good couple of minutes. Word finally went around the table that the staff was performing *room searches*. My stomach sank.

My first thought went to my phone. I have it tucked away in my school bag. *Will they go searching in there? What is going to happen if they find it? Should I surrender my phone before they find it in hopes of lessening my punishment?*

My second thought went to the bags of candy my mom brought me whenever she came to visit. I have them stashed away between my bed and the wall. It's a strange place for them, but the only people I have to worry about finding them are the cleaning people who come by every other day to change my sheets. I'd have been happy to share some of my snacks with them if they were interested. I would probably get into way more trouble for the food than for my phone.

As the nurse and I began walking to my room, followed by two other nurses, we stopped in my doorway.

"Before we proceed with the search, is there anything you would like to tell us? Will we find anything in your room that you are not allowed to have? Have you been hiding food, restricted media, such as magazines or books, or any electron-," the nurse began.

"I'm sorry! I have my phone with me. I'm sorry. I'm so sorry," I said, cutting her off mid-sentence. I ran to grab my phone from my backpack and handed it to her. She looked taken aback.

"That's alright, Chris. Thank you for telling me. Please understand that our rules regarding phones are in place for a reason. Don't worry. You are not in trouble," the nurse said, replying much kinder than what I had expected.

I breathed a big sigh of relief.

"Now, can you tell me how long you have had your phone for? And how'd you get it here in the first place?"

Crap. I hadn't thought this far through. I thought for a second before replying.

"Only a few days. I asked my mom to bring it in for me earlier this week. It's kind of a long story. My mom told me that I received a text message that she thought I'd be interested in seeing, so I asked her to bring it in for me to see," I lied. Little did she know that I had had my phone for *weeks,* only using it under the covers in half-hour intervals to avoid being caught by one of the night nurses.

I had to laugh remembering my first few days on the unit with David. He was more careless with his phone than I was. He would always leave it lying on his bed and use it throughout the day. It boggles my mind to think that he was never caught. He would even dance in front of the cameras in our room with his phone in his hand. We never knew if the cameras were on or not, but I would tackle him to the ground before we could find out.

"I'm sure you could talk more about that with Connor," the nurse replied, seeming disinterested in my explanation. "Is there anything else you would like to tell us about before we continue with the room search?"

Yes. I have a whole stash of outside food from my mom hidden by my bed.

"No," I hesitantly responded, hoping that the transparency with my phone helped to add a little bit of trust between us.

It worked.

The nurses half-assed the rest of my room search. I'm not sure what would have happened if the food I'd been hiding in my room was found. It would've been bad. It's not like I've been removing and hiding food from my trays during mealtime, but I'm still switching up my meal plan without anyone else's knowledge.

The nurses confiscated at least twenty alcohol wipes from Emmanuel's bedside table. We receive a wipe after every one of our meals, and he had been collecting them for a few weeks. He never told me why, but it was endearing. I'd give him mine sometimes, too.

4:15 PM

I wasn't allowed to go on my fifteen-minute walk outside of the unit today. I was getting prepared to go out when the same nurse who searched my room came up to me and told me I had lost those privileges. I'm also bumped back down to Phase Two, but that should only last the day.

8:45 PM

To my surprise, my uncle did come to visit me tonight. We've never had a super close relationship, and I figured he wouldn't exactly care to visit me. However, it ended up being a nice visit. He had many questions regarding my day-to-day life on the unit. As I have done with every visitor I receive, I showed him my schedule and went over everything I do each day.

He seemed interested in learning about what mealtimes were like and the many guidelines we have to abide by. I happily showed him the list of mealtime and table rules I was given on my first day. I wanted him to understand just how serious of a situation I was in. He seemed to think that many of the rules were counterintuitive.

"I probably break a handful of these rules every time I sit down for dinner, and I sure don't have any problems eating!" he joked.

I then tried to explain why each rule was in place, but he kept interrupting me, so eventually, I stopped. He even tried offering me a Jolly Rancher, which I quickly shooed away because we were in the multipurpose room and not in the privacy of my own room.

"Wouldn't I be helping you by giving you this candy? It's bound to have a couple of calories in it. Isn't that the whole point of you being here—to *eat more?!* I'm trying to help you!" he said, laughing.

Maybe the visit wasn't so good, after all.

Friday, February 21, 2014
DAY 25 OF RECOVERY

9:50 AM

I feel sick this morning. My nose wouldn't stop running during breakfast. It was so embarrassing. I ended up saving both of my chocolate Boost drinks and my bowl of pineapple for snack time. I can usually always finish my pineapple.

Burton saw this as an opportunity to make it seem like I had been slipping back into old habits. During our morning meeting, he suggested that many of the nurses have noticed me cutting my food into tiny pieces and eating at a slower than normal pace. Does it ever cross these peoples' minds that *maybe* I just do not feel well? How is that not even a possibility? Naturally, how I am physically feeling will affect the way I eat. But noooo, that's just my eating disorder putting in extra work.

1:40 PM

You'd have thought I saw a ghost by the look on my face after finishing my lunch. I don't think I'll ever be able to look at quiche the same way again, let alone eat it.

Needless to say, I didn't feel too hot walking into my family meeting today. Connor and I hadn't prepared much to talk about with my parents, so the hour went by slowly. Connor began the meeting saying the same old things—that I'm "doing great" and having an easier time speaking in groups. We talked a bit about the whole seating situation and my relationship with Casey, but I wasn't sure how talking about that with my parents was supposed to help. Nevertheless, I didn't miss the opportunity to say, once again, how lame it all is.

Connor now suggests that I become more "assertive" with my language. He noted that if I truly believed the whole situation with Casey was a bunch of baloney, I should be using my voice to counter it.

He then spent the rest of the hour asking my parents questions about my "passive attitude" at home. I guess I never really noticed it. Going forward, he wants me to tell them what I need from them regarding my recovery and life at home, even if it's uncomfortable or hurtful. I can't seem to think of anything more uncomfortable than any event that occurred within the past month, so that shouldn't be a problem.

10:45 PM

My mom came back to the hospital this evening to visit me, even though we only had the family meeting a few hours prior. She told me that before the meeting began, Connor spoke to her and my dad at length about how he has seen tremendous growth in me through our daily meetings, and he is proud of how far I have come in such a short time. He added that the strides I have taken in bettering my mental health are ones that he has seen other patients take months to do. Burton even came into the room to say how excellent my recovery has been going, which is apparently a big deal. He never says that about any patient.

I have to say, it is nice to see others take notice of your success, especially if you can't see it yourself. I know I still have more weight to gain, but I'm glad to see that the status of my mental health is being taken just as seriously. I don't know if I'll ever be physically healthy enough to meet Burton's standards, but that's not important to me. I came into treatment to find myself again—to free myself from the hold of my eating disorder. There is nothing more horrific than feeling submissive to your own mind. It is something I will never be able to put into words.

At the same time, I can't help but acknowledge the fear I have of losing that part of me. It is all I have ever known. I am scared of losing myself, and I am scared of how my family, my friends, and the world will react to the new me. I'm barely ready myself.

Saturday, February 22, 2014
DAY 26 OF RECOVERY

9:03 AM

Alright. I'm up another four pounds. I tried my hardest to act pleased when Burton told me this number, but I couldn't help from thinking otherwise. Why am I letting a silly number dictate how I am supposed to feel for the rest of the day? The good news is that I am still inching towards my discharge weight. Things are starting to pick up around here. And by "things," I mean my weight. That scares me.

1:35 PM

I have some good news and some bad news. I'll begin with the bad news. My maroon jeans are becoming tighter and tighter on me. They were always one of my safer pairs of jeans, ones that were always slightly baggy on me. They fit me perfectly whenever I wanted to hide my legs. I never enjoyed wearing them much since I thought I looked heavier in them; however, I can barely fit into them anymore without giving everybody who I walk by a detailed, anatomical glimpse of everything going on between my legs. It's embarrassing. The hospital isn't exactly the place I'm trying to find my next hookup.

Let's move on to the good news. My mom has been doing a lot of research on outpatient programs. Our hope is that we would be able to find one closer to home *and* that accepts boys into their program. Believe it or not, a large portion of treatment and residential centers are female-oriented. They are mostly run by women, and they do not accept boys into their programs. Connor warned my parents that they may not have a choice other than to send me back to Cherry Oak for outpatient. It wouldn't bug me too much if that were the case, but I'd feel bad for my mom who would have to drive me every day. I'm not even sure how that would be possible. She'd probably have to quit her job.

However, my mom was able to find an eating disorder clinic only a couple of towns over from where we live. They offer intensive outpatient, outpatient, and a few other tiers that I have never heard of before. Boys are only allowed in the outpatient program. The clinic is called The Warner Center for Eating Disorder Recovery, and there are at least twenty locations throughout the country. They have a few women-only inpatient and residential centers, but the location nearest to me is outpatient only. The only thing my mom warned me about was Warner's many requirements for a person to begin their program. I forget the specifics, but I have to be within a certain age group and weight bracket. You can't be "too sick" where they would turn you away for inpatient, but you have to be "sick enough" to even be considered. It makes zero fucking sense. I'm also not sure if my insurance will be accepted there.

And finally, Burton told me I should begin thinking about where I want to go on my pass next weekend! My heart skipped a beat when those words came out of his mouth.

"Really?" I asked in disbelief. As much as I have been hoping for a pass, I wasn't expecting it anytime soon.

"Yes," Burton replied with a grim smile. "Really."

I practically shit my pants.

After nearly a month of being confined in the hospital, I will take my first steps back into reality. What should I do? Where should I go?

"This is your first pass, so it will be five hours long. And with that, you are required to have one meal out on your own," Burton said. He handed me a sheet of paper that resembled one of the food journals that we keep a record of our meals on.

"This is the fun part," he looked at me sternly. "It is up to you to convert your meal into starches, proteins, fats, et cetera. It's what you're going to have to do at home."

I looked at him with a blank stare. *How the fuck am I supposed to do that?*

"Don't worry. I'll give you a little cheat sheet with some common food items and their exchanges listed."

Phew.

Since Cherry Oak is an hour away from home, spending two hours in the car doesn't seem like such good use of my time. My parents and I will probably just stay in the area and grab something to eat at a restaurant nearby. I wish I could research what else there is to do in this town besides live in a hospital. I'm sure my mom will find a nice place for us to go.

For the past month, I have seen just about everyone, with the exception of Casey and Dandy, go out on a pass. It is discouraging to see patients who have come after me get a pass so soon. Connor tells me not to compare my recovery to others', but it is hard not to.

<u>*6:25 PM*</u>

I have spent the latter part of my afternoon reading a new book my mom brought for me. It's a fiction novel about a middle school class who started a recycling program in their town. I laughed looking at the cover of the book where it clearly states that the book is recommended for children eight years and older. My sixteenth birthday is in three days! I wondered if my mom knew she bought me a book that is meant for a child. My guess is that she didn't because she acted awfully shocked to learn I finished the read in about twenty minutes.

Reading has been my favorite hobby for as long as I can remember. Stories allowed me to feel a sense of belonging and friendship. In a way, words were there for me when nothing or no one else was. The connection I would feel to a plot or a character allowed me to forget about everything else besides the story I was currently captivated in. My favorite and most meaningful memories from my childhood all have one thing in common: a story. Whether it was listening to my mom hold back tears as she read the final Harry Potter book to me and my sister or traveling across states to meet the author behind the *Series of Unfortunate Events*, books always found themselves tucked in between the greatest moments of my childhood.

I couldn't even tell you how many books I have read throughout my lifetime. I think I read around 250 during seventh grade alone, some of which included my favorite books to date, like Ellen Hopkins's *Crank* and Anne Edwards's 600-page biography on Barbra Streisand. That book was so big, my teachers always assumed it was the class textbook I was reading. Little did they know I was studying the life and discography of Barbra Streisand. Coincidentally, my seventh and eighth-grade years were also some of my hardest.

This may sound silly, but I hope I read less once I come home. I just hope I won't need to as much. Part of me will always associate reading with the times in my life when I was desperately trying to escape my reality.

8:45 PM

We went to a different location for our evening walk tonight. Past the maternity ward is a quaint little courtyard area that overlooks a side of Cherry Oak I had never seen before. It was a nice change of scenery. It was packed with nervous-looking fathers and soon-to-be grandmothers. For a moment, it felt like I, too, was awaiting the arrival of someone new in the family. Everybody looked so happy. It made me happy, too.

Sunday, February 23, 2014
DAY 27 OF RECOVERY

2:40 PM

Sundays are the worst days on the unit. There is not much structure to the day, so people do their own thing. I haven't seen Casey since breakfast, and everyone else is either taking a nap or calling up friends. Time moves so slow, and it leaves you with ample time to overthink everything that has crossed your mind in the past few days.

I talked to my mom earlier. She is going to call Warner tomorrow to get a bit more information about their outpatient program. She cannot wait for me to come home. She told me that if I make it to March and gain as much weight as possible in the next week, she'll sign the forty-eight for me. At this point, I hesitate to get my hopes up about that anymore. I know Connor and Burton would be angry to see me leave without their approval. I brought up the possibility of my mom signing a forty-eight with Connor, and he told me that I would not be permitted to use any further treatment facilities or recovery programs at Cherry Oak if she did. For example: every Tuesday at eight o'clock, the hospital holds a free Eating Disorders Anonymous meeting open to the public. I wouldn't be allowed to go. I think that was meant to intimidate me, but something about the idea of never returning to Cherry Oak makes me almost salivate. Maybe that's just the scrambled egg from this morning coming back up.

10:20 PM

Burton told me earlier today that I weighed a half pound more than I did yesterday. It's easy to get lost in all the numbers I hear each day. They appear meaningless but hold stronger significance when I'm given a moment to process what they mean. For example, it's almost ten-thirty at night, and all that has been on my mind since this morning is my weight. I have nothing else to distract me.

With each pound I gain, I feel myself slowly slipping away from who I am. I'm gaining almost a pound a day, and I am struggling to find the time to rediscover parts of my body that I haven't touched since I was fifteen pounds lighter.

It's hard to think that I will never be that thin again. Actually, I will never be thinner than what I am *right now*. Well, I shouldn't say *never*, but I also shouldn't be predicting my next relapse anytime soon. I am aiming for the day that these urges completely end.

Monday, February 24, 2014
DAY 28 OF RECOVERY

12:00 PM

I'm finding less and less time to write in my journal. It's already the afternoon, and this is the first time I've sat down to write down my thoughts for the day. Some may say that's a good thing. If I have no time to write in my journal, it most likely means I am busy doing other things, like spending time in the multipurpose room with other patients. Who knew I'd have such a social life here in the hospital?

We have received a few new patients on the unit over the past week. One is named Shelby. She looks like she's in her late 50s, and she has curly brown hair that she is always nervously twirling with her finger. She does it all the time during meals and groups. It is quite distracting.

Shelby has not completed a single meal since she has been here, and it's already been a few days. She was given a warning about a feeding tube, though I'm not sure how likely they are to follow through with it. It is hard to watch her *just* not finish her meals. The other day, she was given an incomplete for leaving half of a piece of penne pasta on her plate. Everybody at the table was rooting for her to finish. She couldn't.

This isn't Shelby's first time at Cherry Oak. She has told me a few horror stories about roommates she has had here in the past. This one woman had someone sneak her in over twenty knee-high socks. She would use them during the night to purge into. She pleaded with Shelby to keep it between them until the stench coming from her bedside dresser became too strong.

Shelby even confirmed that rumor I heard during my first few days about the girl whose anus kept falling out. I suppose it's not something one would easily forget. If that's enough of a cause for someone to begin his or her recovery, then let it be.

When I think back to what was going through my mind when I chose to begin my recovery, all I can remember is the feeling of never feeling human. I didn't know myself anymore. Every part of my life felt foreign to me. I was a stranger in my own skin. Waking up was a chore, and everything afterward felt unbearable. My eating disorder forced itself to the forefront of my mind through every motion I took, and there wasn't a single second when my decisions and actions were not directly influenced by my illness. I used to think to myself: "If everything in my life just *stopped,* would I truly care?" The answer was always no. I would think of my family and imagine myself living on an isolated island in the middle of nowhere with nothing but my thoughts. Even the closest of people I had in my life felt foreign to me. It's like I didn't care about them anymore.

There are times that I regret seeking help. I often think about how little I could have weighed right now if I were still home. It's as if the years of suffering and restricting were all for nothing. It could've been so much simpler.

1:45 PM

Lunch was awful. My tofu stir fry was so over-seasoned that I thought they had served me meat. I barely finished it, so I ended up saving three things on my plate for snack time.

My school counselor sent over a ton of work for me to get

finished. She noted that it all should take about two weeks to complete, but I reckon I'll need a bit more time, especially if I need to do my art homework. The assignment is to draw a portrait of yourself through the eyes of a stranger. Connor said this could be problematic for me, so he's going to try to get me exempted from the project. If drawing my body isn't part of the assignment, I should be fine. I've had to do enough of that here in therapy. However, if Connor is set on me not doing the assignment, I'm not going to argue. My eating disorder has taken so much away from me. The least my lazy ass could do is get something out of it, like skipping out on an art assignment.

<u>*8:40 PM*</u>

My birthday is in a little over three hours. I should feel excited. I'm not. Like Christmas, birthdays tend to feel less and less significant as you grow older. Economies become tight, family drama ensues, and you find yourself counting down the hours until you can lie down in your bed and call it a day. The more aware you become of the world around you, the more difficult it is to find joy in places you once had.

Still, birthdays are special, and it hasn't exactly sunk in that I will be spending mine—*here*. I have expressed these feelings to Connor and during group, and in other words, I'm always told the same thing: that it is my fault I am spending my birthday in the hospital. If I hadn't let my eating disorder get so out of hand, this wouldn't be happening. I wouldn't be where I am right now.

It sounds awful writing that down on paper. Professionals in a hospital should be the first to understand that eating disorders are not a choice. It is not *my* fault I am in the hospital for my birthday. Besides, I didn't think I would be here for this long. I was taken aback by what Connor said.

Embarrassingly enough, one thing most kids my age look forward to on their birthday is how many tweets and Instagram posts their friends make for them. We look to see who the first person will be to text us "Happy Birthday!" at exactly 12 am. I hate social media for those reasons. It has trained me to believe that my worth depends on the attention I seek from others. Without it, I feel lost and invisible. It's unfortunate that in order to gain some sort of freedom from my social media, I had to end up in an eating disorder hospital. Silly how that works.

With all of that being said, you can still expect to find me in my bathroom at 11:55 pm tonight, staring at my phone, curiously waiting to find out which of my friends are still thinking of me.

Tuesday, February 25, 2014
MY SIXTEENTH BIRTHDAY

9:02 AM

Bonus points to Ashley for being the first to message me last night. Aaaaand for hyping up my rugged yet obligatory birthday selfie I posted on Instagram. She told me I looked like a model. She is an idiot. The response to the photo has been amusing. For most, this is the first time they have seen my face in weeks. As of this morning, the photo has already garnered over fifteen comments.

> "Happy birthday Chris! I love you sooooooo much. From our late-night convos to making faces at each other when we pass in the halls, we've gotten so close, and you mean so much to me. I hope you had a great day today, and hopefully, I'll see you soon!"
> - Ashley

> "happy birthday chris <3 i've known you since freshman year and you were one of the first few people i met on the first day of school :) our lunch table is not the same without you. when we sit next to each other we always end up laughing at some point like crazy psychopaths. but i miss you so much and

hopefully see you soon <3" - one of my friends who I haven't yet told where I am. Whoops.

"I loveeeee you so much best friend!! words cannot describe how much you mean to me. you're always there for me to matter what. you always know how to put a smile on my face and we have so many inside jokes ;) I cannot wait to see you soon!!!!" - Arielle

"so....you have time to post on instagram but not answer my text lol" - some random girl from my class whose text I ignored

The infamous birthday selfie I posted from my bathroom

The last one made me laugh. Hey, I gotta keep some air of mystery. Besides, half of the comments I received were from people at school who never gave me the time of day. I don't owe them anything. Whatever. Ashley told me she'd keep a tab on what people at school said about me. I expect a full report by tonight.

It was a good thing I spent more than a few minutes deciding on my outfit this morning because all eyes were on me the minute I stepped into the multipurpose room for breakfast. Everybody on the unit broke out into song, and "Happy Birthday, Chris!" was written all over the large dry eraser board at the front of the room. Junko even blinged out the nurse's station with birthday signs and decorations. I couldn't stop smiling.

I feel like I have been inducted into a special society of people who have spent their birthdays in the hospital. I want to ask Junko how commonly it occurs. It's probably more common than I think. I'm more interested to see how my visit with my mom goes tonight. She told me she has a few cards from family members to bring in, in addition to a couple of other surprises. If only I could unwrap a signed forty-eight form. *That* would be the greatest birthday present ever. On the other hand, now that I am sixteen, at least I know that I won't be in here for more than two years. If I turned eighteen today, I'd be on the bus home already. The thought is absurd yet comforting. One day at a time, Chris. One day at a time.

2:30 PM

I was given full reign to play whatever music I liked during our meals so far today. For breakfast, I chose to play Lorde's *Pure Heroine* and, at lunch, Ellie Goulding's *Halcyon*. Casey told me the songs were too sad to be playing during mealtime, so I quickly switched it to *ARTPOP* by Lady Gaga halfway through. I was surprised to see Shelby sing along to some of the songs. She doesn't come across as the type to enjoy the genre.

It's awkward seeing people react to records that mean so much to you. Music has played such a big role in my life and my recovery, and each song I listened to throughout my day-to-day life has had a purpose. I wish there were a way for me to give back to the art form that quite possibly saved my life, but I don't see that in my cards.

I've always dreamed of becoming a performer. One could argue I was one for almost half of my life. I was a part of a dance team for nearly eight years. We would travel around the state performing at street fairs, hotels, and nursing homes, and one year we even performed at Disney World in Orlando, Florida. I was the only boy on the team, and my teachers always told me how good I was at tap. Sure, I was a bit out of my element being in an advanced tap-dancing class at the age of eleven, but it felt unreal being in the same room as high school seniors learning the same steps I was.

I quit dance when I was twelve years old, and it is something I still regret to this day. The eventual insecurities I found in my body got in the way. Whenever I was asked for a reason why I quit, I would jokingly say that I grew too tall and couldn't perform as well. Anyone who knew anything about dance knew that was complete rubbish, but I felt trapped in a body that I couldn't find the means to feel confident in.

Once in a while, I still find myself squeezing into my old tap shoes and dancing in my garage. The sound of my shoes hitting the floor was almost therapeutic for me. I would dance pretending that the entire world was watching me and encouraging me. I felt invincible.

Will I ever seek out dance lessons again? I guess only time will tell. I'm convinced that my time has already come and gone, but I know it's never too late to chase something you love. I would hate to think of it as another thing my eating disorder has taken away from me.

8:45 PM

I awoke from my routine after-dinner-digestion nap to my mom, dad, and sister bustling into my room with two of those ginormous balloons you see on display on the walls of Party City. One was of a sun, at least two feet in diameter, and the other was a round, black balloon with "Happy Birthday" printed in the middle. I couldn't believe they were even allowed through the doors of the hospital!

We spent the evening together in my room, playing a few rounds of Jenga and Blokus, one of my mom's favorite games. I kept nudging her about the forty-eight. If it's going to happen, what exactly are we waiting for? My mom told me that she would like for me to at least finish inpatient here at Cherry Oak. I wouldn't be forced to continue any further outpatient programs if I didn't want to. It's not exactly what I wanted to hear, as transferring to outpatient wasn't something I was too concerned about.

In other words, I have come to the conclusion that I cannot depend on a forty-eight being signed anytime soon. My heart is telling me to drop the subject completely. I know it is not good for me. I'm not stupid. I should trust my doctor. I should trust him when he tells me that it is imperative I start taking my weight seriously and focus on how I can change my perception of my body. I should trust Connor when he tells me the most important thing for me to do is concentrate on differentiating my eating disorder's voice from my own, which entails allowing myself to get triggered in order to learn more about the dynamics of my mental illness. I should trust Stacy when she tells me challenging fear foods and mealtime rituals are the first steps in creating an anxiety-free food environment. I should believe in my treatment team. They know what they're doing. Why is it so hard for me to trust that they have my best interest in mind? I mean, I know the answer to that. There are strong voices in my mind telling me exactly the opposite.

10:50 PM

Casey made me blindfold myself as I walked into the multipurpose room for snack time tonight. Waiting for me at my seat was the piece of carrot cake I saved from dinner with four candles inside. Except, they were not candles. They were rolled up plastic straw wrappers. It was hilarious, pathetic, and perfect all at the same time. Everybody at the table sang to me again as I dramatically pretended to blow the "candles" out. It felt like we were a big family, and we all found ourselves a good excuse to complete whatever remaining cake each of us had for the day. My heart felt warm.

Once I walked back to my room, I called Ashley to see what the response was at school to the picture I posted online. Arielle made a point to let the entire school know that *she* knew where I was but wouldn't be telling anyone out of respect for me. I can tell she's going to expect my gratitude for that. She's the kind of person who needs some sort of recognition for doing something right.

Each morning during the morning announcements, any student birthdays for that day are read. Apparently, when mine was read, some of my teachers laughed and thought I had transferred schools again. They didn't even act like I was still one of their students. That doesn't make sense considering they send me homework to complete every week or so. I'm just glad I wasn't there to see that.

Anyway, it has been a long day, and I am ready to get some rest. My sixteenth birthday surely wasn't my best, but it is one I will never forget.

Wednesday, February 26, 2014
DAY 30 OF RECOVERY

<u>1:25 PM</u>

Connor told me that there is no way I'd be able to be discharged in time to go to the Ellie Goulding concert next month. It would be way too much on my body physically, and hospital rules wouldn't allow me to spend a night outside of the unit. Even though the concert would end around eleven, it would still take a couple of hours to get back to Cherry Oak from New York City. I understood that, but what got to me was the fact that Connor basically confirmed I'd still be in the hospital for at least two more weeks.

I still have eighteen pounds to gain before I reach my discharge weight. The concert is fourteen days away. If I gain almost one pound every day for the next two weeks, I'll be walking into the Theater at Madison Square Garden to see Ellie. Considering my average daily weight gain is half a pound, sometimes less, I'm going to have to start getting creative. Would it be inappropriate to ask my mom to bring me in some quarters or fishing line weights to store in my underwear? Those would probably do the trick.

2:50 PM

The unit got a bit of a cleansing today. Almost everyone who was around for that "clique" drama has been discharged, including Stephanie and that random girl who brought the whole issue up. A weight has been lifted from my shoulders, and I can tell Casey feels the same. There will be no more awkward mealtime moments or disputes over assigned seats. Best of all, group therapies will no longer seem so tense, and the room will feel more accepting of more important topics than whether or not Casey and I are playing "Footsies" underneath the dinner table. Yes, Connor once accused us of doing just that.

To keep things interesting, we have had a few newbies come in. Emmanuel and I were especially excited to see another boy walking around the unit. He was wearing a dark green beanie and had curly, coarse strawberry blonde hair. We haven't seen him since this morning, so we weren't exactly sure who he was or whether he was being admitted. He looked about our age. Emmanuel is being discharged from inpatient early next week, so I wouldn't be surprised if this new kid took his place, and with that, my dream of having a room to myself.

8:40 PM

Earlier this afternoon, Connor gave me an assignment to write a letter to my sister. It's sometimes difficult for me to say what I want to say when I'm face to face with a person, so Connor recommended I write a letter to her to let her know how I have been impacted by her and her boyfriend's actions over the last few months. *Seriously, Connor? The day after my birthday?* I could think of a thousand other things I'd rather be doing. Here is what I have so far:

Dear Ava,

I know these past few months have been extremely difficult for you, but I want you to know that some things at home have greatly affected me. Ever since your boyfriend moved into our home, we haven't felt like a true family. Personally, I am nervous and worried and scared every minute I spend in the house. Every night, I feel like I am waiting to see what the argument will be about that day, and I'm only half-talking about the arguments between you and your boyfriend. The yelling I hear between you and our mom makes me want to rip my ears out. I feel so guilty whenever you two argue. I don't know what to do. Our parents provide endless support for us, and it breaks my heart to see you respond with hateful language and threats, ones that we know are influenced by your boyfriend.

Speaking of your boyfriend, the loud, aggressive sex at four o'clock in the morning has to stop, along with the violent abuse and arguments that follow. Our walls are paper-thin, and I hear every word that is said between the two of you. Hearing your boyfriend throwing up after every meal in my bathroom also needs to end. I don't think I need to specify why that is hard to hear.

When I get home, I hope things will change. I hope I won't feel the need to lock my bedroom doors every night, fearful that your boyfriend may snap and hurt me. I hope I won't have to sit back and listen to you and mom argue about the silliest things that end in suicidal threats and screaming. I hope I no longer have to fear for your safety, and that you can find it within yourself to see your relationship is as toxic as it gets. I just hope we can go back to feeling like a family, and every single one of us is responsible for doing our part.

I might have to tweak it a bit in the morning, but I think it's a pretty good outline of everything that I want to say. Once I'm finished with it, Connor recommends that I read the letter to Ava during my next family meeting. I think I'd need to be medicated to get through that one.

Thursday, February 27, 2014

DAY 31 OF RECOVERY

<u>2:45 PM</u>

The other day, I convinced myself I was done obsessing over the possibility of my parents signing a forty-eight. This morning, my mom called me to let me know they were going to do just that. I couldn't believe my ears. She told me she'd like to see me get through one more week.

Without the forty-eight, I'm not sure how much longer I would be here. I can remember Cori, the therapist I saw before coming to Cherry Oak, promising me that this program wouldn't just be all about me gaining weight, but lately, that's what it has felt like. Meetings between Connor and me have become so repetitive, not to mention that the topics of our daily group therapies have started to loop. I swear I have been given the same pamphlet on "Improving Your Body Image" at least three times. I honestly wouldn't know. They all end up in the trash the minute I return to my room.

I don't know how else to say this, but I feel like each day I am here, things are only worsening for me. I know I have only been here for a month, but it feels like a lifetime compared to some of the newer patients. Sitting next to them cutting up their food into tiny pieces during mealtime is triggering, to say the least. It's difficult to progress in your own recovery when every person around you seems to be doing worse than you are.

I have tried to explain this to my family, but they do not understand. I don't believe Connor does, either. He returns to the old argument I've heard a thousand times before—that in the real world, outside of the hospital, we don't always get to choose who we sit next to when we eat. Therefore, we must be prepared to take on any challenging situation that comes our way. We must learn how to overcome any triggers that may pop up and face them head-on.

I know all of what he says makes sense. I guess the fact that I continue to get upset over it is just one of the many reasons I am still here. The hospital doors are a constant carousel. People come in. People go out. I feel stuck. I feel every force pushing me further and further away from freedom. It feels like no one is on my side.

4:00 PM

I just made the awful mistake of telling Stacy that I would consider eating fish. Ugh. That was enough evidence to convince herself that my vegetarianism *is,* in fact, a part of my eating disorder. In reality, I said those words just to shut her up. I thought it'd blow over after a few weeks here, but the topic of meat-eating still comes up almost every single day. Burton tells me I'd gain weight faster if I did so, and I can just tell Stacy doesn't believe me when I say my choice to avoid meat is not influenced by disordered thoughts. I thought maybe if I said that I would consider trying fish, she'd give me some time to breathe. Turns out it is just the opposite. She changed my dinner tomorrow to salmon and rice.

I am 120% done with this place. I'm tired of false narratives being pushed toward me and not having a treatment team who understands anything about me or my recovery. It is not fair.

And what's the greatest thing about me being given fish tomorrow? To go on my pass on Saturday, all three of my meals the day prior must have been completed. Let's just forget about everything I have done in the past month to get to where I am now and give me the task of eating a piece of *fish* in order to see the world outside of my dirty, depressing windows. I won't do it. Stacy claims that the timing for the fish was not intentional, but I am not so sure I believe her. Can't it at least wait until Monday? I'm not going to eat it regardless of the day, but they're going to give me fish the day before I go out on pass? Seriously? I think I might be sick.

I cannot wait to leave this place. I am not going to miss one bit about it. Maybe Casey, but I'll get over it. My only concern right now is getting out of here as soon as possible. I am so upset. I have the biggest urge to start packing up my things.

8:45 PM

It's ironic that I wrote about packing a few hours ago because that's what my mom and I just spent the last hour doing. My bedside table and its drawers are practically empty, and I gave my mom a bunch of shit to take home. She reassured me the forty-eight will be signed next week. I can cry thinking about returning to school. I didn't think I'd ever say those words. It's more so my average day-to-day routine that I'm looking forward to returning to the most.

Coming home, some things will have to change, and some things will change naturally. Two months ago, I didn't think I'd be alive to see my life transform the way it has in the past month. Sitting here today, I can almost guarantee that I am ready for any changes in my life that may come my way, and those changes will not come if I am locked up in a hospital with a bunch of people doing far worse than I am.

Friday, February 28, 2014
DAY 32 OF RECOVERY

1:40 PM

Burton said I've been making steady progress with my weight, but it's not enough. I must gain weight quicker. Though I am banking on leaving next week, I can't risk not doing everything I can to reach my goal weight while I'm here. That includes completing the brick size quiche I forced down my throat for lunch today.

Burton took some time with me to go over a few of the logistics about my pass this weekend. Or, should I say *passes?!* Tomorrow, I'll have four hours outside of the hospital, and on Sunday, I'll have five! I'll also have the responsibility of having one meal out on my own. I am required to bring my journal along with me to jot down everything I eat, and I shouldn't do much walking. This will be a big test to see how well I eat on my own. I'm going to ask my mom to do a little research on what there is to do around here and where we can eat on Sunday.

Contrary to what I previously thought, Burton told me that my ability to go out on a pass would not be affected by whether or not I eat the fish, which is reassuring, though I can't lose any weight by tomorrow. Burton recommended I eat a few snacks and extras on my passes to make up for any calories lost. The last thing I want is to lose weight on my pass. That would be awful. Once I expressed this to Burton, he told me he would talk to Stacy about pushing the fish until Monday. At least that buys me a little bit of time. I just barely made the weight requirement to go out on pass this weekend, and I cannot risk losing a single ounce.

With that being said, I lay in my bed at night and dream of breaking out of the hospital doors and running halfway across the country. All disordered behaviors aside, I have not jogged, let alone walked for more than fifteen minutes, in a month. I want to feel my heart rate rise once again. I want to be reminded that I am still human, and I must take care of the things keeping my body alive. I took for granted the opportunity to go outside for a morning run or do a few sit-ups in my room. Not only did I take it for granted, but I took advantage. I overexercised my body for so long, I don't know if I'll ever be able to perform any physical activity without the voices of my disorder returning. I don't know if I'll ever be able to exercise again without losing a massive amount of weight, now that my body is dependent on four times the amount of calories I would eat at home.

It is dismal to look at your past and think about how your actions have altered your future. It's even worse to know that some things may never go back to the way they were intended to be. And I'm not only talking about the ability to exercise. I'm talking about my relationship with food and my body. I'm talking about the association of my eating disorder with Oliver and the fear of falling for someone again. I'm talking about the friendships and opportunities I have lost because my selfish mind convinced me they were insignificant.

I don't know what my future holds anymore. I never thought I'd be alive to see it. Turns out, I am currently living in the future I was so afraid of. It's not any less scary than I thought it would be, but maybe that's a good thing. Maybe that means that I have finally seen life without my eating disorder. It hurts to let go of something that has been a part of you for so long. I think that's one of the scariest things about recovery—letting go of who you thought you were.

Saturday, March 1, 2014
MY FIRST PASS

8:55 AM

It is officially the day of my first pass! I cannot believe this day is here. I got practically no sleep last night. I was way too excited.

My parents are coming to pick me up as soon as lunch is finished, so I still have a few more hours to waste before then. I'm not sure what I'll do. I have changed my outfit three times since I have woken up. As excited as I am for the pass, I can't help but feel slightly nervous about this being the first time the rest of the world sees me since my weight gain. I wonder if anyone will notice. I'm also having trouble finding a pair of pants that I'd be comfortable enough to walk around outside in. I wear the same couple of sweatpants every day on the unit, and I sure would like a change. My parents and I have yet to decide what exactly we want to do today, so maybe we can stop somewhere to purchase some new clothing. There must be a mall around here somewhere. Then again, shopping for clothes for my new body doesn't seem like the most exciting thing, either.

Before I spend the next few hours staring at the clock, I thought I'd update you on a few things happening on the unit.

That boy Emmanuel and I saw on the unit the other day has officially been admitted to inpatient. His name is George, and I think he is a year or two older than I am. If I'm being honest, he's actually pretty cute. Well, he was cute until his girlfriend came to visit him last night. It was a little awkward, to say the least. They walked around holding hands for a while until one of the nurses told them they had to sit down. Emmanuel swore he saw them making out in his room. I had to laugh. How anyone could be doing that in a place like this is beside me. Is there anything about this environment remotely romantic? The various codes constantly being announced through loudspeakers on the ceiling? The overwhelming stench of hospital food seeping through the vents? The likely possibility of having your therapist or a nurse walk in on you? I mean, I guess there's got to be someone into that...

However, it is great to have another male voice and perspective during groups. I never imagined I'd ever meet another boy who has suffered through the same things I have, let alone three. The connection George, Emmanuel, and I feel is very real.

8:35 PM

Something I wasn't exactly prepared for on my pass was to see people...just...*living*. People living normal lives, running normal errands, concerned and focused on *real-life* normal problems. My eating disorder seemed so minimal. Everything I accomplished over the past month seemed almost irrelevant. None of it mattered. The world seemed so big outside the doors of Cherry Oak Hospital, and I was a fool to think I was somehow ready to face it all on my own.

I caught myself wondrously staring at the eyes of people through the glass of my mom's car window, thinking: *What is going on in your head? What is going on in your life?* It was inspiring. It was inspiring to see people living their everyday lives without knowing their deepest roots of fear and frustration. It gave me hope that someday I can explore the world and give outsiders the same impression that I had my life together. Everybody else seems to do it just fine.

All doctors, therapists, and nutritionists aside, all I have in this life is myself. No one is going to watch and make sure I eat for the rest of my life. No one is going to call me out and hold me responsible for any disordered behavior I may do. It is up to me to hold myself accountable and find a life worth living that isn't bottled up in anxiety and angst.

Going out on pass today gave me a little glimpse of what that will be like. It isn't until tomorrow that I will be permitted to eat a meal on my own outside of the hospital, so I had to be conscious of my movements—how much I walked and stood—and how well I reacted to being in an environment where trigger warnings aren't given before every word. For what it's worth, I think I did fairly well. My parents and I didn't do much besides take a drive to a nearby mall and do a bit of shopping. We stopped in Forever 21 where I purchased a pair of camouflage skinny jeans and two varsity sweaters. One has "NOPE" plastered across the chest in red and blue patches and the other reads "THANKS FOR NOTHING." I think they both do a pretty good job of explaining my mood.

I ordered some extras for tonight. I won't know how much I weigh until Monday, but I am a little concerned about all of the walking I did today. All I can do is get a good night's rest and hope tomorrow runs even smoother than today did.

Sunday, March 2, 2014
MY SECOND PASS

9:00 AM

Pass number two begins in a couple of hours! I think my mom and I will go to Panera Bread for lunch. My family and I go to Panera a lot whenever we go on small trips up to New York to visit family. The place feels comfortable to me. Their macaroni and cheese is great, and I know it's got to be full of calories. I'll probably end up getting some bread and chips on the side. I remember the days when the only thing I'd have was one of their mango smoothies. They were so good. I'd always be sure to order them without any whipped cream or fatty milk.

Some say they saw a new girl being interviewed near the nurse's station for admission, and she's a little, err, *odd*. Casey, whose room is right across from all the action, swears she heard the nurses talking about this new girl being an "emergency patient." I can only imagine what that means. It almost feels like high school here. First, you have the freshman who just began their journey and walk around like a lost puppy. Then, you have the seniors who are ready to move on but can't exactly do so yet. I'm somewhere stuck in the middle, but honestly, it feels strange that I'm given the same attention and therapy as a newcomer. I talk like I've been here for years, but that's certainly what it feels like. I don't know.

Alright, I'm going to relax a bit before my pass. Wish me luck.

5:00 PM

A few hours and two bowls of macaroni and cheese later, I am back home! Oh, gosh. Did I really just call this place home?

My mom and I had a very nice day. My dad decided not to come. He was probably upset over all the talk about the forty-eight we had yesterday. My mom swears she will still sign it by the end of this week, but my dad is not convinced that I'm ready to go. I have done and said everything I possibly can to convince him otherwise, but I'm afraid his psychologist ego disables him from looking at my situation through any other lens than what he would use to evaluate his own patients. If it weren't for him, I would have probably been home weeks ago. I resent that very much.

I can just imagine him talking to my mom, feeding into every concern she may have about me leaving and convincing her that I should stay. My dad has always been one to go by the books.

My mom and I first stopped at Panera, where, yes, I ordered two large bowls of their macaroni and cheese! I can't wait to tell Stacy. Not only that, but I actually enjoyed them. We then walked around Barnes & Noble—a store that my mom and I used to visit almost four times a week—and we finished the day by seeing the movie *Nonstop* in the theater. We figured seeing a movie was a smart choice since it does not involve much physical activity. It sure did get my heart racing, though.

And with that, my eventful weekend is over. I would say I'm looking forward to the next, but I'm honestly hoping there won't be another one while at Cherry Oak.

Monday, March 3, 2014
DAY 35 OF RECOVERY

1:35 PM

Emmanuel is being discharged in about an hour or so. We exchanged phone numbers and social media handles, though I doubt we will keep in touch beyond today. He doesn't seem like the type. We both had a pretty good run in here together. Still, it's hard to see yet another person leave who started after me.

George will become my roommate once Emmanuel leaves. He seems really cool, from what I can tell, so I am looking forward to getting to know him and his story a little better. His parents came in to visit him the other day, and they looked like two fish out of water. They seemed sweet and accepting of their son's condition, but it was obvious they hadn't the slightest clue about it probably just one week ago. His mom looked surprised, yet relieved that there were two other boys on the unit with her son. She spent about fifteen minutes asking me questions about the meals, groups, protocols, logistics, and the program's all-around environment. She talked to me like I was five years old. I don't blame her. I imagine it can be difficult to know what to say to somebody like me.

> Goals 3/3/14
>
> **Short term**
> 1) complete all my meals for this week
> 2) regain some motivation on recovery that I lost over the last week
> 3) catch up on school work so I'm caught up when I go back
>
> **Long Term**
> 1) go to a college of my choice
> 2) be a good uncle for my sister's baby
> 3) travel around Europe with friends.

<u>*3:00 PM*</u>

Stacy just informed me that my caloric intake has increased again. If that weren't bad enough, today is the day that I will be given fish for dinner. Yes, *the fish*. I'm not going to eat it. I told Stacy.

The only thing that irks me is that I will have another incomplete on my record, and considering how high my caloric intake is, I cannot afford to waste opportunities to incomplete. Stacy says that my eating disorder won today.

11:05 PM

Spoke with my mom. Forty-eight tomorrow. New roommate. A lot happening. I'll tell you more tomorrow.

Tuesday, March 4, 2014
DAY 36 OF RECOVERY

11:15 AM

I lost an entire pound from that whole fish mishap from yesterday. It's crazy how skipping just one meal affected me so much. Not that it matters anyway. My mom is signing the forty-eight this afternoon. My heart is pounding.

I have yet to tell Connor, Burton, or anyone on my treatment team. I'm not even sure they knew about this battle my parents and I have been having about signing it for the past couple of weeks. Connor is going to be so pissed. I'm so nervous to tell him. At the same time, I could not care less. The hardest part of today will be saying goodbye to Casey. I've been meaning to write her a letter to give her when I leave. It's kind of a tradition around here to do so.

Breakfast this morning was not exactly the wholesome experience I had hoped for. The mealtime dynamic is vastly different. It feels like just yesterday Casey and I were reprimanded for "behaving like a clique," yet we are now the ones left out of many discussions and mealtime games. We're a bit burnt out. I guess we deserve it. So many new patients have come along over the past few days that it's getting difficult to remember their names. There is the one new girl who bragged during breakfast about her mom buying her a $150 five-foot statue of a giraffe from the hospital gift shop in exchange for her to go into treatment. There is the emergency patient girl I mentioned the other day who walks into every mealtime with the same blank expression on her face as she shouts, "I knew I'd be the fattest one in the room!" And there is George, who I totally caught jerking off last night after dinner.

I honestly feel like I am on some sort of reality television show or starring in some low-budget rendition of *Girl, Interrupted*. There are certainly days when it feels more like I am in a mental institution than not. Today is one of those days, and it reminds me of what I thought treatment would be like prior to entering. You tend to think about it as a truckload of misfits in white gowns wandering the floors like ghosts. The only sounds you hear are the distant wails and thuds of patients bashing their heads against the walls, desperately seeking any way to escape their dreadful, heavy minds. I'd be lying to you if I said days like those don't occur, but it's less often than not. Regardless, today just feels a bit *off*. Maybe I'm overthinking things. Am I truly ready to return home later today? I don't know. I think I am. I hope I am. So many things have gotten in the way of the forty-eight being signed that it still doesn't seem real. I'll believe it when I see it. I will talk to you in a bit.

Wednesday, March 5, 2014
DAY 37 OF RECOVERY

11:20 AM

Surprise! I am still here.

The second I told Connor that my mom would be signing me out yesterday, his eyes began to twitch, and his face turned bright red. I had never seen him so angry.

"Well then," he began, as he stood up from his seat. "You do realize you would be leaving against medical approval, yes?"

"I know."

"You would not be permitted to take part in any further treatment at Cherry Oak."

"I know."

"Well, in that case, the hospital has no other choice but to call the Department of Children Protection and Permanency."

I didn't know that.

Connor continued. "It's child negligence. You are underage. You are sixteen years old. You are not legally an adult. If your parents sign you out now, well, they are technically withholding medical treatment from their sick son."

"That's fine." I hadn't processed anything he told me.

"Alright then, Chris. You're wasting my time by talking to me right now. As of today, you are no longer my patient. We are done. Good luck."

I was stunned. Our session didn't last more than five minutes, and in that time, Connor brushed me off as just another one of his probably hundreds of patients he has seen come and go through Cherry Oak. And that's really fucking shitty. Every personal spark and human connection I felt toward Connor vanished. Connor didn't care about me. He never did. He was only ever doing his job. All hospital logistics and forty-eight aside, it felt terrible having the one person you are supposed to trust throughout the entire recovery process dismiss you the *second* you are no longer under his care. Where is the humanity in that? My worst fears about treatment became true. *I am only here to gain weight and nothing else.*

And that's exactly the reason why I am still here. I am up three pounds from yesterday. Most of that can likely be attributed to me holding in my pee for my morning weigh-in. I have been doing it for a couple of days now. We are not allowed to have cups in our rooms, so I use my hands to drink as much water as I can from my bathroom sink every night. Sometimes, I'm in there for half an hour. My dick feels like it wants to fall off every night before I go to sleep. We are required to use the bathroom every morning before we get weighed, and a nurse does check to make sure we do. However, as long as the toilet water is slightly yellow, you're good to go. I now realize what a mistake it has been. From now on, I have to drink the same amount of water I had the day before in order to maintain my weight. It's all a big guessing game, and I wouldn't be surprised to see my weight fluctuate a lot from now on. There's no turning back now.

Anyway, back to the forty-eight. After Connor stormed out of my room, he called my mom and told her everything he told me. She obviously isn't signing the forty-eight anymore. It is completely off the table. The last thing our family needs is for me to be on some government list of neglected children. I also wouldn't be medically cleared to return to school, and that leaves me nowhere. That's just great.

Thursday, March 6, 2014
DAY 38 OF RECOVERY

11:10 AM

I had a long chat with my mom last night. We were both upset about the whole forty-eight situation and had to talk a few things out. Now that I'm guaranteed to be here for at least a few more weeks, I have to start worrying about the Ellie Goulding concert again. It'd be a miracle if Connor let me go. I'd feel like such an ass for even asking him. My mom convinced me to talk to Burton about everything that I have done and accomplished while I am here. In other words, I should sell myself as the most qualified patient to go out on an unprecedented pass to New York City to attend a completely unnecessary but necessary concert. You know, the usual.

Well, *it worked*. According to Burton, he doesn't have a problem with me going on the pass, and he seemed strangely casual about it. It is the hospital rules that may prohibit it from happening. Nevertheless, I have Burton on my side for once, and it feels great.

"Frankly, I'd really like to see you go, Chris," he told me. "And I'm going to do everything I can to make sure that you do."

I sat there without any words.

"I don't make the ultimate decision. That's up to Cherry Oak."

"Right," I muttered out.

"But I don't see why they wouldn't approve," Burton said. "It would almost feel wrong not to, considering how far you have come. You deserve it."

"Yeah," I said with a slight chuckle.

He told me he'd let me know as soon as possible if there were any updates. I'll hold my breath on that one. My hopes know better.

4:05 PM

...I got the pass. I got the pass. I GOT THE PASS. Holy shit.

Today was the first time I talked to Connor since our, uh, dispute, and he kept referring to the concert. He kept referring to the concert *like I was going.* I was so confused. After everything that happened the day before, I didn't exactly see this coming. However, Connor told me everything was set for me to go. Both he and Burton approved me for the pass, and the only hospital rule I needed to keep in mind was making sure I was back before midnight. Apparently, that triggers some sort of "patient runaway" protocol that gets a bit messy with my insurance company. Connor said not to worry. When I sign back into the hospital after the concert, I can just write down that I arrived at 11:55 pm, even if it's later than that.

I haven't told Casey yet. I haven't even told my mom! I'll call her as soon as I'm finished here. I cannot believe this is happening. And it's all happening so quickly. The concert is in only six days! I knew it would all work out in the end. I just knew it would. The only thing I had to give up was one of my passes for this weekend. I told Connor I'd give up both! Nothing will compare to what I will be feeling that day.

Before I go to sleep tonight, I have to call my friend Ivana.

Unless my mom has told her anything, she is very much out of the loop. Once I leave the hospital, my mom and I will drive an hour to Ivana's house, pick her up, then take the train into the city. That in and of itself should take almost two hours. If I miss a few songs of the opening act, I won't be upset. Listening to just one of Ellie Goulding's songs live will make everything I've done over the past month worth it.

11:05 PM

It was tough to function properly for the rest of the day. All I wanted to do was blast my Ellie Goulding CD through the hospital intercom and dance around my room in my underwear. George was discharged earlier today, so I might be able to do that last part.

Today was a big day for me. I know that going to a concert seems so insignificant to some, but this is all I have been thinking about for months. This is all I think about whenever I have a bad day. This is all I think about when I get the urge to restrict or use some other disordered eating behavior. Ellie Goulding's music saved my life. And I am so grateful.

Friday, March 7, 2014
DAY 39 OF RECOVERY

12:00 PM

We had group today in the conference room, which is not technically on the unit. We walked past the outpatient patients having a meal in one of their rooms, and I saw so many familiar faces. Emmanuel was there, along with Taissa and a few others. Hospital rules say we aren't allowed to have any communication with them. We aren't even supposed to wave. I didn't care. I ran ahead and gave Taissa a big hug before one of the nurses in the room gave me a stern look.

1:35 PM

I just found out that I have a seven-hour pass tomorrow! It is from 12-7 pm. So much has been on my mind that this weekend completely snuck up on me. Different than last week's pass, I will be responsible for completing *two* meals on my own outside of the hospital. That's two-thirds of my meals for the day. I would love the chance to go home, but I am not sure I'm ready for that. It might be a little triggering. Everything in my room is sure to remind me of *something*—my bed, my sheets, my mirror, even the color of my walls. And how can I forget my closet full of clothing that will no longer fit me? That's going to be fun to clean out.

A seven-hour pass is a long one, though, and I want to be sure to take advantage of every minute of it. I'll see if my mom has any ideas about where we can go.

9:00 PM

I never thought I'd say this, but there are some disadvantages to not having a roommate. For starters, it is undeniably easy to isolate yourself. After meals, especially dinner, Emmanuel and I would sluggishly walk back to our room together and lie down, fighting the urge to puke it all up. Not because we wanted to, but because it was simply too much food for our stomachs. We understood not to talk to one another for at least fifteen minutes and let out a big sigh of relief once we knew we were in the clear. It was nice having that support. Without a roommate, a bit of that is missing.

That's why I am now so grateful when my mom comes to visit me. In the past, I sometimes felt funny about having visitors every night. It became overwhelming and exhausting. Not anymore.

Saturday, March 8, 2014
DAY 40 OF RECOVERY

9:10 AM

I had a cup of coffee this morning for the first time in a long time. I forgot to order any cream or sugar, so it was pretty strong. I hope that's not the most exciting thing to happen to me today. I go out on pass in a few hours, but I am feeling tired. I would always get upset with Emmanuel whenever he would say that he would rather stay on the unit than go out on pass. *How could that be?*

I understand him now. Some days, all one feels like doing is resting. Maybe I can take a nap in the car. I have a long day ahead of me.

7:45 PM

My mom and I started our day by going to lunch at Panera Bread again. I ate two orders of the macaroni and cheese, a side of bread, a seasonal greens salad, and a mango smoothie. During our meal, we talked all about the Ellie Goulding concert. My mom is so proud of me for being able to show Burton and

Connor that I am healthy enough to go. She convinced me that I deserve this. I do deserve this. After everything that has happened, *I deserve this*. My mom and dad are going to accompany Ivana and me to the concert. I called her the other day to confirm, and she was totally on board.

After our lunch at Panera Bread, we shopped at the nearby Barnes & Noble and went back to the mall for a few more sweaters. I picked up a new journal because this one is almost finished. I still cannot believe I have written as much as I have. In a few years, I know I'll be happy that I had.

My pass wasn't even halfway finished, so we decided to drive an hour away to my grandma's house! It was a happy medium instead of going home. It was great to see my grandma and aunt outside of hospital visiting hours. We ordered pizza, played a couple of games of Scrabble, and talked about our upcoming trip to Columbus, Ohio to visit family. We tend to go in the summer, typically around the Fourth of July.

My mind raced from the overwhelming urge to text David and see how he was doing. I ended up texting him. From what I garnered, he is not doing particularly well. He told me that he had been living at his friend's house for a while because he was kicked out of his mom's apartment. She somehow found out that he was gay. He didn't sound too troubled by it, but I texted him paragraphs of support nonetheless. There was a little voice in my head that told me he was lying. He spent the rest of our conversation talking about all the men he met online and had sex with after leaving Cherry Oak. I'm not sure why he felt the need to tell me. Whatever the case, I regretted texting him and will hold my breath before doing so again anytime soon.

I also called up Jodi for a quick talk. She was so happy to hear that I'm going to the Ellie Goulding concert. We didn't talk about much else. I told her Casey and I are still going strong and that we both miss her very much. I struggled to find the best way to ask her how she was doing. By that, I mean how she was *really* doing. Has she binged? Purged? Restricted? There is no easy way to ask.

    I ended up not asking at all.

Sunday, March 9, 2014
DAY 41 OF RECOVERY

10:14 PM

There is something oddly comforting about hospitals. In various ways, they serve as a safe haven for many people. Help can be found around every corner, and your well-being is likely at the forefront of every decision. I'm not going to lie; I've always wanted to work in a hospital. Medicine and science have always interested me, but I never thought I was intelligent enough to pursue such a path.

In many ways, being in treatment has inspired me to weigh what matters most to me and what future I can dedicate a passion to. The nurses and doctors I meet with every day have dedicated their lives to bettering others. That is something that takes a lot of selflessness and drive. I can see how fulfilling it would be.

I want my life to be worth something. I want it to be worth something even when I'm gone. I want to make an impact on the world. I know I have to better myself first. I need to take whatever remaining time I have here at Cherry Oak and remind myself that every aspect of my future depends on *me* and what *I* choose to do from this day going forward.

Monday, March 10, 2014
DAY 42 OF RECOVERY

1:40 PM

Do you remember that girl I told you about who made her mom buy the giant giraffe statue in the gift shop in exchange for going into treatment? She signed a forty-eight today. Her mom is not happy about it. Apparently, she lost one pound and got so upset by how Burton spoke to her that she decided to leave. It's another one of those you're-only-hurting-yourself-by-doing-that cases. At least she got a piece of zoological home decor out of it.

This seemed to trigger more negative feelings across the unit. There were at least five incompletes during breakfast and lunch —each. One girl had a family meeting that went so badly she never even showed up for the meals.

10:55 PM

I forgot to mention that my caloric intake was increased today AGAIN. Saying the number out loud almost makes me laugh. There is no way I am going to be able to keep this up at home. I just don't see how it'd be remotely possible. I doubt there are that many calories in my refrigerator to begin with.

> March 10, 2014
>
> <u>Short term goals</u>
>
> - have a fun, organized pass this Wednesday by figuring out times for trains
> - complete all my meals
> - open up to my parents on Friday on one thing that really triggered my relapse
>
> <u>Long Term Goals</u>
>
> - possibly get discharged in the next like 3 weeks...?
> - be home for my sister's baby shower on the 29th
> - be a good uncle for my sister's baby that's due in less than a month.
>
> **

The only way I can come close to that number would be by drinking the same dietary supplements we are given here, like Boosts and Ensures. Drinking them makes me feel like a child, not to mention that they are so calorically dense that you feel like you're consuming a gallon of two-month-old whole milk.

I should go to sleep soon. Tomorrow is Tuesday, which means the Ellie Goulding concert is right around the corner. I don't think that'll sink in until I'm standing in the Theater at Madison Square Garden itself.

Tuesday, March 11, 2014
DAY 43 OF RECOVERY

1:40 PM

I told my mom to have a cooler full of food in the car for tomorrow. I'm talking junk food, chips, soda, candy, Boost drinks—everything. If I'm going to have any chance at not losing weight during the concert, I'm going to have to drink those up the ass. I know my metabolism is wild, but I don't know what it's going to be like once we are walking around the city and standing for hours. I'm preparing for the worst. I'm preparing to lose a few pounds, but after tomorrow, it won't matter. I'll regain whatever I lose, and I'll gain even more.

Since coming to Cherry Oak, this concert has *always* weighed on my mind. *Will I be out in time? Will I be able to go?* It has driven me nuts. Once it's over—which makes me sad to think about—I know I will be able to focus more on my recovery and what I have to do going forward. I won't be gaining weight for the sole purpose of getting a pass. I won't be spending my time with Burton convincing him to let me go. It'll be done. In many ways, I believe seeing Ellie tomorrow will inspire me to do even better. I need to look at the bigger picture.

10:30 PM

If someone were to ask me what I accomplished today, I wouldn't know how to answer. Does lying in bed all day staring at the clock count? Or how about putting together a giant 400-piece safari puzzle? At least that's something. I have been distracted all day. What am I supposed to do? Tomorrow is going to be life changing. It's going to be unreal.

Wednesday, March 12, 2014
DAY 44 OF RECOVERY

2:15 PM

Well, today is the day I have been waiting for. I cannot believe it is finally here. I am currently sitting in a hospital room more than an hour away from home, and later tonight, I'll be in New York City. It's funny to think about it like that. I'm pretty sure everybody on the unit is sick of me talking about this concert. I'm sure you are, too.

Connor talked to the hospital cafeteria, and they agreed to bring my dinner up at five o'clock. That should give me ample time to complete my meal and get together whatever it is that I need to bring with me. Part of that will be every dollar of my birthday money that has been sitting in my bedside table drawer for almost a month. The last thing you want when attending a show of your favorite performer is an empty wallet. A simple tour shirt can go for at least thirty dollars.

My goal for tonight is simple: get lost. Lose myself. Lose every ounce of anxiety and hatred that my mind has been harboring for way too long. I want to enjoy the concert and not remember that I'll have to return to a hospital's eating disorder unit later on. For those few hours in New York City, none of that will exist. Cherry Oak will not exist.

Thursday, March 13, 2014
DAY 45 OF RECOVERY

1:15 AM

I thought I'd have a special way of beginning my first journal entry after the concert, but I got nothing. It's super late—or early, I should say. It has been a long night, and I need to get some rest. I also need to place my focus on not regurgitating those five Boosts that I chugged in the hospital parking garage.

11:05 AM

My body is still recovering from all the activities of last night. I feel like I completed a triathlon and then had to jog back to the starting line once I was done.

Once my parents picked me up from the hospital, we drove over an hour to pick up Ivana from her home. Seeing her felt unreal. It had only been a little over a month, but that didn't stop me from jumping out of the car once we pulled up to her house to greet her with the biggest hug I could give.

After the initial high of reuniting with Ivana, I spent the remainder of the car ride answering every question she had. *What do they make you eat? Is it any good? Do you hear anyone throw up afterward? Who's the skinniest one there? Are any of your roommates hot?*

With every question she had, I cringed a little harder. Didn't she have any common sense? However, I couldn't help but laugh at half of them. *These are the types of dumb things teenagers should be gossiping about,* I thought. And so, I went into great detail about every mildly inappropriate thing that had happened while on the unit, from the time I pooped six times in a day to every oddly sexual conversation David and I had during his weeks on the unit. She was bummed to hear that David and I never hooked up, but I was very relieved to give her *that* news.

We drove to Secaucus Junction, a train station just outside of New York City, and hopped on the next train straight to Penn Station. Luckily, the Theater at Madison Square Garden is just outside of the station, meaning we wouldn't need to walk much or take the subway to get there.

The night couldn't have gone better. Ivana and I entered the venue through the general admission entrance and got spots near the right side of the stage. I've learned to never go toward the center of the floor because that's where everybody else runs first. People tend to forget about the sides.

The crowd mostly consisted of adults. Ivana and I stood out as some of the youngest there, but it didn't bother us. Once the opening acts were finished and Ellie opened up her show, *nothing mattered.* Everything felt right. At that moment, it felt like every aspect of the universe fell directly into place. The lights were dimmed, the air was hot, and there was no place I would rather have been.

Almost halfway through the show, I looked up at my hand waving in the air and noticed my hospital wristband slowly creeping up my arm. I wondered if any people around me saw it. *Did anybody know what it was? Did anybody know what it meant?* Surely it would be difficult for anyone to see it in the dark, but that didn't stop me from ripping it off my wrist. I pulled so hard that a red band appeared down my arm from the bracelet. I thought that I'd probably have some trouble reentering the hospital without it, but I refused to let that wristband hold any weight over me.

As the show came to a close, my parents, Ivana, and I walked back to Penn Station and took the next train back to New Jersey. It was getting late, but I remembered what Connor told me about signing back in at the hospital. As long as I wrote down that I returned by 11:55 pm, I'll be okay. We chose to drive Ivana home first, and then we took the long drive back to Cherry Oak. I fell asleep the minute I walked back onto the unit.

8:30 PM

We got a situation. During dinner, Burton called me out to the hallway. No, literally. He *called me* called me. Junko handed me her personal phone while he was on the other end. He told me that he had been on the phone with my insurance company all evening, and they want to transfer me to Cherry Oak's partial hospitalization program as soon as possible. And get this—the last day my insurance covered my inpatient treatment was yesterday. Burton said that I might have to be discharged later tonight. *Later tonight? It's practically bedtime! What are they going to do, drop me off on the streets?* I have no idea what is going on right now. Burton told me he'd get back to me with any updates.

Friday, March 14, 2014
DAY 46 OF RECOVERY

1:40 PM

Connor confirmed with me that I'll be leaving after my family meeting this afternoon. I must be off of hospital grounds before dinner, or insurance is likely to charge for another night. This is all happening so quickly. I'm not ready to leave. Why is this happening?

10:20 PM

Monday. I am being discharged on Monday. Partial hospitalization is still a "maybe." I don't know what is going on anymore. Everybody here is telling me something different.
"Your insurance granted you three more days."
"Your insurance stopped paying for your treatment two days ago."
"You might be transferred to partial. It's up to you and your parents."
"Your insurance may not cover that either."
"You need to plan for your pass tomorrow!"

"Don't fill out pass requests for this weekend—you'll be gone."

"Here are your menu orders to fill out for the next two weeks!"

I am so exhausted.

Saturday, March 15, 2014
DAY 47 OF RECOVERY

10:20 PM

I went home today on my pass. I felt a bit bad about it. My room was decorated with "Welcome Home" signs and balloons that I clearly wasn't supposed to see until I was discharged. On my bed were some of my favorite snacks and magazines that I had missed out on from the previous two months. I promised my mom I wouldn't look or touch anything else until I was home for good. And no, it isn't getting any easier to say that.

Everything felt so small. And I felt so big. I felt big walking up the stairs to my front door. I felt big stepping into my room and hearing a slightly louder creak coming from my wooden floor. I felt big looking in my closet and knowing I'd have to buy an entirely new wardrobe once I leave Cherry Oak.

I was consumed by an overwhelming feeling of not belonging. I did not belong there. Every awful memory from my life spurred back into my mind with each step I took into that house. I heard the hours-long arguments between my mom and my sister. I heard the threats, the crying, and my own heavy breathing as I'd sit curled up on my bed waiting for it all to be over. I saw the same old furniture in the living room, the same piles of cluttered, months-old mail on the kitchen table. I saw images of each door in the hallway closed shut, reminding me again of the contrast in our family dynamic now from what is used to be. Nothing much in the house had changed, and I think that was what I was most afraid of.

It became clear to me that I was not ready to return home. I tried to smile and reassure myself that I was. As far as I am concerned, there is nothing I or anyone else can do to counteract my insurance's decision to discharge me. Yet, the last thing I need is for anybody, especially my parents, to walk on eggshells around me. I didn't want to give the impression that I was not ready to go home or that in my mind, I knew I needed to stay in treatment. I have to act strong, like I didn't just spend the last three weeks trying to convince my mom to sign me out of treatment. I wish I could take it all back. I have to act brave, even if I am faking it.

Sunday, March 16, 2014
DAY 48 OF RECOVERY

10:55 PM

Junko gave me a survey to fill out about my experience at Cherry Oak. Honestly, should someone with an eating disorder be trusted to give a praising review of the place where they first received treatment? It seems a little twisted. I didn't give the place such a terrible review. I did leave two notes at the bottom of the page that I hope the staff pays extra attention to. The first thing I wrote about was the passive-aggressive attitude that I felt from many people. I don't think I'll ever be able to forget Connor telling me that it is, essentially, my fault that I have an eating disorder and that I am in treatment. I also don't think I'll ever forget the way that bitch Barbara talked to me about missing Ashley's sweet sixteen.

I also recommended Cherry Oak brainstorms some new content and topics for group therapies. That shit was getting a little repetitive.

I certainly did not meet my exchanges today on pass. My mom and I ate at a California Pizza Kitchen nearby. I couldn't even finish half of my pizza. I was so anxious the entire time that all I wanted was for the pass to be over. That's something I never thought I'd say.

I have so much to get done before I leave tomorrow. I need to write letters to everybody. Casey's will be the hardest. I'm sure our goodbye will be filled with promises of talking on the phone every night and reconnecting in person now and then, but we both know that is unlikely to happen. People come in and out of your life, and that's okay. Closing a chapter in your life is difficult, but the anticipation is even worse. I'm grateful for the connections I have made here. They are truly what has kept me alive.

I don't know what is going to happen tomorrow. I feel completely numb.

Monday, March 17, 2014
DAY 49 OF RECOVERY

1:45 PM

I sound like a broken record. I'm not leaving today. I'm leaving tomorrow. It's definite. Burton has been on the phone with my insurance company all morning. They are refusing to pay for *any* further treatment for me whatsoever. In fact, I learned that I should not have been admitted to Cherry Oak in the first place. Eating disorders aren't covered under my plan, and it was a mixture of miscommunication and misunderstanding that my insurance paid for any of my treatment at all. My case was classified as an emergency, and that was part of the reason I slipped through some sort of loophole.

There is nothing Cherry Oak can do for me anymore. There is nothing Burton or Connor can do for me anymore. Stacy bumped my caloric intake up once more, stressing how important it will be for me to continue such a high-calorie meal plan once I am discharged. Realistically, that is not going to happen. I entered treatment knowing that I needed someone to sit down and tell me what to eat and how much to eat. Without that, I don't know what I'll do. I have learned a lot about my body and nutrition, but I don't think it'll be enough. That many calories? Daily? On my own? I could barely reach that number after chugging three Boost Plus drinks every meal.

My mom will be coming over later to help me finish packing. I want to do as much as I can tonight to make tomorrow run as swiftly as possible. Junko told me I'd be leaving after lunch—basically, in twenty-four hours.

Okay, let's be honest. I cannot wait to go home. I miss my home, my bed, my school, my friends—I miss everything that I knew. I miss the freedom of waking up and going to sleep whenever I want. I miss the freedom of going to the bathroom and not having a nurse check the toilet once I am finished. I miss fast food, soda, and my favorite brand of jalapeño-flavored potato chips. I miss showers that last more than ten minutes. I miss my life.

Once I am home, I'm afraid its environment will only push me back where I started. Nothing around me will have changed, yet I am returning as a drastically different version of myself. My eating disorder had been the most important thing in my life for so long. It was the only way I ever found any sort of identity entering my young adulthood. I was afraid of who I really was and felt that disappearing was the only way to mask those feelings.

I am a changed person. No, let me rephrase that; I am me. It's who I have always been. Each day for the past two months, I have worked to find that person again. For that, I feel changed. Who I am now feels foreign compared to the person I have been for the last couple of years, but I know I've always been this person.

I'm beginning to confuse even myself now. I know I have more work to do. I know there is a stronger relationship with my body and with food to be developed. I know I still have weight to gain in order to be classified as "healthy." In a perfect world, my discharge tomorrow wouldn't be happening. In a few weeks, or months, I'd enter partial hospitalization, then intensive outpatient, outpatient, and so on. The one thing I have heard countless times here at Cherry Oak is that recovery is a process. It doesn't end after inpatient. It's a long, gradual process that involves a decreased amount of treatment as time goes on. That is a best-case scenario, of course.

DISCHARGE CHECK LIST

Meal plan for discharge day ☐
Meal plan for day one (home & PHP) ☐
Meal plan for 1st week home ☐
Grocery list ☐
Nutritional questions/concerns to discuss with my dietitian:

1. _____

2. _____

3. _____

4. _____

STARCHES	
Bagel, lenders	
Bagel, regular	
English muffin	
Rice	
Pasta	
Cereal; types	
Sliced bread	
Cookie/dessert	
Sherbet	
Ice cream	
Fruit yogurt	
Hot chocolate	
Graham crackers	

PROTEIN	
Deli; cheese	
Tofu	
Tuna fish	
Cottage cheese	
Eggs	
Beans, chick, kidney	
String cheese	
Deli meat	

MILK	
Yogurt: vanilla, plain *(Low fat only, no non-fat)*	
Milk: 2%, skim, whole, chocolate	

FRUIT	
Apples	
Grapes	
banana	
Fruit juice	
Dried fruit (raisins, etc)	
other	

FATS	
Cream cheese	
Peanut butter	
Butter or margarine	
Nuts: almonds, peanuts	
Regular salad dressing Type:	
Mayo	

Tuesday, March 18, 2014
DAY 50 OF RECOVERY

10:10 PM

My last few hours at Cherry Oak were heavy. Burton was on the phone with my insurance company until the moment I stepped off the unit, pleading for just one more day. Junko provided me with a month's worth of food journals to fill out and a stack of papers about every diagnosis, medication, and form of medical treatment I had been given at Cherry Oak. Trust me, there was a lot on there—from every Tylenol I took to a daily report of how many times I went to the bathroom. The most daunting? The terms *"Diagnosis: Anorexia Nervosa"* plastered on the top of every page. This is now something I will live with for the rest of my life.

Casey and I hugged for what felt like thirty minutes. Any form of physical contact is not permitted on the unit, but I would have liked to see the staff of nurses and doctors watching our dramatic goodbye try to tell us otherwise. I love Casey so much. I will never forget what she has done for me.

I am home. Somehow, none of this feels real. I don't think it will for a while.

Once my mom picked me up from Cherry Oak, we went to

the mall where I picked up some more clothes. I needed some new khaki pants to wear to school.

School. I'll be returning to school next week.

What am I doing now? I'm sitting on my bed. I'm reliving every moment of the past two months in my brain as if I can somehow change certain things if I focus hard enough. *Did I say goodbye to everybody that I needed to? Did I forget anything in my room? Did Connor and I leave on good terms? Will I ever see him again? Do I care? With everything that I have learned about myself throughout the past two months, will it be enough to translate into newfound respect for food, my body, and the value I place on my life?*

It's hard to tell.

I had dreamt about the day I'd be discharged from Cherry Oak. I imagined locking myself in my room for at least a week and promising that I wouldn't come out until I lost all the weight I gained in treatment. I was determined to have no trace of my time at Cherry Oak on my body whatsoever.

My body.

I hadn't looked at myself in a full-length mirror in nearly two months. Now, there is one standing three feet away from me. Who I see looking back at me isn't a person I'm familiar with. He isn't necessarily happier. He isn't sad, either. He's just different. The same, but different.

Now what?

I may not love my body yet. I may not have the confidence to be my authentic, complete self yet. I know I am not yet the best version of myself that I can be, but every day, I am fighting to be that person.

I have the power to take my life back.

And I think that's the most important lesson I've learned so far in my recovery.

END OF JOURNAL

Thicker Ice

It can seem impossible to notice the forces that are trying to help you. And when you do, your eating disorder will most likely translate that help as something quite the opposite. The most difficult part of anybody's recovery journey is admitting that help is needed and pushing aside the stubborn ego of the eating disorder to accept it.

Cherry Oak Hospital saved my life. Connor saved my life. Dr. Burton saved my life. Every individual on my treatment team, every nurse who woke me up at five in the morning to check my vitals, every heart-wrenching therapy session, every person that I encountered, and every event that occurred during my two-month stay at Cherry Oak Hospital saved my life. Most importantly, I saved my life.

Returning home was bittersweet. I was there only a few days prior on a pass, yet things still seemed foreign to me. I forgot how my mattress felt against my back as I laid down my first night home. I couldn't remember which way to turn my shower faucet to make the water warmer. Simple things, like sitting in my kitchen, spending time on my phone, and walking through my house felt strange. Yet, I couldn't expect anything different. I couldn't go back to the way I once lived my life. I couldn't repeat the same behaviors that brought me to Cherry Oak in the first place. I had to learn how to live my life without the feeling of things around me being tainted by my eating disorder. I was given the opportunity for a fresh beginning, and I planned to take every advantage of it that I could.

My first days back at school went better than I could have ever expected. My friends were waiting by my locker and swarmed me with hugs the second they saw me. Even some kids who I had only talked to a handful of times approached me. Seeing Ashley for the first time made me especially emotional. I will never be able to repay her for reminding me that beyond everything that happened before and while I was in treatment, I was still the same, silly me. If only she knew how much I clung to every conversation we shared over the phone during my stay at Cherry Oak, one would think I owed her the world.

Ariel, on the other hand, was a different story. Though I trusted her enough to call her up in the hospital and tell her about my eating disorder, that didn't stop her from using that information against me. Whenever we got into a minor disagreement, she'd bring it up and remind me how loyal to me she had been while I was away. She eventually began bullying me and my other friends online, and we cut ties almost immediately.

The principal and other staff from my school acted surprisingly supportive towards me. A few of my teachers even stopped me in the hallway to welcome me back. I still was not sure what they knew and what they didn't know about where I was. I spoke with my guidance counselor almost daily who reminded me that she and the school nurse had gone around to each of my teachers and told them to stay away from any topics regarding weight, food, or calories. A few of my teachers seemingly forgot. There were a few days during my first month back that my mom picked me up from class due to certain conversations I overheard. It was difficult trying to explain to the school nurse how listening to the wrestling team complain to my history teacher about how much weight they needed to lose upset me. It was clear to me that I had to look out for myself in ways I had never done before.

The teacher I got the most questions from was my physical education teacher. On my first day back, I handed her a letter from Burton exempting me from all physical activities for the year. She was tough on me at first, but I gave a few hints throughout the year as to why I could not participate in her class. Instead, she assigned me a ten-page paper on the origins of football.

I also became close buddies with the school nurse. Each day in my art class, which was two periods before lunch, I went to her office to have a supplemental drink. They were similar to those I was given in the hospital to gain weight. The only difference was, now, I wasn't required to announce to a room full of people when I was finished.

CONTRARY TO WHAT I hoped during treatment, issues with my sister never truly subsided. Less than two months after I returned home, my sister, her boyfriend, and their newborn baby girl left our home amidst a sea of red and blue flashing lights. My mom and I heard what sounded like my sister getting beat up in her room. My mom finally decided that it was time to get involved. She knew doing so was putting her relationship with her daughter at risk, but there was no other choice.

My mom began shouting and pounding at my sister's door until it finally opened. My sister was naked and hysterically crying in the doorway. The words and threats my sister used against my mom were vile. My sister and her boyfriend stormed out of our house, promising that no one in our family would ever see them or their new baby for as long as they both lived. If even one person attempted to contact them, my sister said that she'd slit both of her wrists and jump into the nearest river.

As they were halfway out of the front door, my sister came

rushing back into our house to pick up the one thing she forgot: her newborn baby. My sister was in no state of mind to care for a baby, so my mom told her to come back tomorrow and take the baby then. That proposal didn't sit too well with either my sister or her boyfriend. A few moments later, the police showed up to our front lawn amid shouts from my sister's boyfriend that my mom kidnapped his baby.

Once the police became involved, there wasn't much my mom or I could do. We told the cops what happened, certain not to leave out the months of abuse we witnessed. The policeman explained that without my sister wishing to press charges against her boyfriend, it was not up to us to determine what would happen next. With a signal from the police, my sister and her new family left, never to be seen or heard from again for nearly eight months.

I STRUGGLED a lot when I came home. I lost more than half of the weight I gained in treatment almost immediately. My body had become so conformed to living in a secluded, sanitary environment that I grew glaringly ill once home. I couldn't hold anything down, and it seemed like my digestive system was declining as each day went by. The worst part was that I couldn't eat for nearly three days. The thought of even doing so was enough to make me nauseous. Leaving Cherry Oak, all I wanted was to prove to myself and my parents that I *could* eat on my own, but I just physically couldn't. *That* was the worst feeling in the world.

Over time, my initial, post-treatment sickness subsided, but the lack of food I was able to eat during that time made it difficult for me to return to eating the amount of food I should have been. I became so overwhelmed with the idea of reaching the almost four thousand-calorie meal plan I was on at Cherry Oak, that most of the time I wouldn't even reach half of that number. I found myself constantly counting every nutrient I was putting into my body and tracking whether or not any physical activity I did was too much. Though I was now in recovery, my eating disorder was still the only thing making itself present in my mind. It was clear to me that I hadn't been given the proper preparation one needed to return home from treatment, but I couldn't blame anybody at Cherry Oak for that. If only my insurance had allowed me to continue with lower levels of treatment, such as partial hospitalization or outpatient therapy, then I feel I would have been provided with a smoother transition back home.

Yet, I couldn't go a day without recognizing how privileged I had been to be given even a day in treatment. Millions of individuals across the globe suffer from eating disorders, and only a fraction of those will ever be given the opportunity to receive the same level of care that I had been given. For that, I consider myself very lucky. The individuals who took part in my treatment were some of the most qualified professionals. Very few people will ever be given that experience, not to mention having the ability to be in a safe and healthy environment where concerns over a possible eating disorder can be made.

BEFORE ENTERING TREATMENT, I had spent most of my nights watching videos on YouTube of individuals recounting their stays in different eating disorder inpatient hospitalization programs. Some of the videos included the dietary specifications of the meal plans they were put on, the table rules that they encountered during each of their meals, and the themes of certain group activities and therapy sessions that the entire unit took part in. Other popular videos dealt with outsiders' various misconceptions about eating disorders, side effects one may encounter due to the prevalence of certain eating disordered behaviors, and how to progress in life post-treatment while inhabiting a pro-recovery lifestyle. In those videos, there was a constant attribute that I couldn't help but notice: nearly every person who made videos online about their eating disorder was female.

On April 9, 2014, just under a month after leaving Cherry Oak, I sat in my backyard with my old digital camera and a broken tripod I found in my closet from my childhood. Not knowing if the video I was about to film would ever be seen by the public, I decided to introduce myself by partaking in an eating disorder "tag"—a video answering a series of questions regarding a set topic. Tag videos like these were popular on YouTube at the time, though most of them dealt with relationships, books, or which drinks at Starbucks were the greatest. Yet, shyly and awkwardly, I answered questions regarding the current state of my recovery, how long I had been in recovery, and the diagnosis of my eating disorder.

In the weeks to come, I'd film videos such as *Anorexia Hospitalization: What to Bring*, *The Effects of Anorexia*, *My Anorexia Story*, and *Eating Disorder Hospitalization: A Boy's Experience*. I quickly found that sharing my story online was a positive way for me to still hold myself accountable for my own recovery and connect with others around the world who were struggling with the same things. I looked at it as a form of therapy, and the community I soon found reminded me of the one I had in Cherry Oak.

Having a strong support system is a crucial and necessary piece of anybody's recovery from an eating disorder. For many, this includes family members, close friends, and a team of professionals pointing you in the right direction. Mine just so happened to largely exist online. Creating a space where connections can grow and conversations can be had in a safe environment was a priority of mine. As the years went on, I discovered that was the most important and influential decision I ever had the privilege to make.

Recovery is possible. It is something you can choose each day of your life. It will not be easy, and it certainly will not be instant. For every few steps you take forward, it is expected to then take a couple of steps back. What're important are the choices you make afterward. If your eating disorder is unhappy with a decision you make, it probably means that you made the right one.

Lessons from Recovery

There isn't a "right" time to begin recovery.
 Before I entered Cherry Oak, I struggled to determine when would be the "perfect" time for me to start my recovery and receive treatment. I had many concerns about missing school, holidays, birthdays, and family events. I felt that receiving treatment for my eating disorder was a selfish and inconvenience in my life, and I wasn't convinced that it was necessary.
 Ultimately, I learned that my eating disorder would make an excuse for any day of the year to not be the day I chose recovery. Recognizing those excuses was hard, but it was what led me to initially begin to understand the patterns, behaviors, and voices of my eating disorder. Choosing recovery is a daily, sometimes hourly, decision.

BE honest with your therapist and tell them as much as possible.
 I quickly learned that being as upfront and honest as I can with a therapist would only further benefit myself. Your therapist cannot help you if you don't tell them what is wrong. The anxiety and nervousness I'd feel going into a meeting would almost instantly vanish the moment I spoke up about something I was holding in. Remember that your

therapist is on your side, and you are the only person who can let that help in.

IT IS important to recover for yourself.

I can remember one day in group therapy being asked what made me want to recover. I mentioned the same things I told Cori, stating how poorly I felt every morning and how I felt too tired to do anything. I also remember mentioning my mom, which was an answer that was met with unexpected groans from across the table. I was confused, not to mention slightly offended. I thought to myself, as long as I'm recovering, what does it matter why or for whom I am doing it for?

It took me a while to recognize the risk you take when placing the reason for your recovery on someone or something else, even with that someone being your mom. Reading these excerpts from my journal, I was reminded of who I really needed to recover for: myself. Looking back to middle-school-me, there is little I want more than to be able to comfort him and tell him that everything will be okay. Whenever I am having a rough day or wishing to use a behavior, I think of him and I want to make him proud.

NEVER JUDGE a book by its cover.

I notice my narrative change a lot throughout this book. One thing I initially observed was my inability to introduce a new patient to my journal without giving some type of description as to the way they looked. Whether it be the way they styled their hair, what clothes they wore, or even a random part of their body that stuck out to me, it was my eating disorder that thrived on comparing myself and my body to others'. When I first saw Casey, my mind didn't initially acknowledge her as someone who was struggling. Seeing her, all that I wanted was to be her. This desire was based on nothing except her appearance in comparison to mine.

Eating disorders are extremely competitive, and they work to remove the humanity and identity that is in each of us. A difficult part of recovery is deconstructing the way that we view ourselves in comparison to others and being able to recognize these patterns in our own thoughts.

STEP outside of your comfort zone.
It's a common piece of advice, but one that I found especially relevant during my time in treatment. Asking to play Hedbanz with the other patients at Cherry Oak is a silly example, but I can still remember how I felt after I did. Though I was nervous to join them, I felt a sense of confidence after doing so.

Eating disorders are incredibly isolating. They make you feel alone and almost incapable of living a life without them. Accepting support from friends and family sometimes felt like a burden, but ultimately allowed me to think critically about my eating disorder and how its thoughts affected me. Differentiating my voice from those of my eating disorder proved to be one of the most logical and constructive steps in beginning my recovery.

A "BAD DAY" isn't as bad as you think.
It's expected to have a bad day in recovery every once in a while. That doesn't make your recovery weak or vulnerable. In fact, it is through those tough days that give me the most insight into my eating disorder and the ability to pinpoint what may have triggered my bad day. I find that the more I'm confronted with my triggers, the more I learn about them and how to cope with them.

YOU CAN'T EXPECT everybody to know what you're going through.
This was something I learned early on in my recovery. When opening up to someone about anything deeply personal to you, you run the risk of that person not responding in a way that you hoped. Opening up to someone about your eating disorder is no different, especially given the

number of stereotypes and misconceptions about them that can infiltrate any conversation.

Remember that it is your recovery, and it is up to you to decide who you want to share parts of your story with. What's most important is protecting your peace and your health. Take your time in deciding how you want to approach the topic of your recovery with others.

TRUST THE PROCESS.

Beginning recovery is a journey of reestablishing the trust that you hold within yourself, your body, and those around you. It's also about giving yourself permission to embrace the unexpected, to grow, and to acknowledge those times when it's right to welcome guidance from others.

I didn't know what to expect upon entering inpatient at Cherry Oak. I thought many of the activities and meetings that filled my days were silly and had little to do with my eating disorder. I remember Connor telling me that two people could be sitting in the same group therapy session and take away entirely contrasting points from it. Being in recovery doesn't just mean attending groups and going to therapy. Recovery is about the active work that a person puts into themselves and their mental health. Recovery is what you make of it, and part of the journey is trusting the process despite any intrusive thoughts and setbacks from your eating disorder.

DON'T COMPARE YOUR RECOVERY.

For the majority of my time at Cherry Oak, it was all I essentially did: compare my weight to others, compare my meal plan to others, and compare certain advances others made in their recoveries before I did (i.e. being taken off of Fall Risk). I grew particularly frustrated when it seemed like those around me were taking strides in their recoveries quicker than I was, while I struggled to make any progress at all.

If I could go back in time, I would remind myself that just how every person's eating disorder is different, the same can be said about every person's recovery.

Seven Years Later
JANUARY 28, 2021

The first excerpt from my journal was written seven years ago today, but it wasn't until mid-2017 that I decided it was ever going to be published. *On Thin Ice* has been in the works for nearly four years, and it has felt like a never-ending cycle of edits, self-doubt, and pain. Revisiting the events written about in this book was no less painful than the events themselves. There were days I'd write just a few words then find myself unable to concentrate on anything else. Other days, I'd find the very voices written about in this book creeping back into my mind like an old friend. It was isolating and, at times, unbearable.

I had many reservations about publishing *On Thin Ice*. An overwhelming part of me thought, "Who would want to read the journal of a teenage boy beginning his recovery from an eating disorder?" I didn't believe anybody would care enough to understand the development of my disorder, how it permeated my life, and how I ultimately chose to overcome it. There are millions of stories similar to mine out there. What makes mine so special? Why should I share my story?

The answer was simple: not enough people do.

The pain caused by putting this book together developed

into something else. Power. Strength. Healing. And the ability to take something that happened in my life and turn it into something meaningful.

I chose to publish this book for a few reasons, and each of those reasons stems from my now seven-year-long mission of providing a voice to those who most need it. I often think about myself when I was younger and what it would have felt like for me to see an openly queer guy talk about his eating disorder and his recovery with the world. While my eating disorder isn't necessarily something I feel pride in, the journey I have taken to reclaim my life is.

One of the most common questions I receive on social media is, "Do you consider yourself recovered?" I've talked with many who began their recovery after me or during the same time, and I am amazed with how many of them answer yes to that question. I know for a fact that I am not, but that's the thing about recovery—it isn't linear. What takes one person a year to overcome may take others a decade. And that's okay.

There isn't a deadline on recovery, and it is still something that I have to consciously choose every day. That doesn't negate the fact that I still struggle. There are still days when I hate my body. There are still times when I restrict and convince myself that a relapse is what's best for me. I haven't attended a family or holiday dinner in years for the fear of something being said about my food or my weight that will take me back to a place of insecurity. The thoughts of my eating disorder still linger in the back of my mind, but instead of giving them any more attention, I'd like to take some time to tell you how my life has been since beginning recovery.

Making videos and publishing content online about my story and my experience as a boy in recovery from anorexia proved to be something that I loved to do. My audience has grown to over 550,000 across all platforms, and my videos have accumulated tens of millions of views. I have shared my story with news outlets, such as Good Morning America, Teen Vogue, USA

Today, and BuzzFeed News, and I receive messages every day from people on the Internet who see themselves in my story. For the past seven years, nearly every moment of my life has been spent spreading awareness for eating disorders in one way or another, and it has been the best and most rewarding decision of my life.

My life will forever be divided into two parts: before recovery and after.

In my journal entry from March 3, 2014, I mentioned that one of my long-term goals was to travel around Europe with a group of friends. Though the friends may be lacking, I have found joy and fulfillment in traveling alone. Back in 2017, during my second year of college, I studied abroad with a program called Semester at Sea. It was as adventurous and outlandish as it sounds. I lived on a German cruise ship for four months with nearly 700 other students, earned college credits, and traveled the world. We visited nine countries in total, including Ghana, China, Japan, Myanmar, and Vietnam. Once I arrived home from four months at sea, it was official—I caught the travel bug. I have since visited seventeen countries in total, and I discover a piece of myself everywhere I go.

Besides that, I got my first job, graduated from college with a bachelor's degree in Political Science from Southern New Hampshire University, adopted an adorably stubborn Shiba Inu named Chad and a sassy cat named Lannah, and became an uncle —twice!

If you're looking for an update on any of the characters written about in this book, unfortunately, I do not have much to share. I still see Cori every single week. Oliver is a distant memory that almost doesn't feel real. My sister and I have gotten closer, but nowhere near where we once were. I do not keep in contact with anybody from Cherry Oak Hospital. We were all there for one another during the most challenging time in our lives, and for that, we will forever be bonded.

I suppose this is where this story ends. Now that I am in

recovery, my true story is just beginning. I hope that reading *On Thin Ice* has broadened your understanding of eating disorders.

If you see something, say something. You may save a life.

Thank you for reading.

Acknowledgments

My mom—you are the strongest person that I know. And thank you—for everything. You deserve the world. I love you so much. I don't think anybody else could have dealt with all my crankiness throughout this entire publication process. You are the best. Thank you for taking the time to understand me and thank you for sneaking me in all those gummy bears and cake pops onto the unit.

Karin—thank you for fighting for me. And thank you for being my cheerleader through every single thing I have been through in the past almost ten years. You are one of, if not *the*, reason why I am here today, and that is something that I will never forget.

Nichole—you are my best friend, and I love you. Thank you for being one of the first to read the original draft of *On Thin Ice*. I couldn't ask for a better friend than you.

Chad, Lannah, Mr. Norris, Charles, Snuggles, and Harold—thank you for providing me with endless cuddles when I needed them most. Working on this book, that was quite often.

My editors, beta readers, and every YouTube video I watched that helped me to publish this book—thank you for your broad and honest insight, and thank you for working with me to make *On Thin Ice* the best that it could be.

Robbie—the love of my life, whose support and encouragement allowed me to revisit this story. Thank you for being by my side throughout it all.

And finally, my online family & supporters—thank you for giving my life purpose.

About the Author

Chris Henrie is a dedicated advocate for eating disorder recovery whose story has garnered attention from major media outlets including Good Morning America, Buzzfeed News, USA Today, Scholastic Choices Magazine, and Teen Vogue. With a strong social media following exceeding half a million, Henrie has emerged as a leading voice in the field to help represent the male and LGBTQIA+ populations within the recovery community. Beginning activism at just sixteen, Henrie has collaborated with several mental health nonprofits and organizations to advance his work.

Henrie currently resides in New Jersey with his antique doll collection of over two hundred and works as a content creator full-time.

www.ingramcontent.com/pod-product-compliance
Lightning Source LLC
LaVergne TN
LVHW041247080426
835510LV00009B/630